Women, Islam, and Resistance in the Arab World

Women, Islam,
and Resistance
in the Arab World

Maria Holt
Haifaa Jawad

LYNNE
RIENNER
PUBLISHERS

BOULDER
LONDON

Published in the United States of America in 2013 by
Lynne Rienner Publishers, Inc.
1800 30th Street, Boulder, Colorado 80301
www.rienner.com

and in the United Kingdom by
Lynne Rienner Publishers, Inc.
3 Henrietta Street, Covent Garden, London WC2E 8LU

Library of Congress Cataloging-in-Publication Data
Holt, Maria.
  Women, Islam, and resistance in the Arab world / Maria Holt and Haifaa
Jawad.
      pages cm
  Includes bibliographical references and index.
  ISBN 978-1-58826-925-6 (alk. paper)
  1. Women—Arab countries—Social conditions. 2. Women and religion—Arab
countries. 3. Women and war—Arab countries. 4. Political
participation—Arab countries—21st century. 5. Arab Spring, 2010–
I. Jawad, H. A. II. Title.
  HQ1784.H65 2013
  305.40917'4927—dc23
                                    2013014679

British Cataloguing in Publication Data
A Cataloguing in Publication record for this book
is available from the British Library.

Printed and bound in the United States of America

The paper used in this publication meets the requirements
of the American National Standard for Permanence of
Paper for Printed Library Materials Z39.48-1992.

5   4   3   2   1

Contents

Preface

In an increasingly interconnected global community, the continuation of violent conflict in the Middle East has implications for everyone, and one could argue that the exclusion of women from peacemaking processes is likely to have a negative impact on social stability and well-being. The study of Middle Eastern women is still a relatively neglected area, and little substantive work has been done on Arab women and conflict. The unexpected victory of the Islamist party Hamas in the Palestinian legislative elections of January 2006, together with Islamist successes in Iraq and other parts of the Arab world, adds fresh urgency to our need to understand the Islamist trend in Arab politics. Finally, in light of the 2005 *Arab Human Development Report,* which identifies the empowerment of women as one of the key reforms needed in the Arab world, and United Nations Security Council Resolution 1325 of October 2000, which highlights "the importance of bringing gender perspectives to the centre of all United Nations conflict prevention and resolution, peace building, peacekeeping, rehabilitation and reconstruction efforts," both scholars and policymakers need to have a better understanding of the priorities and concerns of Arab Muslim women. Hence, this book brings new perspectives to existing literature on women and Islam and on women and conflict: it provides a comparative perspective; draws on firsthand accounts of women involved in conflict, whether as active participants, victims, or bystanders; places Islamic belief and ritual into a practical framework and considers how religious faith influences women's responses to crisis situations; and advances theoretical understandings of women's participation in violent conflict.

In the book we illustrate some of the struggles taking place in the Arab world, with a particular focus on three Arab countries, from the perspectives of women. We make extensive use of personal testimonies from a wide range of women of all ages and backgrounds; they tell engrossing, often painful, and sometimes inspiring stories. By examining some of the factors that contributed to women's modes of participation in conflicts and by investigating how religion, patriarchy, traditional practices, and revolutionary forms of activism influenced the choices they made or were unable to make, this book adds to our knowledge not only of how women in the Arab world are affected by violent conflicts but also how their involvement begins to change the rules that govern their societies.

In addition, the book investigates how women negotiate violence and patriarchal structures in order to make sense of an otherwise fearful situation. It tests assumptions of female powerlessness and victimization by looking at women's own strategies of resistance, and it offers evidence both of how conflict disadvantages women and how they deal with disadvantages, whether through faith or the internalization of traditional roles or by challenging existing gender hierarchies. Their experiences of conflict make clear that many of these women were not only victims but also agents. In an atmosphere of violence, they have located appropriate strategies to counter the pressures of conflict. Some of these strategies have included direct involvement in the waging of conflict.

The three case studies chosen illustrate how women in Lebanon, Iraq, and the Palestinian territories have participated in the Islamist political project, including Islamist resistance against foreign invasion and occupation, and what implications their involvement in Islamist movements has (or will have) for future democratic trends. Evidence (gleaned from the interviews) of women's choices in these three countries, as well as other states in the region, throws into question assumptions of female powerlessness in Muslim societies. In most cases the research results indicate that the Islamization of the struggle has led to greater involvement of women in violent conflicts; this happens through personal choice but also coercion, when they have no other alternatives. Despite the risks involved in such activities, their participation in violent conflicts, according to women's own testimonies, has given them a sense of empowerment that helps them to address the male-dominated character traditionally attributed to Islamist movements. This is important in view of the recent increasing centrality of Islamism in the electoral processes of a number of Arab states and the likelihood that this trend could have a great impact on women in these areas.

This book was commissioned by Elisabetta Linton of Lynne Rienner Publishers, and it might never have been completed without her encouragement. Our warmest thanks go to her. The publisher's two anonymous readers provided valuable suggestions and criticisms and tactfully put us right on many points. We are also grateful to Salwa Ismail for her constructive comments on the first draft of the book. Warmest thanks and debts of gratitude go to Reza Shah-Kazemi and Nureen Kazemi for their support and helpful suggestions. The same gratitude must go to Tansin Benn for reading certain chapters of the book and constructively commenting on them. Our abundant thanks and appreciation go to all the women in Jordan, Syria, Lebanon, and the Palestinian territories who shared with us their inspiring and painful personal stories. Last but by no means least, warm thanks are due to Muhammad Bashar al-Fadhi and Abdulhamid al-Ani of the Information Office of the Association of Muslim Scholars in Amman and Damascus, to Hana Ibrahim of the Women's Will Association, to Kholoud Hussein and Nadia Abu Zaher, and to the many individuals and organizations who facilitated the fieldwork elements of our research for their valuable time and efforts and for their willingness to go the extra mile to help us in the task we set for ourselves.

—Maria Holt and Haifaa Jawad

1

Women and Islamism
in the Arab World

Even when we are in mourning, we still need to behave according to the expected codes and male orders.[1]

When I interviewed Umm Hassan in 2007, she was fifty-five years old.[2] She was married to her cousin at the age of thirteen. Her family came from the town of Bint Jbeil in southern Lebanon, in the area that was occupied by Israel until 2000. Her husband was a personnel manager. The couple had two sons and three daughters. They now live in Kuwait. When I interviewed her, she told me about the death of her eldest son, who worked as a mechanical engineer in Kuwait. During visits to Lebanon in the 1980s and 1990s, she said, he became inspired by and involved with the "Islamic resistance," which was fighting a guerrilla war against the Israeli occupation. He was caught by the Israelis making bombs and imprisoned in Khiam prison; they brought his mother to intimidate him, but he refused to talk. In early July 2006, Umm Hassan was in Bint Jbeil with her son and, when the resistance captured two Israelis on the Lebanese-Israeli border, she said, "he was crying with happiness." Following the subsequent Israeli invasion, he went away "to do an operation" but did not return; he was killed on August 12, 2006. They were very proud of him. The resistance, she added, "is a source of pride for the country."[3]

Umm Walid also lost her son under violent circumstances. She was fifty-one years old when I met her in 2007 and lived in Hebron in the Palestinian West Bank. She was born in Jerusalem, was married, and had three sons and one daughter. Her husband was a tailor. Her eldest son, Walid, was killed by the Israelis in 2003. He was a fighter with the Islamist movement Hamas. Umm Walid supports the Islamic resistance movement, she said, because "they work against the Israeli occupation." She also believes strongly that Palestine should be an Islamic state. She and her husband had been unaware, she said, of their son's activities. Nonetheless, they felt "very proud" of him. Walid, she recalled, often talked about becoming a martyr. Another of her sons, also a fighter, is in an Israeli prison.[4] Umm Sarah, forty-one years old and a native of Iraq, lost her brother during the invasion and was forced to flee Iraq with her husband and four children, first to Yemen and then to Jordan, where they currently live as refugees in difficult conditions. She affirmed, "We support the Islamic resistance; they are defending our homeland and families and I do not mind if my son wants to fight with them." In response to a question on the role Islam should play in Iraq, she answered, "We want Islam to rule our lives and land, we are Muslims."[5]

The narratives of these three women, their pride and their anguish, provide some idea of the popular support in Lebanon, the Palestinian territories, Iraq, and also in the wider Arab world for Islamic resistance movements. They are a source of empowerment for populations who feel they are victims of injustice. Their stories also reveal that their natural sense of sorrow, be they mothers, sisters, or daughters, at the loss of their loved ones, is tempered by the positive concept of martyrdom that continues to sustain Muslims, especially Muslim women, in times of tragedies and difficulties.[6] It is a "politics of piety," in which "men are associated with martyrdom [and] women mainly with mourning."[7] But their stories raise questions about the meaning of resistance in conflict situations, how it is understood by the women affected, how it contributes to articulations of modernity in Arab societies, how power and powerlessness are expressed, and how the resistance includes, or fails to include, women. Can the positive feelings of these three women and many other women in Lebanon, Palestine, Iraq, and elsewhere in the region translate into more active forms of female participation in Islamic resistance movements? What implications does the involvement of women have for future democratic development in the Arab world? These questions highlight "some of the conceptual challenges that women's participation in the Islamic movement poses to feminist theorists," one of which is whether their roles, as nationalist agents or active resisters, are likely to be inhibited or empowered by the ideological influences of Islam.[8]

Power and Empowerment

According to popular misconception in the west, Muslim women are oppressed and mistreated by men and by their religion. In this view, they lack power, both political and personal, and enjoy few of the rights or freedoms to which women in the west are accustomed. Simplistic generalizations of this kind have proved unhelpful in understanding the complex reality of Arab societies, specifically the ways in which women's experiences vary over time and place and the strategies they adopt to negotiate on their own behalf. Where there is power, as Michel Foucault tells us, there will be resistance, and as we are focusing on resistance in this book, we must also explain what we mean by power, and especially the empowerment of women. We ask how women can feel empowered in a situation rigidly structured by patriarchy and how they subvert patriarchy in order to play a part in both national and more private struggles.

It should be acknowledged, first of all, that knowledge and the pursuit of knowledge are also forms of power. To know, as Bryan Turner argues, "is to subordinate."[9] The orientalist discourse, as explored by Edward Said in his influential 1978 book, was "a remarkably persistent framework of analysis," which also "constituted a field of political power."[10] To avoid, or at least minimize, such power relations, we have been careful to privilege the voices of the women we interviewed, to highlight their concerns over our own theoretical preoccupations, and to accord respect to points of view we may not necessarily share.

We agree that it is misconceived to classify women as "a coherent group across contexts, regardless of class or ethnicity."[11] According to this view, power relations "are structured in terms of a unilateral and undifferentiated source of power and a cumulative reaction to power. Opposition is a generalized phenomenon created as a response to power."[12] As Judy el-Bushra and others have argued, to equate men solely with power and women with powerlessness creates a false dichotomy. On several levels, even though men are usually the formal holders of power, "women exercise agency in the pursuit of self-identified goals."[13] Beyond the arenas of the state and the family, many women in Iraq, Lebanon, and Palestine perceive themselves as powerless vis-à-vis the west and its local ally Israel. Their response, as outlined in this book, is to resort to various forms of resistance.

Questions of Identity and Belonging

Our objective is to challenge assumptions of powerlessness and victimization, and we will do so by referring to Islamic texts and exploring how Islamic activism enables women to play constructive roles in violent conflict, by reviewing Arab women's involvement in war and conflict in the present period, and by focusing on how women in several Middle Eastern societies experience and are being empowered by their participation in Islamic resistance movements and revolutions in the Arab world.

In this book, we seek to address the issues mentioned above by (1) defining "resistance" in the context of national and anticolonial struggle, (2) assessing how forms of resistance enhance an Islamic emancipator project, and (3) considering how Arab Muslim women engage with legitimate

and illegitimate violence in order to resist oppression both inside and outside their societies. We are primarily concerned with resistance against perceived external enemies by Muslim communities who choose to organize
their struggles within an Islamic framework. But we cannot altogether disregard how women and men are differently affected. Although the language
of political Islam is one of rights and Islam supposedly gives women "all
the rights they need . . . what this actually means for women is, for all practical purposes, the same patriarchy."[14] But it is also a language of identity
and belonging that has not, we argue, been altogether hijacked by "the
patriarchy."

Women's "gendered identities are constructed through the discourse of
religion and nationalism."[15] This has positive and negative connotations
because "Islamic movements themselves have arisen in a world shaped by
the intense engagements of Western powers in Middle Eastern lives," and
therefore it is likely that the primary concern of women and men is to
express communal solidarity in the face of threats from outside.[16] Constructed, historically and symbolically, as "mothers of the nation," women's
status has meant that the nation has been frequently identified through "the
iconography of familial and domestic space."[17] This idealization—or
restriction—of women's role has meant that nationalist activism has tended
to take place outside the private sphere, thus excluding women.

Following the attacks of September 11, 2001, on the United States by
self-proclaimed Muslim "jihadists" and the emergence of what has been
called the "new terrorism,"[18] the tendency of uninformed public opinion in
the west to demonize Islam, without distinguishing between the vast majority of law-abiding and peaceful Muslims in the Arab world and the small
minority that has opted to use Islam as a weapon of violence, increased dramatically. It also placed under the spotlight the activities of Arab women
and raised urgent questions about proper female conduct; although "the
mother of the martyr" (*umm shahid*) is a respected role, as Umm Hassan's
and Umm Walid's narratives demonstrated, the woman who chooses to act
violently on behalf of her nation or people tends to be treated with more
ambivalence. However, as we will argue, the increasingly popular practice
of resistance within an Islamic framework is enabling some women both to
access sources of dignity and empowerment and also to adopt more active
roles.

But it is also clear that a tension exists between women's engaged and
committed participation on the one hand, and their symbolic and relatively
restricted role on the other. We address this tension by exploring how the
strength of Islamist movements affects women's rights and entitlements in
the Arab world, in the context of non-western versions of "modernity"; we
also ask whether the trend of Islamic resistance, in the face of gender
stereotyping by many in the west, is capable of empowering women;

finally, we evaluate some of the ways in which Arab women are throwing into question or, in some cases, subverting the male-dominated character frequently attributed to Islamist movements and whether their efforts can be described as a type of "feminism."

Female Forms of Resistance in the Arab World

One of the key arguments we make in this book is that women in the Arab world, in response to oppressive practices from outside and discrimination within their own societies, are performing various forms of resistance. They are inspired by anticolonial movements, nationalism, and, of particular note in the context of this book, religion. We suggest that resistance is adopted by women to protect them from patriarchal excesses or traditional patterns of behavior that appear to relegate them to second-class status. However, resistance is a broad concept and difficult to define. As Foucault argues, resistance is a response to the exercise of power; and power clearly takes many forms in women's lives. In Arab societies, "many women willingly participate in the dominant power relations (patriarchy), accept socially designated roles, and internalize and use various socially constructed discourses to explain why things are and to give meaning to their experiences."[19] This, we argue, is a form of resistance. It implies not simply "acting in opposition" but also reflects the "potential for subversion and contestation in the interstices of established orders."[20]

Although Rose Weitz asserts that "the term resistance remains loosely defined,"[21] Jocelyn Hollander and Rachel Einwohner focus on two recurring themes: "recognition and intent."[22] An important issue, as they say, is "the *visibility* of the resistance act" (emphasis added).[23] It may be oppositional or unrecognized, overt or deliberately concealed.[24] Although some argue that the concept of resistance should apply only to "visible, collective acts that result in social change,"[25] others are of the opinion that it is equally applicable to what Scott calls "everyday" acts of resistance,[26] the "ordinary weapons of relatively powerless groups."[27] As el-Bushra notes, "everyday forms of resistance within existing gender relations frameworks provide scope for women to exercise political influence."[28] Any discussion of resistance "must detail not only resistant acts, but the subjective intent motivating these as well."[29] However, as Hollander and Einwohner observe, assessing intent may be problematic; oppressed people "may intend to resist [oppression] in some fashion, but this resistance may occur privately because public resistance is too dangerous."[30]

For Arab women suffering oppression, resistance occurs on several levels and takes a variety of forms. As women, they may resist the patriarchy, but this is likely to be a concealed form of resistance. The women in our case studies see themselves as part of a resistance project against the colonizing power of Israel and the hegemonic power of the west. They tend to regard themselves, in some respects, as marginalized; however, rather than identifying marginality as "a site of deprivation," they find that it is preferable to re-conceptualize it as "the site of radical possibility, a space of resistance."[31]

Resistance, as we argue, can be expressed in subtle and more obvious ways. It is very often nonviolent but can also become violent. It can take the form of dress: for example, the veiling movement in Egypt from the late 1970s and in Iran following the 1979 Islamic revolution has been described as an expression of resistance, in this case against the neocolonial project of the west.[32] The women in our case studies have also used dress to express their opposition to prevailing narratives, especially Shiite women in Lebanon who consciously adopted Islamic dress as a visible form of protest in the early 1980s. Some of the women we interviewed, who often conceptualized their own activities in terms of resistance against the enemy "other," preferred not to discuss more complex internal dimensions of resistance, such as coercion and lack of choice, although some asserted that, once national liberation has been achieved, women's "liberation" is likely to follow. They rarely used the language of "women's rights" but the meaning was implicit in their words.

Overview of the Book

We have selected four key areas to illustrate our arguments. First, in the context of the rapidly evolving study of Middle Eastern Muslim women, we discuss the dangers of essentializing women; colonial feminism, as Abu-Lughod notes, belongs "in the past."[33] Second, we assess the impact of violent conflict on women in the Arab world in terms of identity, national belonging, and modernity. Third, we consider the various effects that Islam, as a faith, a tradition, and activism, has on women involved in violent conflict. Fourth, in the case studies we explore the significance of women's own agency. While acknowledging the complexity of the topic, we argue strongly that, without analyzing all relevant elements, it is impossible to draw meaningful conclusions about women's lives. Our project took place against a background of violence, insecurity, and uncertainty; it is essential to bear in mind that the women interviewed for this project exist in similarly insecure conditions, which is likely to have an effect on the framing of their narratives.

We test our arguments by referring to three case studies—of Iraqi, Lebanese Shiite, and Palestinian women—all of which present very persuasive models of both intense oppression of women and women as "liberatory subject."[34] We chose these three groups of women because (1) all of them have consciously embraced an Islamic form of resistance against oppression imposed on them from outside; and (2) they embody significant differences, both in the performance and perfectibility of their resistance. In all three cases, women have assumed a diversity of roles that highlight victimization but also demonstrate that "their lack of formal power does not deprive them of their capabilities of resistance."[35] To explore the influence of Islamic resistance on women, we analyze the Lebanese, Palestinian, and Iraqi conflicts from the perspectives of some of the women involved, in their own words. We ask how Islamic teachings, including the modern ideology of political Islamism and Islamic resistance, prevent, constrain, or encourage female participation in the defense of the nation and the formation of personal identity. We argue that, far from being excluded from the dominant discourse, many Arab women are finding their "voice" through the modernizing processes of Islamic resistance. For many, especially in the west, the presence of women (sometimes in leadership positions, as is the case with the Yemeni activist Tawakkol Karman, who won the Nobel Peace Prize in late 2011) on the streets has been surprising and has caused some to reevaluate the stale stereotypes of silencing and powerlessness. Indeed, their efforts, determination, and dynamism seem to have created a model for others to emulate.

In this chapter, we discuss some of the theoretical underpinnings that inform our understanding of Arab women's resistance in situations of violent conflict, with a view to challenging preconceptions. We also describe the methodology used to conduct research. There is a great difference, as Nadera Shalhoub-Kevorkian observes, "between those who invert the patriarchal order by putting women in the centre and those who deconstruct that order and perceive women *as* the centre," and we certainly support the notion of women's centrality.[36] In order to construct an appropriate analytical framework in which to locate the research, it is necessary to decolonize feminism[37] and, by doing so, to destabilize some of the founding assumptions of modern theory.[38] Our work touches upon the question of control, in the sense of who controls the research process, who controls the agenda, and who controls the outcomes.

In Chapter 2, we consider the theological elements of the debate: What are the religious foundations of "Islamic resistance" and women's role in it? How does their activism challenge the patriarchy? As we were writing this book, a sequence of events of far-reaching significance began to unfold in the Arab world; since the end of 2010, many watched in amazement as women and men in states across the region poured into the streets to demand reform and the overthrow of dictatorial regimes. Although these events can by no means be attributed to Islamic activism, they are a natural progression of a resistance trend of which Islam is a key constituent. The so-called Arab spring is continuing still, and it is impossible to make meaningful claims about its outcomes. However, we felt it important to refer to the various Arab revolutions in terms of women's participation that, we argue, has parallels with the case studies explored here; in Chapter 3, therefore, we present an overview of women's activism. The final three chapters focus on the particular experiences of women in Lebanon, Iraq, and Palestine and are based on substantial fieldwork carried out in the countries concerned. Our aim, overall, is to link the discourse on gender and national identity with discussions of women's role in national liberation and Islamic resistance movements.

Research Method: An Exploration of Difference

In order to analyze Arab women's experiences of violent conflict and resistance in the latter part of the twentieth century and the early twenty-first century, we address the questions of how best to study women in societies other than one's own, in this case the Arab Middle East, and, more broadly, why a separate study of women is necessary at all. We need to consider, in other words, to what extent it is possible to generalize about "women" as a category. Clearly, discussions about "difference" cannot be separated from questions of identity[39] and these in turn "cannot be resolved outside those of gender."[40]

Fieldwork research for this book was conducted in Lebanon, the West Bank, Syria, Jordan, and Yemen in 2002–2003, 2006–2007, and 2010–2011.[41] It took the form of questionnaires and semi-structured interviews with a wide range of women of all ages and classes and, in certain cases, of communication by email. Suitable (and willing) participants were identified with the help of local organizations and individuals, who also advised on the content of the questionnaires. In addition, we interviewed some prominent male figures who have links to the resistance. The primary objective of the interviews was to assess each woman's personal experiences of violent conflict, her relationship with and feelings toward the national/Islamic resistance as a form of activism and liberation (both personal and political), and her own particular methods of coping. On the whole, the interviews tended to turn into conversations; in some cases, other women were present and contributed to the discussion. Our interviewees included professional women (university lecturers, teachers, doctors, lawyers, etc.) and women who had no schooling at all; women living in towns, villages, and refugee camps; political activists; women involved in welfare activities; students; Islamist women and secular women; the widows and mothers of martyrs; and women who refer to themselves as "feminists."

Each interview lasted, on average, one hour; most were conducted in Arabic and took place either in the woman's home or in a community center or the office of a nongovernmental organization. In every instance, the research project's aims were clearly explained to the woman so that she could give her informed consent; she was assured that she need not answer any question that made her feel uncomfortable and that her identity would be protected. We wanted the participants to appreciate that the project gave them space to express their own views, hopes, and experiences, both positive and negative, rather than fearing that an artificial agenda was being imposed on them.

By and large, the women were forthcoming about shared goals of national liberation and nation building and their own reasons for participating in what often appeared to be a bloody, chaotic, and frequently hopeless conflagration. What emerged from these encounters was a strong sense of pride on the part of the majority of the women in their contribution to the struggle; they made it clear that they had no choice but to involve themselves. Forms of participation were described in creative and sometimes even humorous detail. One gleaned a feeling of a broad and vital objective shared by all members of the community. On the fringes of the consensus, however, we sometimes sensed an element of discontent and began to be aware of areas in which women had experienced dissatisfaction, though these were rarely articulated openly to us. We sensed that some of our interlocutors were disappointed that, although they too had risked their lives for the national struggle, their male-dominated society was still reluctant to give women a voice in the business of postconflict reconstruction, if and when it began.[42]

Our experiences convinced us that it was impossible to arrive at any definitive version of the "truth," or perhaps the women with whom we spoke simply did not wish to share their truths with us. Conversations were often simply that: an opportunity to exchange views and to establish where we all stood. At the same time, despite the problematic nature of the relationship between us, the women revealed—deliberately or inadvertently— something of the complexity of their situation and the ways in which they were coping with it. At the end of the period of fieldwork, we both felt we had learned a great deal. But new questions had begun to take root in our minds, specifically, what happens when the mask of consensus slips?

We must acknowledge the difficulties of addressing these problems because there is no shared understanding of what constitutes resistance or how to deal with the fluid boundaries of dissatisfaction. The problem of conceiving difference "in ways which are not restrictive but liberating remains a key theoretical and political question for contemporary feminism."[43] One engages in the exploration of the lives of women who are "different" with two distinct objectives: to locate points of convergence and to enrich one's own understanding of the world. However, as this introduces complex issues of self-positioning and a notional postcolonial methodology, it should be undertaken with caution. There has been much discussion among feminist researchers about "non-hierarchical research relations," which, it has been argued, can "only be met by an *escape* from reality" (emphasis in original).[44] Our aim here is to engage consciously and deliberately in research that is not only nonhierarchical but also hands over part of the power involved in the research process to the women who are the subjects of the research.

One should beware of equating difference with deviation from the norm. It is preferable to acknowledge "change, complexity, and interpretative privilege in cultural formation. . . . This enables us to locate and condemn the particular historical formulations of culture that oppress women . . . as well as to understand and support women's ability to wrest freedom from amidst these oppressive conditions."[45] There is a danger, too, of reinforcing "the notion of difference as objectified otherness. . . . An abstract anthropological subject deemed 'oppressed' is thus created. Studying this constructed subject is not for the purpose of understanding her as such as it is to gather documentary evidence of her 'oppression.'"[46] We have taken care to avoid labeling the subjects of our research as "oppressed" except in terms that they themselves apply to their situations. Although it is unrealistic to ignore "difference," it is equally unhelpful to pretend we have nothing in common. Difference "has been a stumbling block for western social science from its very inception."[47] A division is drawn not simply between the private and the public spheres of life but also between western and nonwestern societies. By extracting particular categories of individuals—in this case, Arab Muslim women—one is intimating that there is something special and different about them, whereas in reality it is an artificial distinction. It is pointless to take "Muslim" or "Arab" women as an undifferentiated group and to assert that what they have in common is greater than what divides them from each other and from women elsewhere. At the same time, western researchers recognize that definitions of feminism may differ in fundamental respects, that objectives and ways of achieving these objectives may also be different, and that everyday life for women in Arab societies—on the whole—contains symbols and patterns of behavior that are more or less unfamiliar to women in western societies.

We have also consciously tried not to fall into the trap of orientalist stereotyping. In the writings of orientalists, the Middle Eastern woman, if she is mentioned at all, is usually considered in terms of a series of crude contrasts or contradictions: from colonial fantasies of "the oriental woman," on the one hand a voluptuous harem dweller and on the other a beacon of progress; to the national liberation ideal of the Arab woman, a symbol of purity and traditional values and, at the same time, a representative of the modernist aspirations of the new nation. Although scholarship has, by and large, moved beyond such simplifications, the starkness of "modernity" and "nonmodernity" remains an issue fraught with difficulties and requiring further exploration.

In the context of postcolonial scholarship, feminist researchers are adopting new and innovative approaches to the study of women and gender. Nadje al-Ali, for example, in her work on the Egyptian women's movement, speaks of "multiple allegiances," in the sense that the researcher is likely to experience a variety of involvements or relationships with the research community. She admits that she felt "torn between my wish to engage in a more reciprocal relationship where I was not the only one asking questions and a fear that I could too easily slip into an act of indiscretion."[48] Her dilemma goes to the heart of the problematic relationship between the researcher and the research community, particularly when the individuals one is researching are "different." As far as we are concerned, the point is not "to dismiss the role that Islam plays in women's lives" but rather "to study the historical conditions under which religion *becomes significant* in the production and reproduction of gender difference and inequality" (emphasis in original).[49] We are aware of the challenges this endeavor poses.

There is a gap between how Islamic resistance is generally perceived in the west—as "a medieval political party using religion as an attractive shield behind which to hide their real intent"[50]—and its attraction for many men and women in the Middle East, who regard it as a "new way of living and a new vision of modernity . . . that fundamentally differs from what the West terms "modernity."[51] Many Arab citizens fear that Islam is "under siege"; they regard western attitudes, and in particular the west's uncritical support of Israel, as hypocritical and unjust. Their articulations of dissatisfaction and frustration at their inability to be heard lie at the heart of our research project.

Islam and Feminism: The Debate in the Arab World

We believe that it is impossible to consider women's activism in the Arab world without some reference to feminism as a motivation or a methodology. Defining feminism, however, is not at all straightforward. To begin with, feminism "must stop conceiving itself a nation, a 'natural' political destination for all women. . . . Rather than adopting a politics of inclusion . . . it will have to develop a self-conscious politics of partiality, and imagine itself as a *limited* political home, which does not absorb difference with a pre-given and predefined space but leaves room for ambivalence and ambiguity" (emphasis in original).[52] In any case, thanks to the efforts of female scholarship, women "have been rendered visible"[53] to some extent, and the focus has been shifted from the universal male subject. Feminists have begun "to question and challenge the implicit male perspective of the dominant paradigms, methodological strictures, and theoretical assumptions of the various disciplines."[54] Although this approach might be theoretically persuasive, how can it be effectively linked to the lives of the women we are studying?

What, in other words, does "feminism" mean to Arab and Muslim women? Definitions of feminism, both in the west and in the Middle East, are highly contested. Chandra Talpade Mohanty speaks of "imagined communities" of women "with divergent histories and social locations, woven together by the *political* threads of opposition into forms of domination that are not only pervasive but also systemic."[55] However, the historical literature "is full of all kinds of feminists who would surely have had a hard time finding common ground," and the term "feminism" remains problematic today.[56] Badran suggests that the various revolutionary upheavals in the Arab world are "inscribing a new feminism . . . which does not go by the name 'feminism,' but by its spirit—redefines the words freedom, liberation, justice, dignity, democracy, equality, and rights."[57]

Margot Badran and Miriam Cooke state that feminist scholarship in the Middle East first arose "in a pre-colonial context following the rise of capitalism and the modern state. . . . From the start women grounded their feminism first in Islam and later in nationalism."[58] In Deniz Kandiyoti's view, it "has followed a distinctive trajectory reflecting both its engagement with local debates and its dialogue with broader currents of thought, from the turn of the century to the present."[59] The first wave of feminist writing in the Middle East "is associated with movements for social reform and modernization during the era of post-colonial state formation spanning the periods between the nineteenth and early decades of the twentieth centuries . . . nationalism was the leading idiom through which issues pertaining to women's position in society were articulated."[60] The second wave occurred during the 1950s and 1960s. This period "witnessed . . . the incorporation of questions about the family and women's roles into broader discourses about social transformation."[61] A third wave emerged after the 1970s, when we began to see "more significant inroads being made by Western academic feminism into Middle Eastern scholarship."[62] One result was "a selective and uneven incorporation of the various concepts of feminist theory into Middle East studies and the emergence of distinctive, local styles of polemic and scholarship."[63] In the 1980s, the consensus that assumed "women" were a category sharing a particular form of oppression broke down, which "set the scene for what might be characterized as an internal crisis about 'difference.'"[64]

The concept of feminism has encountered mixed reactions in the Middle East. Denounced by some as an inappropriate or irrelevant western import, it has been welcomed by others as a tool of female advancement. It is evident that notions of a globalized and unspecific feminism have proved unhelpful to many Middle Eastern women, who dislike the term "feminist" and prefer to engage in a "new women-friendly and gender-sensitive Islamic discourse" that they do not regard as part of a feminist project.[65] In Egypt, for example, some women are reluctant "to identify themselves with feminism," not only because of "its negative image in society" but also because of a belief that it detracts from more important issues, such as gender equality within the public sphere.[66] Others, in contrast, use the word and its connotations as a call to action.

Yet, taking into consideration the fact that both the term and the practice of western liberal feminism have appeared unsatisfactory to some Arab women, we need to ask ourselves exactly what it might mean in a non-western setting. By deconstructing the concept into its component elements, one can extract at least three meanings. The first, often used by conservative Muslims to criticize those who advocate greater equality for women, dismisses feminists as "agents of Western cultural imperialism"[67] who encourage Muslim women "to abandon home life and its responsibilities . . . and make their lives miserable by running after political, economic, social and other activities."[68] A second usage applies to Muslim women who use the tools of western feminist scholarship to reappraise "the theological justifications that have been offered for restricting women's rights."[69] A third understanding of feminism has been adopted by some Muslim women who would definitely not describe themselves as "feminist" in a western sense, but who are pushing forward the boundaries of women's rights by action and example. Islamic feminism "burst on the global scene as a new discourse or interpretation of Islam and gender grounded in *ijtihad*, or independent intellectual investigation of the Qur'an and other religious texts."[70] In other words, even as many women engage in the practice of feminism in terms of women's rights and development, they may prefer not to adopt the label, whereas others choose to align themselves deliberately with western feminist tradition. We should, finally, take care not to confuse "Islamic feminists who articulate an egalitarian mode of Islam" with "Islamist women who promote political Islam and its patriarchal version of the religion."[71] The women interviewed for this book fall into the various categories outlined; although some defined themselves as "feminists," to others the term was alien and inappropriate. And yet, the actions of some of these women had the characteristics of feminist praxis in the sense that they expressed agency and a clear intention to effect change; in other words, they represent a self-recognizing form of resistance.

"Empty Modernity": Challenging the Colonial Narrative

There is no doubt that European colonialism "profoundly transformed the everyday lives and discursive terms of the colonized" and had a particularly disruptive effect on women.[72] In her study about "remaking" women in the Middle East, Lila Abu-Lughod suggests that the question arose "as to how new ideas and practices considered 'modern' and progressive implanted in Europe's colonies or simply taken up by emerging local elites might usher in not only forms of emancipation but new forms of social control."[73] She poses an important question. It is certainly the case that one cannot understand contemporary gender relations in the non-western world—or indeed the roles played by women in national liberation movements—"without some analysis and discussion of the colonial period."[74] Although colonial discourse was "highly gendered," the impact of colonialism on gender relations was diverse and contradictory.[75]

Under its influence, women tended to be "treated more as symbols than as active participants by nationalist movements organized to end colonialism and racism."[76] In the case of Arab societies, religious practices were taken to illustrate the barbarism of those subjected to colonial rule. The Euro-Christian gaze upon Muslim culture, "whether expressed by word or picture, has been a gaze of violence, dominance, distortion and belittlement."[77] Europeans have looked upon the Middle East with fascination, focusing in particular on "the two characteristics perceived as essentially Oriental: sensuality and violence," and there is no doubt that the legacy of such attitudes continues to affect the region.[78]

At the same time, while "many women suffered increased burdens as a result of the changes which were part of colonial rule . . . the colonial state was also a site of gender struggle and some women attempted to use the limited spaces which had opened up to their advantage."[79] Thus, although some have argued that colonialism was wholly negative and served only to increase women's subordination, it may also be the case that some of the changes brought by colonialism "did allow some space for some women to resist, use and challenge both new and existing patterns of gender relations."[80] In their complex reactions to colonialism, Arab women engaged in multiple forms of resistance, some of which took religion as a source of protection and opposition. In this way, many women were able to assert their own nationalist identity.

This pattern continued into the Arab nationalist period. While nationalist projects "consistently favor the standpoint of men and privilege the masculine,"[81] gender has been identified as central to the phenomenon of nationalism.[82] Women are feted and excluded at the same time. In Middle Eastern societies tainted by colonialism, a specific version of nationalism tended to emerge. Created out of an uncomfortable marriage between traditional values and western notions of modernity, it contained a special place for women as agents of modernization and symbols of identity. But, rather than being seen as liberating, this apparent "progress" provoked conflict, confusion, and backlash as women's bodies and sexuality became "a privileged political site for the expression of difference and resistance to Western modernity."[83] It is likely that these battles are still being fought as Arab citizens confront new manifestations of colonialism.

As elsewhere, nationalism in the Arab world was a response to the fragmentation of colonialism and to an ideological crisis that originated "in the intensification of the contradictions and the accumulation of conflictual situations in Arab society."[84] The governments of newly independent states in the region "indicted European imperialism for its invasion and occupation, as well as its policies which divided by creating states and drawing artificial national boundaries, thus debilitating the Arab and Muslim world."[85] At the same time, Arab nationalists drew inspiration from European nationalist models as well as the Islamic *ummah*. Pan-Arab nationalism claimed that since the Arabs possessed a common history, language, and religion, it was "natural" that they should form one nation. From the start, however, Arab nationalism was an ideology mired in contradiction.

Most significantly, in the context of this book, the Arab nationalist vision contained an idealized place for women, but one that appeared divisive. The portrayal of Middle Eastern women by early European travelers "was part . . . of a larger picture of the primitive, Islamic East," and one that Arab nationalists were determined to challenge.[86] In response to the confusing impulses of European colonialism, which dismissed Middle Eastern women as victims of Muslim backwardness, newly independent Middle Eastern states tended to treat them as symbols of nationalist achievement. The creation of a "new Arab woman" was part of the modernizing project for nationalist elites involved in the anticolonial struggle. She "is literate and educated in the nationalist curriculum designed by the respective Arab governments once her country has attained independence. She is even, in many cases, employed."[87] But this woman frequently occupies an uncomfortable position, resented by the traditional classes, struggling to balance paid employment with the responsibility of running her home, and regarded by some as a tool of decadent western feminism. Her situation becomes even more precarious when violent conflict threatens to engulf the society.

In order to understand women's "problematic relationship to the modern nation-state and its construction of subjectivity,"[88] we need to focus on two distinct areas: (1) the debate on "modernity" in the Arab world and (2) gendered aspects of nation building. Modernity, according to feminist scholars, "has brought about an identity crisis among the formerly colonized peoples of the Middle East . . . who may seek a form of alternative modernity that is not contingent on embracing westernization."[89] At the heart of modernity "is the notion of the freely acting, freely knowing individual whose experiments can penetrate the secrets of nature and whose work with other individuals can make a new and better world."[90] However, as Abu Zeid notes, many Muslims "are reluctant to accept contemporary modernity, on the grounds that most of its values either contradict Islamic ones, or stem from human legislation."[91] They regard "modernity" as inextricably linked to the "grand narrative" of western progress, yet, as Alastair Crooke points out, the "grand narrative of Islam has not collapsed. It is revived and in the ascendant."[92] At the same time, Islamist discourse is still structured by that of the west,[93] and "Islamists do not intend to dismantle modernity but to Islamize it, to create an alternative modernity."[94] They insist that "Islam is modern/civilized *and* modern/progressive, as well as superior in certain ways to the empty modernity of the West."[95] Given the evidence of our research, it seems likely that some modern Islamist groups in the Arab world are engaging with modernity in order to create a more inclusive society. If women have felt left out of "nation making," they may be better able to relate to the Islamist grand narrative of resistance, not only to invasion and occupation but also to the empty modernity of the western model. Islamism, as Crooke observes, "is indeed challenging the west. But . . . the revolution is a struggle—a resistance—centred not on killing, but on ideas and principles."[96] From the point of view of many in the Arab world, this is an attractive revolution that, in the words of many of the women we interviewed, fully incorporates them.

For women in conflict situations, a sense of vulnerability is likely to make them ambivalent about their role in the national struggle. Since "the nation" is a largely masculine construct and the "historical patterns of colonialism and other forms of oppression would seem to suggest that there is an apparent affinity between nationalism [and] sexism," women tend not to be treated as full partners in the process of nation building.[97] As we suggested, nationalist symbolism tends to confine women to the domestic sphere. Thus, a cycle may be created, in the sense that men are largely in charge of the communal response to the conflict; they also exercise effective control over the women of the society. In other words, "the very idioms that women use to assert their presence in previously male-defined spheres are also those that secure their subordination."[98] As a result, it is conceivable that women will be less inclined to contribute their efforts to the struggle, and if this is true, their role may become a more passive one, apparently justifying the woman-as-victim mythology. The variables in this scenario are (1) that men do *not* have sole control over the violence that threatens their society—their actions depend to some extent on what the enemy does—and (2) that women very often can and do find appropriate and socially acceptable ways of participating in conflict situations, as our case studies reveal.

Women and National Liberation

In the Middle East, "nationalism and feminism have never mixed very well. Women have been used in national liberation struggles—Algeria, Iran, Palestine, to name a few—only to be sent back to their kitchens after 'independence' was gained."[99] As we argue, although nationalist ideology has played a vital role in liberation struggles in the Arab world, it also "reclaimed many of the patriarchal values of Islamic traditionalism as integral to Arab cultural identity as such."[100] As a result, although it is true that many women have experienced a conflict between national liberation and an anticipated improvement in their own status, others have welcomed a return to greater authenticity. One could argue, of course, that Arab men were also often victims, and some of them reacted to their perceived powerlessness by reverting to the hollow symbols of an imagined golden past and, in some cases, by asserting their power over women.

Palestinian, Iraqi, and Lebanese nationalisms developed in different ways in the twentieth century. Although all of them are rooted in the colonial experience—British in the case of Palestine and Iraq and French in Lebanon—they were influenced to some extent by Arab nationalism. Palestinian nationalism evolved to compete with Zionism for possession of the land, whereas Lebanese and Iraqi nationalisms were more undefined. Indeed, it could be argued that there is no such thing as "Lebanese nationalism" or "Iraqi nationalism." They are more precisely mosaics of competing nationalisms united by a commitment to a shared Lebanese or Iraqi identity; the latter has been further questioned and challenged since the US invasion in 2003. Insofar as Iraqi, Lebanese, and Palestinian nationalisms emerged, at least in part, as reactions to adverse experiences, they may be described as "embattled" forms of nationalism: the Palestinian experience has enjoyed few fruits of success, and Iraq remains mired in sectarian violence, but Lebanon has evolved a distinctive national identity, at least on the surface. If we examine the sorts of actions and activities in which women engage during national liberation struggles, we discover both diversity and creativity. During the first Palestinian intifada (1987–1993), for example, women in the West Bank and Gaza Strip established alternative educational and economic structures, devised ingenious methods of avoiding Israeli interference in order to carry on with their normal lives, and formed political organizations to advance their own interests. During the Lebanese civil war (1975–1990), women of all religious persuasions engaged in courageous peacebuilding activities, such as publicly meeting at the Green Line dividing East and West Beirut in order to express their opposition to the violence. Women in Iraq, across both ethnic and sectarian divides, work hard to protect their communities, oppose sectarianism and division, and call for national unity. In the Arab Muslim context, it is useful to look back at the roles of women in warfare, and to ask, on the one hand, how their participation or nonparticipation affected the ways in which they were treated and, on the other, how broad or diverse was the range of activities permitted to them.[101] As will be discussed, many Arab women today refer proudly to female role models in the early Islamic period. All these actions raise the question of who or what is being resisted and how significant a factor Islam truly is. All three groups are suffering or have experienced some form of foreign occupation; groups within each area have mobilized to confront and remove occupying forces. In all three cases, Islam has been a key factor. There has been a determination, in the Iraqi, Lebanese, and Palestinian cases, to end what they see as an illegal occupation and liberate their lands; it is a matter of honor, keenly experienced by women as much as men. Because diplomacy and passive resistance are perceived to have failed, a more militant form of resistance has been recognized by many as the most feasible solution.[102] Nonetheless, despite some notable successes by the Islamic resistance movement in removing the Israeli occupation from southern Lebanon, Palestinians and Lebanese Shiites are aware that they face a far more powerful enemy. That enemy appears vindictive and seems to respond only to force, and some Arabs argue that Israel has been successful largely because it is supported by a compelling ideology, rooted in religion.

The Palestinian-Israeli conflict can be characterized as a quest for national liberation, whereas the Lebanese Shiite conflict with Israel falls into the category of anti-imperialist struggle. In Iraq, the struggle has been against foreign invasion and continuing sectarian violence. In response to violent conflict, Palestinian, Iraqi, and Lebanese women have adopted several modes of action. They support their male kin in a variety of traditional ways, protect their children, and attempt to maintain the integrity of their communities. On rare occasions, they resort to violence themselves.[103] These activities are broadly defined as "resistance." The majority of Lebanese, Iraqi, and Palestinian women regard the violence, directed against an unprincipled foe, as unavoidable, and it would be overly simplistic in all three cases to link women automatically with peace and men with war. For example, interviews conducted with Palestinian refugee women in Lebanon in July 2011 revealed that, although the women strongly disapproved of all forms of violence, most said that it was acceptable to use violence, including suicide bombing, against the Israeli occupation of Palestinian land. Similarly, most Iraqi women who were interviewed in Jordan and Syria in February and March 2011 accepted violence as a way of liberating their own country, arguing that violence is not only legitimate in the case of occupation, but also a means of precipitating the liberation of their territory. Nonetheless, male and female ways of coping and resisting tend to differ; the roots of these clearly delineated roles, one could argue, are located in their national histories and religious traditions. We explore these differences carefully in Chapters 4–6.

However, we argue that liberation also means the liberation of individuals, in this case women. On the whole, national liberation and women's liberation do not sit comfortably together. Although the assumption is that women will be "better off" once the nation has been liberated, real improvements often fail to materialize or fall short of expectations. Cultural values tend to remain rigid, and notions of "respect" are rarely examined. Indeed, male values, being associated with victory, have a tendency to become entrenched, and the role of women continues to be idealized as a measure of tradition and continuity since, historically, "women have been regarded as the repositories, guardians, and transmitters of culture."[104] Moreover, national liberation struggles are almost always military in style and violent in practice, qualities conventionally defined as "masculine." Islamic resistance movements have also adopted militaristic trappings; they seem to celebrate masculinized forms of heroism, which often includes resorting to overt violence. If women participate at all, it is assumed that they must do so on male terms, either by imitating men, which has connotations of social unacceptability, or by carrying out traditional feminine support roles. While these assumptions are certainly part of the story, we propose to test them through our research and to argue that female forms of resistance represent an authentic expression of women's empowerment.

The Performance and Perfectibility of Resistance

When Umm Hassan in southern Lebanon talked about the violent death of her son, she gave the impression that both his "heroism" and her own narrative of suffering were part of a larger story about the "perfectibility" of resistance. It has grown beyond the simple defense of the country into something, as Crooke says, that embraces "ideas and principles." Although many women feel comfortable with that concept of resistance, has it been able to subvert gender stereotypes? Umm Hassan is still "the mother of the martyr," the one who performs the rituals of mourning. Is that her agency? Where is the agency of Umm Sarah, forced to flee from her country and live as a refugee, or Umm Walid, unaware of her son's activism but proud that he died a martyr?

In this chapter, we have analyzed the literature to show that nationalism and conflict are ordered according to male criteria. They tend to reinforce masculine notions of heroism, which may have the effect of excluding women. One should be cautious, however, when applying such theorization to Arab societies that are caught up in violent conflict. To begin with, there may be no functioning government to enforce the law. Even where there is the semblance of a government, it is constrained in the Arab-Muslim context by sensitivities regarding the private sphere of women and the family. Although the majority of states in the world have signed international treaties guaranteeing gender equality and national legislation may be in place to protect women from the excesses of warfare, prevailing attitudes and an attachment to traditional practices are more difficult to change. Finally, women's own efforts are challenging the conventional discourse of woman-as-victim.

For Palestinians, Iraqis, and Lebanese Shiites, the blurring of lines between the battlefront and the home front has permitted the violence of conflict to spill over into all aspects of their lives. Although women and men are both negatively affected by conflict, their experiences of it and their ways of coping with it vary. For both, "home" is experienced as a site of insecurity. They have grown accustomed, on the one hand, to sudden and violent incursions by the enemy into their most private spaces and, on the other, to the threat and reality of displacement. To ascertain the validity of the assertion that men and women experience conflict differently, it is necessary to separate the strands between (1) Islam as a social system that protects women; (2) patriarchy as a social system that is prevalent in Iraqi, Palestinian, and Lebanese Shi'i society and privileges men; and (3) enemy violence against Iraqi, Palestinian, and Lebanese civilian populations, which, on the whole, does not discriminate against women or men.

The framework we have outlined is intended to highlight women's roles and activities in the context of violent upheavals. Palestinian women have been fighting dispossession, exile, occupation, and repression for well over half a century. Their struggle is for national liberation and self-determination, but it also contains a growing feminist consciousness, which sometimes comes into conflict with nationalist objectives. Lebanese Shiite women, too, have been struggling against injustice. And Iraqi women have been fighting ethnic and sectarian strife and occupation. By examining the construction of national identity for women and men and the emergence of Islamic resistance movements as a form of national assertion and self-respect, we hope to illustrate women's growing sense of belonging to the nation and how that provides a path toward activism.

At the same time, we suspect that wars affect women, whatever their religion or circumstances, in similar ways all over the world. The more we have spoken to women about their experiences and perceptions of war, the more we have discovered a common thread weaving its way through their responses. Women tend to regard war and violence as unnatural, avoidable, and repugnant. We are certainly not claiming that women always reject the use of force or that they are not sometimes themselves violent. In their accounts of conflict, some Palestinian, Iraqi, and Lebanese women express pride in their respective resistance movements: like Umm Hassan, Umm

Walid, and Umm Sarah, they celebrate the martyrdom of husbands and sons; and, in rare and extreme cases, they themselves resort to violent acts against the enemy. But on the whole, although they are very often present in the arena of war, particularly when it intrudes into their personal spaces, women are more likely to seek nonviolent ways of opposing or surviving it.

Because of the diversity of influences on contemporary Arab states, women's lives are controlled by a tapestry of ideologies of which Islam is an important strand. The modern state "not only formalizes politics, it also changes the nature of political conflict, diminishing the forms in which women might previously have participated."[105] According to this hypothesis, female patterns of political participation occur in gender-specific social spaces, such as the domestic sphere.[106] We believe their involvement is growing, as the Arab revolutions of 2011 and the experiences of Islamic resistance illustrate.

One of our key objectives in writing this book was to understand how women's activism becomes "legitimate." For instance, the participation of women in the Iranian revolution was sanctioned by the clergy, and the activism of Palestinian and Algerian women during their respective liberation struggles was condoned by the urgency of popular resistance.[107] As we analyze the narratives contained in the three case studies, we argue that many women in Lebanon, Iraq, and the Palestinian territories have been able to access new arenas of effective activity, despite experiencing forms of victimization. Umm Hassan, Umm Walid, and Umm Sarah have not only been subjected to terrible events in their lives but also have gained access to a new way of conceiving themselves as "resistant" and active subjects. In the next chapter, we explore some of the theological underpinnings of this much-contested debate.

Notes

1. "Umm Riad," quoted in Nadera Shalhoub-Kevorkian, "Liberating Voices: The Political Implications of Palestinian Mothers Narrating Their Loss," *Women's Studies International Forum* 26, no. 5 (2003). 405.
2. The names of all women interviewed for this book have been disguised.
3. Interview, Bint Jbeil, Lebanon, July 27, 2007.
4. Interview, Hebron, West Bank, November 4, 2007.
5. Interview, Amman, Jordan, March 2011.
6. Shalhoub-Kevorkian, "Liberating Voices," 403.
7. Roschanack Shaery-Eisenlohr, *Shi'ite Lebanon: Transnational Religion and the Making of National Identities* (New York: Columbia University Press, 2008), 156.
8. Saba Mahmood, "Feminist Theory, Agency, and the Liberatory Subject," in Fereshteh Nouraie-Simone, ed., *On Shifting Ground: Muslim Women in the Global Era* (New York: Feminist Press at the City University of New York, 2005), 111.

9. Bryan S. Turner, *Orientalism, Postmodernism, and Globalism* (London: Routledge, 1994), 21.

10. Ibid.

11. Chandra Talpade Mohanty, "Under Western Eyes: Feminist Scholarship and Colonial Discourses," in Reina Lewis and Sara Mills, eds., *Feminist Postcolonial Theory: A Reader* (Edinburgh: Edinburgh University Press, 2003), 66.

12. Ibid.

13. Judy el-Bushra, "Transforming Conflict: Some Thoughts on a Gendered Understanding of Conflict Processes," in Susie Jacobs, Ruth Jacobson, and Jennifer Marchbank, eds., *States of Conflict* (London: Zed, 2000), 80.

14. Ziba Mir-Hosseini, "We Need to Rethink Old Dogmas," interview with Yoginder Sikand, Qantara.de—Dialogue with the Islamic World, October 28, 2010, http://en.qantara.de/We-Need-to-Rethink-Old-Dogmas/9555c9654i1p660.

15. Suruchi Thapar-Bjorkert and Laura J. Shepherd, "Religion," in Laura J. Shepherd, ed., *Gender Matters in Global Politics: A Feminist Introduction to International Relations* (London: Routledge, 2010), 270.

16. Lila Abu-Lughod, "Do Muslim Women Really Need Saving? Anthropological Reflections on Cultural Relativism," *American Anthropologist* 104, no. 3 (September 2002): 789.

17. A. McClintock, "Family Feuds: Gender, Nationalism, and the Family," *Feminist Review* 44 (1993): 62.

18. National Commission on Terrorist Attacks upon the United States, *The 9/11 Commission Report* (New York: Norton, 2004).

19. Cheryl A. Rubenberg, *Palestinian Women: Patriarchy and Resistance in the West Bank* (Boulder, CO: Lynne Rienner, 2001), 11.

20. Deniz Kandiyoti, "Gender, Power, and Contestation: Rethinking Bargaining with Patriarchy," in C. Jackson and R. Pearson, eds., *Feminist Visions of Development* (London: Routledge, 1998), 141.

21. Rose Weitz, "Women and Their Hair: Seeking Power Through Resistance and Accommodation," *Gender and Society* 15 (2001): 669.

22. Jocelyn A. Hollander and Rachel L. Einwohner, "Conceptualizing Resistance," *Sociological Forum* 19, no. 4 (December 2004): 534.

23. Ibid., 539.

24. Ibid., 540.

25. Jeffrey W. Rubin, "Defining Resistance: Contested Interpretations of Everyday Acts," *Studies in Law, Politics, and Society* 15 (1996): 241.

26. James C. Scott, *Weapons of the Weak: Everyday Forms of Peasant Resistance* (New Haven, CT: Yale University Press, 1985).

27. Hollander and Einwohner, "Conceptualizing Resistance," 539.

28. el-Bushra, "Transforming Conflict," 79.

29. Lauraine Leblance, *Pretty in Punk: Girls' Gender Resistance in a Boys' Subculture* (New Brunswick, NJ: Rutgers, 1999), 18.

30. Hollander and Einwohner, "Conceptualizing Resistance," 542.

31. bell hooks, "Marginality as Site of Resistance," in Russell Ferguson, Martha Gever, Trinh T. Minh-ha, and Cornel West, eds., *Out There: Marginalization and Contemporary Cultures* (Cambridge, MA: MIT Press, 1990), 341.

32. Fadwa el-Guindi, "Veiling Resistance," in Reina Lewis and Sara Mills, eds., *Feminist Postcolonial Theory: A Reader* (Edinburgh: Edinburgh University Press, 2003), 586–609.

33. Abu-Lughod, "Do Muslim Women Really Need Saving?" 790.

34. Mahmood, "Feminist Theory, Agency, and the Liberatory Subject."

35. el-Bushra, "Transforming Conflict, 80.

36. Shalhoub-Kevorkian, "Liberating Voices," 405.

37. For an exploration of the concept of "decolonizing feminism," see Marnia Lazreg, *The Eloquence of Silence: Algerian Women in Question* (New York: Routledge, 1994), 6–19.

38. Michele Barrett and Anne Phillips, "Introduction," in Michele Barrett and Anne Phillips, eds., *Destabilizing Theory: Contemporary Feminist Debates* (Cambridge: Polity, 1992), 1.

39. Roslyn Wallach Bologh, "Feminist Social Theorizing and Moral Reasoning: On Difference and Dialectic," *Sociological Theory* 2 (1984): 388.

40. Julie Marcus, *A World of Difference: Islam and Gender Hierarchy in Turkey* (London: Zed Books, 1992), viii.

41. Funding for fieldwork in Lebanon, the Palestinian territories, and Yemen was provided by the US Institute for Peace (2007–2008) and the Cordoba Foundation (2010).

42. An example of this was the "Women's Charter," presented by a group of women's organizations to the Palestinian National Authority in August 1994, for inclusion in the new Palestinian constitution.

43. Chris Weedon, *Feminism, Theory and the Politics of Difference* (Oxford: Blackwell, 1999), 12.

44. Jayati Lal, "Situating Locations: The Politics of Self, Identity, and 'Other' in Living and Writing the Text," in Sharlene Hesse-Biber, Christina Gilmartin, and Robin Lydenberg, eds., *Feminist Approaches to Theory and Methodology: An Interdisciplinary Reader* (Oxford: Oxford University Press, 1999), 112.

45. Arati Rao, "The Politics of Gender and Culture in International Human Rights Discourse," in Julie Peters and Andrea Wolper, eds., *Women's Rights, Human Rights: International Feminist Perspectives* (London: Routledge, 1995), 173.

46. Lazreg, *The Eloquence of Silence*, 35.

47. Ibid., 6.

48. Nadje Sadig al-Ali, *Secularism, Gender, and the State in the Middle East: The Egyptian Women's Movement* (Cambridge: Cambridge University Press, 2000), 13.

49. Lazreg, *The Eloquence of Silence*, 14.

50. Tarek Heggy, *The Arab Cocoon: Progress and Modernity in Arab Societies* (London: Valentine Mitchell, 2010), 29.

51. Alastair Crooke, *Resistance: The Essence of the Islamist Revolution* (London: Pluto Press, 2009), 6.

52. Ien Ang, "I'm a Feminist but . . . 'Other' Women and Postnational Feminism," in Reina Lewis and Sara Mills, eds., *Feminist Postcolonial Theory: A Reader* (Edinburgh: Edinburgh University Press, 2003), 191.

53. Gisela Bock, "Challenging Dichotomies: Perspectives on Women's History," in Karen M. Offen, Ruth Roach Pierson, and Jane Rendall, eds., *Writing Women's History: International Perspectives* (Basingstoke: Macmillan, 1991), 1.

54. Bologh, "Feminist Social Theorizing and Moral Reasoning," 388.

55. Chandra Talpade Mohanty, "Cartographies of Struggle: Third World Women and the Politics of Feminism," in Chandra Talpade Mohanty, Ann Russo, and Lourdes Torres, eds., *Third World Women and the Politics of Feminism* (Bloomington: Indiana University Press, 1991), 4.

56. Leila J. Rupp and Verta Taylor, "Forging Feminist Identity in an International Movement: A Collective Identity Approach to Twentieth-Century Feminism," *Signs: Journal of Women in Culture and Society* 24, no. 21 (1999): 363.

57. Margot Badran, "Egypt's Revolution and the New Feminism," *The Imma-nent Frame*, March 2011, http://blogs.ssrc.org/tif/2011/03/03/egypts-revolution-and -the-new-feminism/?disp=pr, accessed March 12, 2011.

58. Margot Badran and Miriam Cooke, "Introduction," in Margot Badran and Miriam Cooke, eds., *Opening the Gates: A Century of Arab Feminist Writing* (London: Virago, 1990), xxvii.

59. Deniz Kandiyoti, "Contemporary Feminist Scholarship in Middle East Studies," in Deniz Kandiyoti, ed., *Gendering the Middle East: Emerging Perspectives* (London: I. B. Tauris, 1996), 7–8.

60. Ibid., 8.

61. Ibid., 10.

62. Ibid., 12.

63. Ibid., 12.

64. Ibid., 15.

65. Margot Badran, *Feminism in Islam: Secular and Religious Convergences* (Oxford: Oneworld Publications, 2009), 9.

66. al-Ali, *Secularism, Gender, and the State*, 5.

67. Ann Elizabeth Mayer, *Islam and Human Rights: Tradition and Politics*, 2nd ed. (Boulder, CO: Westview, 1995), 97.

68. Abu'l A'la Mawdudi, *Purdah and the Status of Women in Islam* (Lahore: Islamic Publications, 1981), 24, quoted in Mayer, *Islam and Human Rights*.

69. Mayer, *Islam and Human Rights*, 97. She names Abdullahi al-Na'im, a law professor in the Sudan, who became executive director of Africa Watch, and Fatima Mernissi, a Moroccan sociology professor and one of the founding members of the Moroccan Organization for Human Rights, as examples (see p. 96 in Mayer).

70. Badran, *Feminism in Islam*, 3.

71. Ibid., 6. See also Haifaa A. Jawad, "Islamic Feminism, Leadership Role, and Public Representation," *Hawwa, Journal of Women of the Middle East and the Islamic World* 7, no. 1 (2009).

72. Lila Abu-Lughod, ed., *Remaking Women: Feminism and Modernity in the Middle East* (Princeton, NJ: Princeton University Press, 1998), 17.

73. Ibid., 6.

74. Georgina Waylen, *Gender in Third World Politics* (Buckingham: Open University Press, 1996), 47. Other relevant works include Edward Said, *Orientalism* (London: Routledge and Kegan Paul, 1978); J. De Groot, "Sex and 'Race': The Construction of Language and Image in the Nineteenth Century," in S. Mendus and J. Rendell, eds., *Sexuality and Subordination* (London: Routledge, 1989); Veena Das, "Gender Studies, Cross-Cultural Comparison and the Colonial Organization of Knowledge," *Berkshire Review* 21 (1986).

75. Waylen, *Gender in Third World Politics*, 49.

76. Cynthia Enloe, *Bananas, Beaches, and Bases: Making Feminist Sense of International Politics* (London: Pandora Press, 1989), 42.

77. Fadwa el-Guindi, *Veil: Modesty, Privacy, and Resistance* (Oxford: Berg, 1999), 23.

78. Billie Melman, *Women's Orients: English Women and the Middle East, 1718–1918* (Ann Arbor: University of Michigan Press, 1992), 60.

79. Waylen, *Gender in Third World Politics*, 68.

80. Ibid., 50.

81. Fatma Muge Gocek, "Introduction: Narrative, Gender, and Cultural Representation in the Constructions of Nationalism in the Middle East," in Fatma Muge

Gocek, ed., *Social Constructions of Nationalism in the Middle East* (Albany: State University of New York Press, 2002), 5.

82. Linda Racioppi and Katherine O'Sullivan See, "Engendering Nation and National Identity," in Sita Ranchod-Nilsson and Mary Ann Tetreault, eds., *Women, States, and Nationalism: At Home in the Nation?* (London: Routledge, 2000), 22.

83. Deniz Kandiyoti, "Islam, Modernity, and the Politics of Gender," in Muhammad Khalid Masud, Armando Salvatore, and Martin van Bruinessen, eds., *Islam and Modernity: Key Issues and Debates* (Edinburgh: Edinburgh University Press, 2009), 95.

84. Issa J. Boullata, *Trends and Issues in Contemporary Arab Thought* (Albany: State University of New York Press, 1990), 152.

85. John L. Esposito, *The Islamic Threat: Myth or Reality?* (Oxford: Oxford University Press, 1992), 71.

86. Ruth Roded, ed., *Women in Islam and the Middle East: A Reader* (London: I. B. Tauris, 1999), 9.

87. Lama Abu-Odeh, "Crimes of Honour and the Construction of Gender in Arab Societies," in Mai Yamani, ed., *Feminism and Islam: Legal and Literary Perspectives* (Reading: Ithaca Press, 1996), 166.

88. Norma Alarcón, Caren Kaplan, and Minoo Moallem, "Introduction: Between Woman and Nation," in Caren Kaplan, Norma Alarcón, and Minoo Moallem, eds., *Between Woman and Nation: Nationalisms, Transnational Feminisms, and the State* (Durham: Duke University Press, 1999), 1.

89. Therese Saliba, Carolyn Allen, and Judith A. Howard, "Introduction," in Therese Saliba, Carolyn Allen, and Judith A. Howard, eds., *Gender, Politics, and Islam* (Chicago: University of Chicago Press, 2002), 12.

90. Joyce Appleby, Lynn Hunt, and Margaret Jacob, "Post-Modernism and the Crisis of Modernity," in *Telling the Truth About History* (New York: Norton, 1994), 201.

91. Nasr Hamid Abu Zeid, "The Modernisation of Islam or the Islamisation of Modernity," in Roel Meijer, ed., *Cosmopolitanism, Identity, and Authenticity in the Middle East* (Richmond, Surrey: Curzon, 1999), 71.

92. Crooke, *Resistance*, 26.

93. Bjorn Olav Utvik, "The Modernizing Force of Islam," in John L. Esposito and Francois Burgat, eds., *Modernizing Islam: Religion and the Public Sphere in Europe and the Middle East* (London: Hurst, 2003), 65.

94. Ibid.

95. Lara Deeb, *An Enchanted Modern: Gender and Public Piety in Shi'i Lebanon* (Princeton, NJ: Princeton University Press, 2006), 25 26; emphasis in original.

96. Crooke, *Resistance*, 16.

97. Nadera Shalhoub-Kevorkian, *Militarization and Violence Against Women in Conflict Zones in the Middle East: A Palestinian Case Study* (Cambridge: Cambridge University Press, 2009), 83.

98. Mahmood, "Feminist Theory, Agency, and the Liberatory Subject," 115.

99. Evelyne Accad, "Sexuality and Sexual Politics: Conflicts and Contradictions for Contemporary Women in the Middle East," in Chandra Talpade Mohanty, Ann Russo, and Lourdes Torres, eds., *Third World Women and the Politics of Feminism* (Bloomington: Indiana University Press, 1991), 238.

100. Mai Ghoussoub, "Feminism—or the Eternal Masculine—in the Arab World," *New Left Review* 161 (January–February 1987): 8.

101. In the early days of Islam, women were present on the battlefield, urging the male warriors on with songs and stirring words. See Chapter 2.

102. The first intifada, which began in 1987, succeeded in placing the Israeli-Palestinian conflict back in the international spotlight. Hizbullah's violent struggle against the Israeli occupation of southern Lebanon succeeded in forcing the Israelis to withdraw in May 2000.

103. Although increasing numbers of young women in the West Bank and Gaza Strip are becoming suicide bombers against Israeli targets and some Iraqi women have also undertaken such actions, there are very few such examples in Lebanon.

104. Rao, "The Politics of Gender and Culture," 169.

105. Suad Joseph, "Women and Politics in the Middle East," *Middle East Report*, January–February 1986, 4.

106. Ibid., 6.

107. Ibid.

2

Islamic Discourses
on Women and Violence

A key concern of ours in writing this book was the influence of
Islam (as a religion, a cultural system, and a form of activism) on the lived
experiences of women in the Arab world. We explore the influence of
Islamic teachings and practices on Muslim women caught up in situations
of conflict, in terms both of their ability to participate in the conflict and of
their private lives. Rather than endorsing "Muslim women's entrapment in
a false debate," we want to start with the voices that have informed this
piece of research, those of Palestinian, Iraqi, Lebanese, and other Arab
women, as a way of questioning some of the misleading generalizations
made about "women and Islam."[1] Some westerners assume that Islam
oppresses women more than other religions do. But, in order to subject simplistic assertions of this kind to more rigorous analysis, we need to deconstruct "Islam" and "oppression." Most of the women who participated in
our research claimed that their religion is meaningful to them, whether as a
source of spiritual comfort or an aid to activism. But they also expressed
resentment and criticism at some of the restrictive practices prevailing in
their societies, which they attribute to cultural baggage rather than to Islam
per se. How, then, are we to distinguish between "pure" Islam, as revealed
to the Prophet Muhammad in the seventh century CE, and the encrustations
of custom and misogynistic tradition that have infiltrated the faith and are
now identified as part of it? With the exception of the early, brief era in
Medina in which the spirit of egalitarianism prevailed, Islamic history generally reveals a patriarchal tendency that promotes or favors the interests of
certain groups and individuals, usually male, at the expense or exclusion of
females. This clearly is a departure from the intentions of the egalitarian

27

spirit and rules established by the Prophet. Having said that, it is important to stress that a microlevel review on this issue might reveal greater complexities of women's struggles at different historical periods.[2] We start with the proposition that Islam, when it was originally revealed, improved women's status. This claim was made by many of the women interviewed for this book. In order to explore more fully the question of the influence of religion on Muslim women's participation in violent conflict, in this chapter we examine some of the basic doctrines of Islam insofar as they affect women; chronicle how Islamic teachings have been interpreted by society and enacted by women over the centuries; and, finally, look at the development of movements in the twentieth century that promote a more politically engaged form of Islam and enter the debate about Islam, terrorism, and resistance. What has been the effect of political Islam on Iraqi, Palestinian, and Lebanese Muslim women? Is it a progressive movement or an antimodern one? How have such movements sought to incorporate women into their nation-building projects? These issues will be addressed as we investigate the relationships among women, Islam, and conflict violence in the three case studies.

Muslim Women and Religion

Although they can be considered only a partial explanation of the dilemmas being experienced by Arab women today, it is worth examining the founding discourses of Islam. We need to know the extent to which the new religion initially improved women's position, the formal legal rights it bestowed upon them, and the underlying themes of male domination that were present when the religion was established and, we could argue, still persist in one form or another in most Muslim states today. Despite the general success of the Islamic message in the seventh-century Arabian Peninsula, in introducing what we might call balance and egalitarianism, male elites continued to exercise power and to use it in their own interests, and they did so by adding Islam to their repertoire of control. Even today, "if women's rights are a problem for some modern Muslim men, it is neither because of the Koran nor the Prophet, nor the (authentic/spiritual) Islamic tradition, but simply because those rights conflict with the interests of a male elite."[3] To assess the accuracy of this claim, it is useful to approach the question (1) by referring to influences that predated Islam and (2) in terms of a power struggle between competing elites. We do this by looking at the work of scholars such as Fatima Mernissi, Leila Ahmed, Amina Wadud, and Deniz Kandiyoti, all of whom have made important contributions to the debate on interpretation in Islam. Although there were some early "feminist" attempts to enter into this field, they were marginalized and prevented from becoming part of the overall mainstream of Islamic thought, chiefly because of political and religious hostilities. Hence, we can see that until the latter part of the twentieth century, this subject was debated almost entirely among men. Now the process is being undertaken by women, which is exciting, in the sense that it brings into question some of the accepted tenets of the religion and subjects them to fresh scrutiny and new understanding.

Islam, in common with the other principal monotheistic religions, Judaism and Christianity, is a system deeply rooted in patriarchal interpretations.[4] Leila Ahmed has produced compelling evidence to show that, in the pre-Islamic Middle East, the subordination of women and the patriarchal family, "designed to guarantee the paternity of property-heirs and vesting in men the control of female sexuality, became institutionalized, codified, and upheld by the state."[5] She cites examples from civilizations that preceded Islam and asserts that male dominance became entrenched with the "growth of complex urban societies and the increasing importance of military competitiveness."[6]

However, she also cautions against a simplistic view of history. Although some scholars claim that, in the centuries preceding Islam, women possessed few formal rights, there is also an argument to be made that "Islamic civilization developed a construct of history that labelled the pre-Islamic period the Age of Ignorance and projected Islam as the sole source of all that was civilized."[7] After all, we know that the Prophet's first wife, Khadijah, whom he married before the Islamic revelations began, was a wealthy and respected trader.[8] According to Ahmed, although pre-Islamic marriage practices "do not necessarily indicate the greater power of women . . . [they] correlate with women's being active participants, even leaders, in a wide range of community activities, including warfare and religion."[9] Of course, this kind of freedom may be assumed to pertain to a particular section of the female population, not all women in those societies.

The Quran—the main text in Islam that is considered by Muslims to be the literal word of God—both reflects and radically modifies the environment into which the new religion was born nearly fourteen centuries ago. Historical accounts indicate "that Islam was initially far ahead of other religions and cultural traditions in its recognition of women as independent persons with rights and obligations."[10] Such accounts, according to Mernissi, "portray women in the Prophet's Medina raising their heads from slavery and violence to claim their right to join, as equal participants in the making of their Arab history."[11] The Quran addresses believers on two levels, one legal and the other spiritual and moral.[12] Although Islam would have had difficulty surviving had it suddenly departed altogether from the mood of the times, and there is no doubt that it took many of the existing customs into consideration, it was certainly "a force that improved the lot of women."[13]

Mernissi, a sociologist, suggests that from the start, there was a tension between two distinct forces: (1) the strongly misogynistic tradition of pre-Islamic Arabia and the determination of men of the elite to maintain their dominant position at the expense of women and (2) the emergence of Islam as a socially and ethically enlightened force that women experienced as positive and beneficial. Nonetheless, the prevailing ethos of the time permitted men to enjoy uncontested control, even though the quranic revelation, clearly, "was never intended as an affirmation of patriarchy, but rather as a denunciation of it."[14]

Islamic perspectives on almost all aspects of human life can be gleaned from the Quran, the *sunnah* (example), and the *hadith* (sayings) of the Prophet Muhammad. The *hadith* were compiled after Muhammad's death and have been subjected to scrutiny and a diversity of interpretations. Nonetheless, although little consensus has emerged when it comes to the position, status, and rights of women, a body of law was formulated that appears to privilege male Muslims over female Muslims. Are we to conclude that the Quran and other sources of Islamic tradition have been interpreted—deliberately and systematically—to create, maintain, and institutionalize the inferior position of women? It is often argued that interpretations of the Quran and religious texts rely, to some extent, on the vantage points of the interpreters and on schools of thought that have developed over centuries. Even though religious texts might be regarded by Muslims as authoritative, they have not been able to avoid human interpretations, which are undertaken, the interpreters claim, to clarify their meanings.

Interpreting the Word of God

For further clarification, we consider several interpretations of what the Quran "really means" with respect to women, conflict, and resistance. There are, of course, many differing views, but we have selected the most prominent ones. On one side of the debate are social conservatives, who regard women and the family as the unchanging foundation of Muslim life. This group maintains that, although it is difficult to separate the words of the Quran from the interpretations derived from them as Islam evolved, the Quran contains precise instructions about how women—and men too, of course—should dress, behave, and interact with others. These are, as it were, "set in stone" and, therefore, not susceptible to change or new interpretations. On the other side stand the modernists who believe that Islam, by its nature, is capable of changing with the times. The modernist school argues that the Quran is an enlightened and progressive document, designed to respond to the needs of Muslims and to the times. Adherents of this trend argue that, since most references to women are unspecific, any attempt to approximate the lifestyle of seventh-century Arabia is not only inappropriate but also impossible.

In the latter part of the twentieth century, a third group, the Islamists, often referred to as "fundamentalists," added their voice to the debate. At present, this tendency is exerting considerable influence in a number of Muslim countries, whether in opposition or as part of the political and religious establishments. In the "new ideological construction of Islamist movements, women are presented as symbols and repositories of religious, national, and cultural identity."[15] Although Islamist movements are controlled by men, significant numbers of women identify with them, and although some observers regard such movements as a potential threat to women's rights, women who call themselves "Islamist" regard this development as potentially empowering.

The real difficulty in this context is the battle between what Khaled Abou El Fadl calls the "moderates" and the "puritans," between those who are pragmatic, tolerant, and inclusive and aim to reconcile universal Islamic principles with current moral and ethical principles, and those who are literalist, reactionary, zealous, and exclusive and reject any progressive and forward-looking voices.[16] The real problem, in our view, is how to represent an extreme variation of Islamist interpretation, described by Mernissi as "fear of the modern world." Is it because, she asks, "the idea of democracy touches the very heart of what constitutes tradition in these societies: *the possibility of draping violence in the cloak of the sacred?*"[17]

Feminists (although many Muslim men and women prefer not to use this term) comprise a final component of the current debate on Islam, and they fall into two categories: those who argue from the standpoint of Islam and those who do not. In the words of one commentator,

> The debate between feminists and neo-Islamists has influenced Middle Eastern feminists . . . and has produced the first signs of what [is now termed] Islamic feminism. It would seem that Muslim women . . . have reached the conclusion that in order to improve the status of Middle Eastern women, and Muslim women in general, they must adopt Islamic discourse instead of Western feminist jargon.[18]

According to this analysis, "it is not Islam per se that oppresses women but, rather, the continuity of patriarchal values within nationalist and religious interpretations that limits women's agency."[19]

Miriam Cooke defines "Islamic feminism" as "a contingent, contextually determined strategic self-positioning," but admits that the term may be problematic.[20] Nonetheless, she believes that Islam and feminism are compatible and, furthermore, this "linking of apparently mutually exclusive identities can become a radical act of subversion."[21] The process, according to Anouar Majid, has already begun in parts of the Islamic world. In Iran, for example, "a country governed by a male clerical elite, there is now a thriving intellectual debate over how to challenge repressive laws from within the Islamic tradition itself."[22] In fact, their success has set a precedent and encouraged other Muslim women to follow suit, giving momentum and sharp focus to Islamic feminism. Islamic feminists therefore

> are claiming that Islam is not necessarily more (restrictive or conservative) than any other identification, nor is it any more violent or patriarchal than any other religion. They are claiming their right to be strong women within this tradition, namely to be feminists without fear that they be accused of being Westernized and imitative.[23]

Haideh Moghissi, however, rejects the notion that a religion based on gender hierarchy could be "adopted as the framework for struggle for gender democracy and women's equality with men."[24] In her view, gender-conscious women in Muslim societies who are active in the women's rights struggle "rarely choose to identify themselves or to be identified by others as feminists."[25] Islamic feminists, whether self-styled or otherwise, take the line that it is not Islam but later additions and dogmatic interpretations that are responsible for women's diminished status. In the beginning, they say, Islam provided enlightened and revolutionary changes in the lives of women, bestowing upon them rights and entitlements that they had not previously enjoyed, and it is this Islam, which is seen as a source of social justice and spiritual liberation at one and the same time, rather than the Islam of the male establishment, that Muslim women should seek to reclaim. As Moghissi admits, the "newly manufactured image of strong Muslim women in active negotiation with a Muslim male elite" might not achieve the end goal because of the dogmatic and conservative interpretations that dominate in the Muslim world.[26]

The non-Islamic, or secular feminist, argument holds that women all over the world are entitled to defendable rights that are independent of religion or tradition. This group insists on the applicability of universal human rights codes and points out that the treatment of women should not be culturally specific. Arguments about "Islamic human rights" pit the cultural particularist position against the universalist approach. The secular perspective insists that all human beings are entitled to certain basic rights, whereas cultural particularists hold that "members of one society may not legitimately condemn the practices of societies with different traditions."[27] Ann Elizabeth Mayer argues that "if all such 'particularisms' mean that violations of women's rights are excused and perpetuated, they are nothing more than disguises for the universality of male determination to cling to power and privilege."[28] We subscribe to the belief that appeals to "cultural relativism" and "difference" should be subjected to more rigorous probing. By the same token, secular feminism need not dismiss the importance of spirituality to women's lives and the role of religion as a source of stability, belonging, and identity for ordinary women. Most important, these two so-called feminist positions are not mutually exclusive. Women struggling to ensure respect for their rights, whatever their faith position, share a belief in entitlement. Whether their actions stem from religious belief or a commitment to the secular standards of legislation, their objectives very often coincide.

The Quran and Women

What is the best way to proceed through territory that contains, if anything, an overabundance of signposts? The obvious starting point is to return to primary sources, of which the most important is the Quran itself, and then to look at the legal systems constructed upon these. The Quran is clear that, if men and women are faithful to the practices of Islam, they will receive an equal reward for their efforts.[29] Many people we interviewed stressed this basic quranic principle. Certainly, the purely religious sections of the Quran are unambiguous about male and female spiritual equality, but the situation is less clear-cut when it comes to social life. Some have argued that male dominance is not only allowed to persist but even encouraged and endowed with divine right. We could argue that Islam, when it was originally revealed, aimed to create a balance between men and women and to miti-gate some of the negative effects of Arabian patriarchal power. However, its formalization was bound to be affected by the prevailing mood of the time.[30] Clearly, managing a large and complex state that incorporated con-quered peoples with varying social attitudes necessitated certain policies. These policies eventually included the formal control of women, which was clearly reflected in law. Nonetheless, this dilemma highlights a conflict between the ideal of the quranic revelation and the reality of a patriarchal ambience that infused the understanding of religious principles. For exam-ple, a central tenet of Islamic thinking and "one of the most important aims of Islamic regulations governing behaviour and human relations is the preservation of the family unit in such a way that the atmosphere of tran-quillity, love and mercy and consciousness of God can develop and flower to the benefit of husband and wife."[31]

A husband "is expected to take care of his wife and show consideration to her."[32] In return, the best role for a wife in "keeping the marital tie intact and strong, is to recognize her husband as the person responsible for the running of the affairs of the family, and . . . to obey him even if his judgement is not acceptable to her, in a particular matter, provided he does not go beyond the limits of Islam."[33] The majority of ordinary Lebanese, Iraqi, and Palestinian women continue to accept this as the natural order of things. Yet nothing "exemplifies more the contradictions of modern state patriarchy than the fact that today Muslim women can aspire to hold powerful positions and to becoming the heads of governments, yet they face often insurmountable difficulties in divorcing their husbands."[34] This assertion does not necessarily represent the general pattern throughout all Islamic historical periods, however: in his work *Marriage, Money and Divorce in Medieval Islamic Society*, Yossef Rapoport challenges these assumptions and argues that marriage and divorce in medieval Cairo, Damascus, and Jerusalem did not strictly follow the patriarchal norms that were advocated by both jurists and moralists. On the contrary, the transmission of the dowries and the clear definition and separation of properties between spouses allowed room for easy divorce initiated by women in the same way and as often as divorce was initiated by men.[35]

When we consider the immutability of the quranic text and the authority of the *hadith*, two key considerations should be kept in mind. First, the *hadith* need to be revisited in order to sift the authentic from the unauthentic and to differentiate the specific from the general. Fatima Mernissi carried out painstaking research in this area, and some of her discoveries were revealing. The sacred texts, she points out, have "always been manipulated, but manipulation of them is a structural characteristic of the practice of power in Muslim societies. Since all power, from the seventh century on, was legitimated only by religion, political forces and economic interests pushed for the fabrication of some false traditions."[36] In other words, from a very early date, interested parties began to twist the words of the *hadith*: sometimes they attributed to the Prophet words he had never uttered, and sometimes they borrowed words he had spoken under specific circumstances and applied them elsewhere.

Second, we must distinguish between the Islamic precedent established by the Prophet Muhammad in his lifetime and the law making that took place after his death. By the tenth century CE, "the body of Sunni Muslim legal thought and practice achieved final formulation in four schools of law, representing in part the different regional origins of the schools and named after major legal proponents—the Hanafi, the Shafi'i, the Hanbali, and the Maliki."[37] Once formulated, this body of law was regarded as final. Future jurists could only "imitate," not "originate" rules and regulations. Consequently, "the vision of society developed by the men of this period, and their understanding of the relations that should per-

tain between men and women, was established as the ultimate and infalli-
ble articulation of the Islamic notion of justice, which has, ever since, been
imposed as finally binding on Muslims."[38] Of course, we must be careful
not to oversimplify history, since micro-investigation sometimes reveals a
complex materiality of women's struggles at different historical periods.
For instance, Rapoport argues that the common assumption about the legal
inferiority of Muslim women and their economic dependence on men is
grossly exaggerated.[39]

These historical developments continue to have an impact on how the
modern Muslim woman lives her life. On the one hand, it is clear that the
status of Muslim women today is by no means a reflection of women's
lives at the time of the Prophet Muhammad and his companions. The
Quran does create an admirable and even visionary blueprint for women,
but Mernissi and others have argued that the circumstances under which
the Prophet uttered his *hadith*, the pervasive conservative mood of the
time, the incorporation of alien customs during the expansion, and the
determination of the male elite during the period of the Islamic empires to
preserve their own privileges have all affected the present position of Muslim women. We must also stress the role of state economic, social, and cultural policies; the power structures at both the state and social levels; and
their impact on the contemporary situation of Muslim women.[40] On the
other hand, efforts by Islamist groups (which are reactions to modernity
rather than pragmatic Islam) to promote a "pure" and utopian version of
Islam have tended to involve pressures on women to practice greater modesty, to follow a strict code of behavior, and, in some cases, to retreat altogether from the public sphere. To justify their position, Islamists have
argued that attempts to equate progress for women with western notions of
women's liberation are misguided, ethnocentric, and alien; they very often
link feminism to western social problems such as drugs and family disintegration. Hence, rather than seeing feminism as a political response to
these problems, they see it as the cause of them. The Islamists' contention
here goes beyond the matter of the veil and the symbolism of the display of
modesty and purity to issues of control and submission by force if necessary. Puritans are using theology to justify aggression against women: "It is
the desire to dominate [women] that causes [them] to so profoundly deform
and mutilate the truth about the role . . . of women in the Islamic faith."[41]

One of the problems with women's Islamic work "is that it is men who
direct it, not women, and men are careful to maintain their grip on it, so
they would not allow female leadership to emerge."[42] This highlights the
central dilemma of power versus interpretation, of an Islam that originally
emerged as a revolutionary movement promising greater equality in the
eyes of God and purporting to enhance the rights of women, and of the gulf

that exists between the conception of the "eternal" word of God and the wide-ranging versions of what it might "mean."

Women in Islamic History

After the Islamic revelation of the early seventh century CE, when rights for all members of society, male and female, were articulated, for a while women did find their situation improved, especially during the early era in Medina. However, thereafter, and more specifically during imperial Islam, what seems to have happened was a backlash by men. By referring to Islamic history, we can gain some idea of "the limitations gradually placed on Arab women's active participation in their society, the progressive curtailment of their rights, and the simultaneous development of practices detrimental to women and attitudes indicating a decline in their status."[43] If we take as a starting point the position of women in pre-Islamic Arabia, there is evidence to suggest that they were visible, active members of the community but possessed few rights and that only a minority of women, among the elite, could exercise those rights.[44] We learn that, at the time of the Prophet Muhammad, women were involved in all aspects of the life of the community, including its battles. War

> was one activity in which women of pre-Islamic and early Islamic Arabia participated fully. They were present on the battlefield principally to tend the wounded and to encourage the men, often with songs and poetry. A number of women became famous for their poems inciting warriors to fight fiercely, lamenting death or defeat, or celebrating victory. Some women also fought.[45]

According to some accounts, women participated in battles that took place during the lifetime of the Prophet Muhammad. In the Battle of Uhud (623 CE), for example, "women took an active role."[46] A witness described seeing two of the Prophet's wives, "their garments tucked up and their anklets showing, carrying water to men on the battlefield. Other women on the Muslim side are mentioned as caring for the injured and removing the dead and wounded from the field."[47] During the same battle, in which the Muslims fared badly and it was even feared that Muhammad himself had been killed, one hears of a woman called Nusayba who "fought with sword and bow to protect the Prophet."[48]

Succession to the Prophet took the form of a caliphate, but even during the period immediately after his death, when the four "rightly guided" caliphs ruled over the rapidly expanding Muslim community (632–661 CE), dissension took root.[49] This reached a crisis point during the reign of the fourth caliph, Ali Ibn Abi Talib, who was married to the Prophet's daughter

Fatima, and resulted in schism within the religion.[50] After the death of the Prophet in 632 CE, A'isha, his favorite wife, became a figure of some influence; having enjoyed close proximity to Muhammad, she was able to attest to the accuracy of some of his *hadith*. In 656 CE, when she was forty-two years old, A'isha "took to the battlefield at the head of an army that challenged the legitimacy of . . . Ali."[51] This incident, known as the Battle of the Camel, was "named after the camel on which A'isha sat while exhorting the soldiers to fight and directing the battle."[52] She and her army were defeated, which vindicated the position of some opponents who claimed "that A'isha's going into battle violated the seclusion imposed by Muhammad, who had ordered his wives to stay at home, women's proper place in this new order."[53] A'isha's participation in warfare "resulted in the creation of a problematic female public example."[54] The question is, "Did A'isha break pre-Islamic or Islamic precedent by participating directly in battle?"[55] On this topic, there seems to be no clear consensus. At any rate, after her defeat, A'isha retired from public life, and her retreat has been interpreted by conservatives "as representative of the future limited role of all women in the Islamic community."[56] Instead of building on this precedent in a way that would give women more freedom, Islamic historians allowed A'isha's legacy to be ignored and suspended.

Significantly, even after A'isha's defeat, women continued to play a role in warfare. For example, Ali's daughter Zaynab took part in the Battle of Karbala in 680 CE, at which her brother Husayn was killed by the Umayyads. Zaynab is still revered as a heroine by the Shiites; many of the women interviewed in Lebanon and the Iraqi women interviewed in Jordan and Syria mentioned her as a role model. Mernissi records that two Shiite women in Yemen, Asma Bint Shihab al-Sulayhiyya, who died in 1087 CE, and Arwa Bint Ahmad al-Sulayhiyya, who died in 1138 CE, "enjoyed the privilege and unquestioned criterion of a head of state: the *khutba* proclaimed in their name in the mosques."[57]

As Islam spread and became established and its survival was no longer at risk, women found themselves increasingly restricted in their movements; they were excluded from warfare, and evidence reveals that even some of their Islamic rights and freedoms were curtailed by men. The contradictory reasons given for the enforced control of women must have had the effect of creating confusion about their roles. On the one hand, there existed a belief that women's sexual power, if not strictly regulated, would destroy society. Muslims, argues Yvonne Yazbeck Haddad, "have always believed that female sexuality is potent with a predilection to create havoc and chaos in the male. Thus it is necessary to control the woman in order to preserve order and well-being in society."[58] On the other hand, in the centuries following the death of the Prophet, women increasingly came to be treated as inferior beings, in need of male protection and guidance; because they were considered to be overly emotional, women could not be entrusted with positions of power or responsibility. Once established, the subordination of women became a habit.

There is relatively little information about women's lives in the Muslim Middle East from the early Islamic caliphates to the beginnings of western penetration of the region in the early nineteenth century, other than their roles as wives, mothers, and concubines.[59] However, as Ali Mazrui argues,

> the gender revolution was intended in Islam but never took off. It was aborted arguably for two reasons: a) mainstream Islam turned royalist from the Ummayids onwards and the harem developed and became more secluded as a more aristocratic version of Islam developed, and b) the doors of ijtihad [intellectual effort] closed and the gender revolution was thereby aborted.[60]

Ahmed, too, believes that the one factor that shaped women's lives in this period was the social ideal of women's seclusion.[61] Although it would be inaccurate to claim that women became entirely invisible and powerless, it would appear that some of the laws promulgated to control their behavior, together with the idealization of female seclusion, had the effect of severely circumscribing their lives.

Wealthy men, besides the four wives allowed them by Islamic law, often amassed large harems of concubines, sometimes totaling several thousand. Some historians argue that under these circumstances, many women were able to develop skills that they could use to exert influence over their powerful husbands, lovers, or sons. For example, the mother of the Abbasid Caliph al-Muqtadir, who came to power in 908 at the age of thirteen, reigned in her weak son's name, together with some of the ladies of the harem, for twenty-five years, although the reign "was marked by riots and the increasing disintegration of his empire."[62]

Rarely permitted to rule in their own right, since women are "wearers of the veil and have not complete intelligence," women were forced to devise strategies in order to play a constructive role in the lives of their societies or simply to survive.[63] For example, there were women in early nineteenth-century Iran who "wrote treatises advising women how to get around their husbands, carry on flirtations, and otherwise subvert strict 'Islamic' rules."[64] Majid reports that, in the pre-colonial era, "traditional, veiled women told stories with what today might be considered pornographic content and, at the same time, made copious references to Islamic texts to bolster their arguments."[65] It seems clear from this and other evidence that many women took steps to ameliorate the restrictions of seclusion.

In the nineteenth century, the Ottoman Empire—the last of the great Islamic empires—began to crumble, and much of the Islamic world fell under the control of colonial European powers, thus exposing women to a number of unfamiliar influences. In Muslim societies, women tend to be closely linked with traditional values, and, thus, their participation in liberation struggles has been problematic. Men believe they are religiously obliged to "protect" their women, that exposing them to the violence of warfare risks corrupting the nation. However, a significant number of Arab women did join in the fight for independence in the twentieth century. For example, "accounts of the Egyptian revolution of 1919 mention the participation of women."[66] Iraqi women were actively involved in the anticolonial movement.[67] Palestinian women, too, played an active role from the 1920s onward in the struggle against the British occupation and Zionist encroachment of their land. During the Algerian war of national liberation in the 1950s and 1960s, women were involved "in a variety of ways"; they worked as nurses and fighters; they planted bombs and also carried messages, money, and weapons. The "Battle of Algiers could not have taken place without these women," and that was true for other conflicts in other parts of the Arab world.[68]

In a number of Arab and Muslim countries, women have appeared in public to demand an end to what they regard as unjust practices. For instance, in 1991, when a western-led coalition attacked Iraq, women poured onto the streets in countries as far apart as Morocco and Pakistan to protest this new form of colonial aggression against the Muslim world; although the western powers were acting to protect the people of Kuwait, their intervention was viewed by many Arabs and Muslims as unwelcome interference. Similar demonstrations of anger by women were witnessed in 2003 when the United States and UK threatened to overthrow the regime of Saddam Hussein. Women have been deployed to represent the symbolic dignity of the nation, as personified by the mother of the martyr and the loyal wife, but also the determination of all members of society to resist foreign interference.

Although male Muslim leaders have been quick to capitalize on the symbolic value of women, they have sometimes, both in the past and in recent times, taken measures to reassert control that involve enforcing specific patterns of behavior and modes of dress. For example, a "Muslim sovereign in a crisis, facing hunger riots or a popular revolt, immediately had recourse to the traditional measures of destroying the stores of wine and placing a ban on women leaving their homes."[69] In 1438 CE, during the famine and plague in Egypt, "the Mamluk sultan Barsbay conferred with the religious scholars about the causes behind these catastrophes, and they agreed that the primary cause was the appearance of women in the streets. A decree was immediately issued ordering women to stay home!"[70] In Ottoman Turkey, after "each national upheaval, military defeat or on the whim of a sultan, the government would issue a decree holding responsible the 'immorality' of women, mandating that they cover themselves more."[71] Veiling, as Daryush Shayegan remarks, is "a perverse way of taking it out on the women, when things are going badly at the front or some resounding defeat has occurred on the battlefield."[72] A similar pattern of repression can be observed in Iran since the Islamic revolution in 1979 and in Hamas's enforcement of dress codes on women in the Gaza Strip in the early days of the first Palestinian intifada.

These restrictive practices seem surprising when one recalls that, in the early Islamic period, women "led armies . . . and earned immortality as artists and writers."[73] These exalted roles, as Akbar Ahmed points out, are "far removed from the lowly situation of women in our times."[74] He attributes the decline in women's status to the impact of colonialism, which, he suggests, "imposed foreign values at the same time as it destroyed or eroded native ones. As a result . . . [m]en retreated into the shell of rigid customs and sterile ritual. . . . They also forced women to hide behind *burkhas* . . . and remain invisible in the courtyards of their homes."[75] His comments raise this question: how accurate is the image of the modern Muslim woman as a victim both of her religion and of men? Is there an element here of western mythologizing? Scholars have spoken about "widespread misconceptions" that "were born mainly out of mythology, including Arabic and Islamic mythology, such as the tale of the 'One Thousand and One Nights,' and information broadcast abroad by early European travellers and orientalists unfamiliar with language and local customs."[76] These tended to create an exoticized image of "oriental" womanhood, of the protected but sexually alluring Muslim woman.

The targeting of women, however, is not simply a means of consolidating male power. There are also reasons that have more to do with powerlessness. For example, in recent decades,

> the national sense of humiliation suffered by the Arab male as a result of the defeat by Israel, and the social sense of humiliation caused by the prospect of class demotion that may result from the reversal of certain socio-economic policies in a number of Arab countries—these two types of humiliation both leading to a sense of lost dignity—may have contributed to a process that turns women into an easy target for the "restoration" of dignity.[77]

Although there may be some truth in this argument, it disregards both female agency and women's changing status in the Arab world. Nowadays, Arab and/or Muslim women are beginning to enter public space in ways that are considered religiously acceptable, under "the shield" of Islam. These women, "like their secularist sisters before them, emphasize the importance of the collective good over the benefit of individual liberation and self-realization"; while they do not entertain the notion of "women's liberation," many are "invading public space in increasing numbers in the name of Islam, and with its symbols."[78] Under this shield of Islamic modesty, women "can legitimately study, work, and act politically and publicly, with their honor and modesty protected within the confines of the 'Islamist' movement."[79] One such Islamist intellectual is Heba Ra'uf Izzat, an Egyptian woman who is both an academic and an activist in the "Islamist" movement. Although, she says, she is not an Islamic feminist, she believes "in Islam as a world view, and I think that women's liberation in our society should rely on Islam. This necessitates a revival of Islamic thought and a renewal within Islamic jurisprudence."[80] There are theological doctrines of Islam that recognize certain situations as so extreme that they demand the participation of all members of society, in order to combat, for example, an external threat. Women are then permitted, and even encouraged, to join in the armed struggle. If infidels invade a Muslim country, "all the inhabitants of this country should go out and fight the enemy. In this situation, it is unlawful for anyone to refrain from fighting."[81] Shaikh Na'im Kassim, deputy secretary-general of Hizbullah in Lebanon, believes that men bear the primary responsibility for defending their country because they are stronger and less emotional than women. But, in his opinion, women also have an important role, as mothers, teachers, and carers for the families of martyrs. By combining their different but equally necessary skills, men and women contributed to the success of the Islamist resistance movement in Lebanon.[82]

On the whole, however, men maintain the exclusive right to use violence, and they do so in ways that seem contradictory: to protect their societies, their groups, and particularly their women and, at the same time, to punish women who misbehave. The employment of violence is accepted as the exclusive preserve of males; it "belongs" to them. Women are generally regarded as being in need of male "protection" against the violence of other men. But these attitudes seem to be at odds with views expressed by, for example, some politically active Shiite women in Lebanon, some Iraqi women who are politically active, and a number of Jordanian women who are active members of the Jordanian Islamic National Front.[83] They appear content with their supporting roles and certainly do not regard themselves as helpless victims of male power politics; as far as they are concerned, violence belongs solely to the enemy outside, against whom all members of the community, according to their ability, are obliged to struggle.

The Modern Islamist Movement

In the face of perceived defeat, loss of land, and the failure of postcolonial states to achieve their promised socioeconomic and political reforms in the twentieth century, many Muslims have turned—with hope or perhaps desperation—to religion. However, since they are seeking a quick and comprehensive solution to a wide range of ills, from economic stagnation and political ineptitude to the defeat of the Arab armies by Israel in the 1967 war, the version of Islam to which they subscribe is often a straightforward, even simplistic one. "Fundamentalist" Islam or "Islamism" offers a seductively uncompromising vision. It has the advantage of being readily accessible to the mass of ordinary Muslims through local mosques and networks that respond to disaster by turning "to the past in order to draw from it the strength that the present denies" them.[84] But it is not simply nostalgia for more pious times. Modern Islamism has a pronounced political tinge. By rejecting the present, the "average Muslim" is advocating a radically different agenda.

As the formal Islam of the *ummah* came into contact with the allegedly "un-Islamic" regimes of modern Muslim nation-states in the twentieth century, a radical religious-political movement emerged that seeks to return to a more authentic form of the religion. The "heightening of Islamic consciousness" has been characterized as "revivalism, rebirth, puritanism, fundamentalism, reassertion, awakening, reformism, resurgence, renewal, renaissance, revitalization, militancy, activism, millenarianism, messianism, return to Islam, and the march of Islam."[85] "Islamic revivalism," according to Moghissi, "is not a new phenomenon."[86] Nazih Ayubi, however, argues that political Islam *is* "a new invention—it does not represent a 'going back' to any situation that existed in the past or to any theory that was formulated in the past."[87] Indeed, it is a response to modernity and a sign of the tension between Islam and modernity that has not been settled either way.

In John L. Esposito's view, "Islam re-emerged as a potent global force in Muslim politics during the 1970s and 1980s." He refers to a worldwide movement of "Islamic resurgence" in which governments and opposition groups use it to claim legitimacy for their policies and activities.[88] "Neo-Islamic movements" aim "to change their own societies. . . . They regard Islam as a superior, eternal and universal faith and way of life. Thus, the path to liberation of Islamic societies from cultural, social and political domination lies in the return of Muslims to the true values of Islam."[89] However, although it is popular with many Muslims, Islamism is

> frequently portrayed [by the west] as an enraged mass movement engaged in a social uprising which abhors the symbols of the West and Western influence in the Arab world. As it is popularly understood, Islamic fundamentalism is an anti-modern trend that champions a return to an uncivilised age with a social and political order based on despotic rule and barbarian practices.[90]

The rise of political Islam has inhibited many Arab states "from promoting, and even sustaining, women's advance." Some Arab governments adopted state feminism, but it was tokenism and in fact denied women the right to be independent of the state and achieve real change.[91] Our research reveals that this situation is at odds with the aspirations of many Arab citizens, both men and women.

Starting with the 1979 Iranian Revolution, "a succession of dramatic events made the term *Islamic fundamentalism* a part of the West's political, scholarly, and journalistic vocabulary."[92] Many in the west have come to regard it as a threat, particularly after the events of September 11, 2001. Although the revival of Islam represents empowerment and authentic renewal to many Muslims, there has been a tendency in the west to delegitimize the process and to demonize those who adhere to it. The clash of worldviews "has reinforced the Western tendency to see Islamic activism as extremism and fanaticism," a tendency that also does not differentiate between various forms of political Islam.[93]

To further contextualize our discussion on women and Islamic resistance, we will now review the characteristics of "militant" Islam in order to arrive at a working definition. We agree with Ayubi that it is a new invention. It emerged in the latter part of the twentieth century as a powerful force in Muslim politics all over the world.[94] It aims to bring new political practices to what Islamists regard as stale and corrupt ruling regimes in Muslim states and has been accompanied by "an Islamic reawakening in personal life."[95] Beneath the rhetoric of the movement, however, lie more prosaic concerns. People from all classes and backgrounds who have a grudge against the system or feel their aspirations are being thwarted have turned to Islam as a way of expressing their opposition.[96] In response to perceived problems in their public and private lives, many Muslims are adopting what they believe to be more "authentic" solutions. Some are trying to use Islam as a way to address injustice. They treat it as an oppositional tool, a means of registering protest. Inspired by the thoughts and teachings of various scholars or religious leaders, such as Hasan Turabi in Sudan, Ayatollah Khomeini in Iran, and Shaikh Yasin in the Gaza Strip, it is expressing itself through democratic means, such as Hizbullah's presence in Lebanon's parliament, or through violence, as in the actions of the Islamic Salvation Front in Algeria and the transnational "terrorist" organization al-Qaeda. In this context, and building on the discussion of resistance in Chapter 1, it is important to stress that our approach and, more specifically, our definition of "Islamic resistance" throughout this book is based on the overall declared aims and sociopolitical objectives of these movements: on the one hand, resistance by all means, including armed resistance, against any forms of foreign encroachment on their homelands;

and on the other hand, struggle, at least from the female participants' perspective, against all patriarchal forms of religious and social customs. The women we interviewed stressed that their overarching theme is to protect, not threaten, and insisted that the movements they support are neither aggressive nor offensive. In this respect, they are distancing themselves from those movements and groups that openly advocate violence and use unjustified and indiscriminate violence against others, in aims, strategy, and approach.

The development of political Islam has had a contradictory impact on women. The movement—although it is by no means a monolithic one—counts a great many women among its supporters, which raises the question of whether they are attracted to its uncompromising ideology or to its anti-establishment, even revolutionary rhetoric. Generally speaking, however, Islamist movements tend to take a dogmatic approach to the role of women. This may include an idealization of female seclusion (as experienced, for example, by women living under Taliban rule in Afghanistan, by the majority of women in Saudi Arabia, and more recently in Iraq), apart from occasions on which women are permitted to participate in religiously sanctioned activities (as a means of swelling the crowd in antiregime demonstrations, for example). It is important to appreciate why women might willingly seek to become part of what many people, in both the west and the Middle East, view as a reactionary trend. For women, exactly as for men, it springs, one might surmise, from a mixture of frustration with socioeconomic deprivation and a corrupt and unrepresentative government and, at the same time, personal piety with its obligation to follow a more Islamic lifestyle. Valentine M. Moghadam comments on the "surprising activism" displayed by Islamist women. They "staunchly defend the veil as liberation from a preoccupation with beauty, call for the education of women in order that they be more competent in raising 'committed Muslims,' and argue that Shari'a and women's emancipation are compatible."[97]

Many women have benefited from the upsurge of Islamic activism in a number of Middle Eastern countries, in the sense that they have not been altogether comfortable with the aggressively westernizing approach of some regimes. Most Arab women have no desire to become inadequate imitations of western women, whom they regard as far from liberated in many respects. A young woman in Beirut, for example, described how she used to leave her home dressed in western attire and, as soon as she was out of sight of her parents, change into the all-enveloping Islamic garb she had come to prefer; she was forced to practice such subterfuge, she explained, because her mother, who had grown up in the "enlightened" Lebanon of the 1960s and 1970s, would not have approved of a "fundamentalist" daughter.[98] This woman, together with many other women and men in Lebanon, Iraq, Palestine, and elsewhere in the Arab world, is actively seeking a more "comfortable," a more respectful alternative. Protest that is approved by religion may be considered safer and more legitimate. It is also regarded, particularly in Lebanon, as being more effective.

According to many male purveyors of militant Islam, woman occupies a central and very special position. References to her role, confusingly, are expressed in terms both active and passive. She remains the receptacle of honor, the lynchpin of the family, the giver of life and preserver of continuity. At the same time, however, against "the onslaught of . . . hostile armies without and within, the fundamentalists see the Muslim woman . . . as a soldier fighting a holy war for the sake of Islamic values."[99] Women are expected to be both protectors of fragile manhood and holy warriors, roles with clear militaristic overtones. There is a risk here of confusion caused, on the one hand, by the "breakdown of the moral universe" and women's quest for a more meaningful order and, on the other, by men's dependence on them as unsullied moral symbols.[100]

The precursor of the modern Islamist movement, the Muslim Brotherhood (al-Ikhwan al-Muslimin), was founded in Egypt in 1928 by Hassan al-Banna. Al-Banna believed, like many thinkers then and now, that "the secret of Muslims' backwardness is their estrangement from the religion, and that the basis of reform should be a return to the precepts and judgements of Islam."[101] Although, in line with the spirit of the times, his movement had a resolutely masculine face, it also developed a female offshoot, the Muslim Sisterhood, which echoed the belief that women's potential could be fully realized within Islam. Egyptian Islamist leader Zaynab al-Ghazali, in her memoir, *Days of My Life*, has written about her experiences in prison after taking part in the Muslim Brothers' alleged plot to assassinate President Gamal Abdul Nasser in 1954. The book "traces out a path that reconciles apparently contradictory prescriptions for Muslim women as opposed to Muslim soldiers by making them mutually inclusive. The ideal Muslim woman must work out, with God's help, priorities for her life: Should she stay in the kitchen or should she go out into the battlefield?"[102] For female supporters of Hizbullah in Lebanon, Hamas in Palestine, and the Islamist resistance in Iraq, the kitchen has become the battlefield in the sense that the enemy has invaded all areas of public and private life. For Iraqi women in particular, the battle continues, and even after the nominal withdrawal of the occupying forces, women still face daily encroachment into both their private and public lives by militias that are financed and controlled by an illegitimate government.

Some of the Islamist movements established since the early 1970s exhibit a pronounced confrontational streak. Their rhetoric is couched in terms of struggle against the neocolonialist west but also against "rebellious" women. To succeed, they must control the female half of the population. Thus, in the name of "authentic" Islam, women are allotted a position that many observers deem inferior. One could argue that because female inferiority is not mentioned in the Quran, this raises the possibility of an entirely new agenda or, to be precise, a struggle for male dominance. But such arguments need to be examined very carefully in the light of women's own narratives. Many women adopt Islamic dress by choice because it is in tune with their sense of identity and self-expression, because they see it as capable of empowering rather than restricting their aspirations, or, most importantly, because it is a religious obligation.

We are confronted with this contradiction: although women, on the whole, have been excluded from formal politics in the Arab world, they have been permitted, indeed actively encouraged, to participate in national liberation struggles.[103] The discord between expediency and the perfected society is clear. Yet even this may be incorporated into official ideology, as happened in Iran during its war with Iraq in the 1980s, and Algeria beforehand, so that women can be returned to seclusion once the need for their services has disappeared.

Islam, Resistance, and Modernity

Against the backdrop of Islamist ideology and the support it enjoys among Arab populations, any ruling regime that wishes to preserve its power, however enlightened it may be, must exercise caution. Women, who possess very little formal political power, lack the means to influence governmental policy or to mount an effective opposition. Some commentators regard Islamism as a temporary aberration on the way to modernization, but such arguments involve assumptions about modernization and the forms it should take that fail to address the possibility that modernity and progress may come in different forms, some more appropriate for certain societies than others. They also disregard the reality of women's complicity in the Islamist political project.

The study of modern Islamist movements has become somewhat polarized in the wake of the September 11, 2001 attacks against the United States. On one side are those who tend to link all Islamist activism with the terrorism of groups such as al-Qaeda and argue that such violence springs from the lack of democracy in the Middle East. According to this understanding, "Islamic fundamentalists" are "a medieval political party using religion as an attractive shield behind which to hide their real intent."[104] Taking the position that the western narrative is universal, critics seek to brand Islamism as "nothing more than a violent, reactionary and transitory kick against the inevitable advance of modernity."[105] But, for many Muslims, western knowledge and civilization are little more than an extension of colonial practices, whereby western scholars and policymakers continue to impose particular versions of the truth on Muslim societies and particular ways of judging what is good and what is bad. This is "a view of civilization and modernity conceived as singular," as opposed to "the counterview of civilization and modernity as not only plural but also as inherently open to contact, interaction and exchange."[106]

On the other side of the intellectual divide are scholars who believe we need to "open new debates about the many ostensibly religious practices and meanings that are lumped together under the category of political Islam."[107] Alastair Crooke describes this process as the west's need "to refresh its own narrative" and "to step beyond the constraints of its fast-fading 'vision.'"[108] Students of Middle East politics need to explore the possibility that the Islamist "grand narrative of history" directly challenges "the western vision"[109] by questioning "the westernized mindset that sees facts as fixed, given and unalterable."[110] According to this argument, Islamist resistance is transformed into a larger project of resisting western truth claims and rejecting culturalist explanations.

It is very clear that so-called modern civilization has left many Muslims "with a profound sense of alienation and injury."[111] They recognize that, for many in the west, Islam is seen as "incompatible with modernity."[112] However, this view is problematic in two ways. First of all, it assumes that western "progress" is desirable and will naturally be the objective of all societies, but this assumption has become increasingly hollow as western models reveal themselves to be hypocritical and frequently aggressive, which casts doubt on the historical development of the western project of modernization. Islamism is regarded by many Muslims "as a tool for liberating oneself from the universalist claims" of the west.[113] Second, it ascribes a monolithic character to Islamist movements that does not, in reality, exist. For example, the Islamists described by Hind, a student at Sana'a University in Yemen, appear to conform to western stereotypes.

> Islamic movements in Yemen are against modernization; they are against the west and globalization. Indirectly, these movements are tools, used by forces in Yemen. Some of these forces are in the government, which uses Salafi ideology against the opposition. The majority of Yemeni women are indirectly engaged with the concepts of these Islamist movements; they do not officially belong to these movements but they do intellectually and therefore promote the Salafi ideology. The structure is very conservative and male-dominated. There is much illiteracy in Yemen. It pushes women to accept such ideologies. Religion plays a crucial role in forming the ideas of ordinary people. It is easy to relate everything to the Prophet and then people will accept it.[114]

Yet the Islamist movements to which she refers do not represent and are not typical of Islamist movements elsewhere. In Lebanon, while "pious Shi'is made an effort to undermine western standards for defining modern-ness, at the same time, they used those same western standards to claim value as equally modern/civilized as the West."[115] However, as Saba Mahmood argues, if Islamist movements "were disliked before for their social conservatism and their rejection of liberal values (key among them "women's freedom"), their association with terrorism—now almost taken for granted—has served to further reaffirm their status as agents of a dangerous irrationality."[116] Islam and Islamist movements "are identified with violence and religious extremism, leading some to speak of . . . a 'clash of civilizations' between the Muslim world and the West."[117]

The linking of Islamist groups, whether moderate or radical (good or bad), with terrorism has become, as Mahmood notes, "almost taken for granted" since the tragedy of September 11. This linkage ignores the legitimacy of Islamic resistance to occupation forces. In her study of Islamist terrorism, Katerina Dalacoura asks why "terrorist methods" were chosen by Hamas and Hizbullah in their struggle against Israeli invasion and occupation. She concludes that repression and political exclusion offer only a partial explanation. Hamas, she suggests, used such methods to undermine the Oslo Accords, "to enhance its prestige among the Palestinians," and "to get the Israelis to do what it wanted in a situation of power asymmetry."[118] Shmuel Bar agrees that "Islamic terrorism" cannot be attributed solely to political and socioeconomic factors, but emphasizes "the significance of the religious culture in which this phenomenon is rooted and nurtured."[119] As we have noted above, there is a conflation of "terrorist methods" with other forms of resistance against foreign occupation, which have been overlooked in the rush to demonize Islamism as violent and antimodern.

Conclusion

There is a contradiction between feminist discourse and the "cultural authenticity" of Islam that reflects the aspirations of Arab women themselves. Even as many women in the Arab world are working toward a relaxation of rigid social codes, others support a return to "original" Islam as a way of achieving these goals but also rejecting western notions of "modernity." We believe, however, that this debate fails to do justice to the reality of women's lived experiences and does not fully take into account the element of choice. The work of anthropologists has revealed that many Muslim women "lead rich, rewarding and meaningful lives behind the apparent limitations set by segregation and that they wield considerable influence and power."[120]

As discussed in this chapter, "feminism" is a fiercely contested term, and most Muslim women do not see their own liberation solely in terms of an escape from family responsibilities. Iraqi, Palestinian, and Lebanese Shiite women have told us they do not feel oppressed by religion. Indeed, many of them have drawn strength, in personal, spiritual, and public terms, from their Islamic faith. Although many Palestinians, male and female, would disagree that Islam has been a motivating factor in their liberation struggle, it is clearly an important part of everyday life and has increasingly affected the ways in which the struggle is being waged as well as modes of female participation. Similarly, Iraqi women interviewed in both Jordan and Syria held the perception that Islam plays an important role in overall female participation in the resistance to the occupation and its appointed government, although many Iraqis (both men and women) might disagree with this assertion and place less emphasis on the role of religion in the national struggle. Many Shiite women in Lebanon, however, regard Islam as a central component of their participation in the Lebanese civil war and the struggle against Israeli occupation in the south of the country. For them, a closer identification with religion has enhanced their national identity and communal pride.

In order to draw conclusions on the basis of religion, one must take into account the words of the Quran, the codified laws of later centuries, and the present situations in Muslim countries. It is clear that, broadly speaking, Islam improved the status of women and gave them rights that they had not previously enjoyed. That these rights are not always honored can be attributed to human interference rather than divine directives. One would imagine, in the event of violent conflict, that some negotiation might be possible. The evidence we gathered indicates that one of the outcomes of the conflicts in Lebanon, Palestine, and Iraq has been an expanded space for female participation. We are aware that the relationship among women, violence, nationalism, modernity, and Islam is a complex subject: if all these factors are taken into consideration, it is very difficult to adequately present a systematic framework that encompasses all women's experiences. But we are also aware of overarching themes that connect all the resistance and protest movements as regards women's participation in and support of the resistance. For example, according to the women we interviewed, their active involvement has certainly given them some power and leverage and allowed them access to a voice that previously they did not enjoy. It has also made those who control the movements (predominantly men) conscious of women's valuable contributions and thus more susceptible to their demands and aspirations for a greater role both in private and public life, making them a force to be reckoned with.

But what is the nature of this power? One might argue that these women have become more assertive and articulate with respect to their rights and decisions. Very often they speak with confidence and pride of what they achieved in the face of occupation and dispossession: they kept their families together, protected their dignity, helped the needy, maintained the struggle of the nation, headed households, and attended to their families' needs. Some of them mentioned that resisting death and being alive is in itself a great achievement and a form of empowerment.[121] Having said that, one might question the real gain for women in this context; in other words, in what way has this activism empowered women beyond the symbolic recognition achieved? Has their activism been linked to improvements in the legal provisions regulating their social, economic, and political rights? These are valid questions, for there are real concerns that little will change beyond rhetoric and symbolism, especially if we take into consideration some of the elements of resistance to real change, not only within the movements themselves but also in the broader society. We consider these issues in more depth in Chapters 4–6.

Notes

1. Anouar Majid, "The Politics of Feminism in Islam," in Therese Saliba, Carolyn Allen, and Judith A. Howard, eds., *Gender, Politics, and Islam* (Chicago: University of Chicago Press, 2002), 69.

2. On this issue see Yossef Rapoport, *Marriage, Money and Divorce in Medieval Islamic Society* (Cambridge: Cambridge University Press, 2005).

3. Rana Kabbani, "Reclaiming the True Faith for Women," *Guardian*, May 23, 1992. She is quoting Fatima Mernissi, who made this remark after finishing her book, *Women and Islam*.

4. Tahire Kocturk, *A Matter of Honour: Experiences of Turkish Women Immigrants* (London: Zed, 1992), 45.

5. Leila Ahmed, *Women and Gender in Islam* (New Haven, CT: Yale University Press, 1992), 12.

6. Ibid.

7. Ibid., 36–37.

8. Muhammad married Khadijah when he was twenty-five years old and she was a widow of forty. She had employed him to oversee her caravan, which traded between Mecca and Syria (Ahmed, *Women and Gender in Islam*, 42).

9. Ibid.

10. Debbie J. Gerner, "Roles in Transition: The Evolving Position of Women in Arab-Islamic Countries," in Freda Hussain, ed., *Muslim Women* (London: Croom Helm, 1984), 72.

11. Fatima Mernissi, *Women and Islam: An Historical and Theological Enquiry* (Oxford: Basil Blackwell, 1991), ix.

12. Fazlur Rahman, "A Survey of Modernization of Muslim Family Law," *International Journal of Middle East Studies* 2 (1980): 452.

13. Kocturk, *A Matter of Honour*, 45.

14. Kabbani, "Reclaiming the True Faith for Women."

15. Valentine M. Moghadam, *Modernizing Women: Gender and Social Change in the Middle East* (Boulder, CO: Lynne Rienner, 1993), 146.

16. See Khaled Abou El Fadl, *The Great Theft: Wrestling Islam from the Extremists* (New York: Harper One, 2005), 11–25.

17. Emphasis added. Fatima Mernissi, *Islam and Democracy: Fear of the Modern World*, translated by Mary Jo Lakeland (London: Virago, 1993), 3.

18. Ruth Roded, ed., *Women in Islam and the Middle East: A Reader* (London: I. B. Tauris, 1999), 17.

19. Therese Saliba, Carolyn Allen, and Judith A. Howard, "Introduction," in Therese Saliba, Carolyn Allen, and Judith A. Howard, eds., *Gender, Politics, and Islam* (Chicago: University of Chicago Press, 2002), 4.

20. Miriam Cooke, *Women Claim Islam: Creating Islamic Feminism Through Literature* (London: Routledge, 2001), 59.

21. Ibid., 60.

22. Majid, "The Politics of Feminism in Islam," 87.

23. Cooke, *Women Claim Islam*, 60.

24. Haideh Moghissi, *Feminism and Islamic Fundamentalism: The Limits of Postmodern Analysis* (London: Zed, 1999), 126.

25. Ibid., 126.

26. Ibid., 50.

27. Ann Elizabeth Mayer, "Cultural Particularism as a Bar to Women's Rights: Reflections on the Middle Eastern Experience," in Julie Peters and Andre Wolper, eds., *Women's Rights, Human Rights: International Feminist Perspectives* (New York: Routledge, 1995), 176.

28. Ibid., 185.

29. See Quran 33:35 and Quran 16:97.

30. Mernissi, *Women and Islam*.

31. Aisha B. Lemu and Fatima Heeren, *Women in Islam* (Leicester: Islamic Foundation, 1978), 17.

32. Ibid., 19.

33. Ibid., 18.

34. Amira El Azhary Sonbol, "Law and Gender Violence in Ottoman and Modern Egypt," in Amira El Azhary Sonbol, ed., *Women, the Family, and Divorce Laws in Islamic History* (Syracuse, NY: Syracuse University Press, 1996), 9.

35. Rapoport, *Marriage, Money and Divorce in Medieval Islamic Society*.

36. Mernissi, *Women and Islam*, 9.

37. Leila Ahmed, "Early Islam and the Position of Women: The Problem of Interpretation," in Nikki R. Keddie and Beth Baron, eds., *Women in Middle Eastern History: Shifting Boundaries in Sex and Gender* (New Haven, CT: Yale University Press, 1991), 60.

38. Ibid., 61.

39. See Rapoport, *Marriage, Money and Divorce in Medieval Islamic Society*. See also Judith Tucker, *Women, Family, and Gender in Islamic Law* (Cambridge: Cambridge University Press, 2008); Tucker, *Women in Nineteenth-Century Egypt* (Cairo: American University of Cairo, 1986).

40. Moghadam, *Modernizing Women*; Moghadam, *Women, Work, and Economic Reform in the Middle East and North Africa* (Boulder, CO: Lynne Rienner, 1998); Laurie Brand, *Women, the State, and Political Liberalization: Middle Eastern and North African Experiences* (New York: Columbia University Press, 1998).

41. Abou El Fadl, *The Great Theft*, 251.

42. Yousuf al-Qaradawi, "Women and the Islamic Movement," Crescent Life, http://www.crescentlife.com/thisthat/feminist%20muslims/women_and-islamic _movement.htm, accessed April 10, 2007.

43. Ahmed, *Women and Gender in Islam*, 69.

44. See Barbara Freyer Stowasser, "The Status of Women in Early Islam," in Freda Hussein, ed., *Muslim Women* (London: Croom Helm, 1983), 14–15.

45. Ahmed, *Women and Gender in Islam*, 69–70. See also Haifaa Jawad, *The Rights of Women in Islam: An Authentic Approach* (Basingstoke: Macmillan, 1998), 21–23.

46. Roded, *Women in Islam and the Middle East*, 33.

47. Ahmed, *Women and Gender in Islam*, 53.

48. Roded, *Women in Islam and the Middle East*, 34.

49. The word "caliph" means leader of the Muslim community. The "caliph is the successor to the Prophet, the one who takes his place as governor of the faithful" in temporal matters only. See Mernissi, *Islam and Democracy*, 23.

50. This dispute in the early Muslim community over who should succeed the Prophet Muhammad as temporal and spiritual leader divided Islam into the majority Sunni branch, which comprises 90 percent of Muslims, and the minority Shiites, the partisans of Ali, who claim that he and his descendants should rule the realms of Islam and serve as spiritual guides (see Nikki R. Keddie and Juan Ricardo I. Cole, "Introduction," in Juan Ricardo I. Cole and Nikkie R. Keddie, eds., *Shi'ism and Social Protest* (New Haven, CT: Yale University Press, 1986), 1–2.

51. Mernissi, *Women and Islam*, 5.

52. Ahmed, *Women and Gender in Islam*, 61.

53. Ibid.

54. Denise A. Spellberg, "Political Action and Public Example: A'isha and the Battle of the Camel," in Nikki R. Keddie and Beth Baron, eds., *Women in Middle Eastern History: Shifting Boundaries in Sex and Gender* (New Haven, CT: Yale University Press, 1991), 45.

55. Ibid., 49.

56. Ibid., 55.

57. *Khutba* is a speech or sermon delivered at Friday prayers. Fatima Mernissi, *The Forgotten Queens of Islam,* translated by Mary Jo Lakeland (Cambridge: Polity, 1993), 115.

58. Yvonne Yazbeck Haddad, "Islam and Gender," in Yvonne Yazbeck Haddad, Byron Haines, and Ellison Findly, eds., *The Islamic Impact* (Syracuse, NY: Syracuse University Press, 1984), 17.

59. See, for example, Ahmed, *Women and Gender in Islam.*

60. Ali Mazrui, "Islam and the End of History," *American Journal of Islamic Social Sciences* 10, no. 4: 1993.

61. Ahmed, *Women and Gender in Islam*, 103.

62. Wiebke Walther, *Women in Islam: From Medieval to Modern Times* (Princeton: Markus Wiener Publishers, 1993), 123.

63. From Nizam al-Mulk's "The Book of Government," quoted in Roded, *Women in Islam and the Middle East*, 121. Nizam al-Mulk (1018–1092) was the chief vizier of the Seljuk sultans, a Turkish dynasty, for over thirty years. He wrote his "book of rules for kings" in 1091.

64. Nahid Yeganeh and Nikki R. Keddie, "Sexuality and Shi'i Social Protest in Iran," in Juan Ricardo I. Cole and Nikki R. Keddie, eds., *Shi'ism and Social Protest* (New Haven, CT: Yale University Press, 1986), 120.

65. Majid, "The Politics of Feminism in Islam," 68.

66. Thomas Philipp, "Feminism and Nationalist Politics in Egypt," in Lois Beck and Nikki Keddie, eds., *Women in the Muslim World* (Cambridge, MA: Harvard University Press, 1978), 288.

67. Haifa Zangana, *City of Widows: An Iraqi Woman's Account of War and Resistance* (New York: Seven Stories, 2007), 8.

68. Cherifa Bouatta, "Feminine Militancy: *Moudjahidates* During and After the Algerian War," in Valentine M. Moghadam, ed., *Gender and National Identity: Women and Politics in Muslim Society*, published for the United Nations University World Institute for Development Economics Research (London: Zed, 1994), 19.

69. Mernissi, *Islam and Democracy*, 154.

70. Huda Lutfi, "Manners and Customs of Fourteenth-Century Cairene Women: Female Anarchy Versus Male Shar'i Order in Muslim Prescriptive Treatises," in Nikki R. Keddie and Beth Baron, eds., *Women in Middle Eastern History: Shifting Boundaries in Sex and Gender* (New Haven, CT: Yale University Press, 1991), 101.

71. Kocturk, *A Matter of Honour*, 16.

72. Daryush Shayegan, *Cultural Schizophrenia: Islamic Societies Confronting the West* (London: Saqi, 1992), 91.

73. Akbar S. Ahmed, *Discovering Islam: Making Sense of Muslim History and Society* (London: Routledge and Kegan Paul, 1988), 185.

74. Ibid.

75. Ibid.

76. Jamal J. Nasir, *The Status of Women Under Islamic Law,* 2nd ed. (London: Graham and Trotman, 1994), 1.

77. Nazih Ayubi, *Political Islam: Religion and Politics in the Arab World* (London: Routledge, 1991), 40.

78. Barbara Freyer Stowasser, "Liberated Equal or Protected Dependent? Contemporary Religious Paradigms on Women's Status in Islam," *Arab Studies Quarterly* 9, no. 3 (Summer 1987): 280.

79. Moghadam, *Modernizing Women*, 148.

80. Karim el-Gawhary, "An Islamic Women's Liberation Movement? An Interview with Heba Ra'uf Izzat," *Middle East Report*, November–December 1994, 26.

81. Fatima Umar Naseef, *Women in Islam: A Discourse in Rights and Obligations* (Cairo: International Islamic Committee for Woman and Child, 1999), 153.

82. Interview with Shaikh Na'im Kassim, deputy secretary general of Hizbullah, Beirut, Lebanon, September 19, 2002.

83. Personal interview, Amman, Jordan, March 11, 2011.

84. Mernissi, *Women and Islam*, 16.

85. R. Hrair Dekmejian, *Islam in Revolution: Fundamentalism in the Arab World* (Syracuse, NY: Syracuse University Press, 1985), 4.

86. Moghissi, *Feminism and Islamic Fundamentalism*, 66.

87. Ayubi, *Political Islam*, 3.

88. John L. Esposito, *The Islamic Threat: Myth or Reality?* (Oxford: Oxford University Press, 1992), 11.

89. Roded, *Women in Islam and the Middle East*, 16.

90. Beverley Milton-Edwards, *Islamic Politics in Palestine* (London: Tauris Academic Studies, 1996), 2.

91. Margot Badran and Miriam Cooke, "Introduction," in Margot Badran and Miriam Cooke, eds., *Opening the Gates: A Century of Arab Feminist Writing* (London: Virago, 1990), xxi.

92. R. Hrair Dekmejian, "Islamic Revival: Catalysts, Categories, and Consequences," in Shireen T. Hunter, ed., *The Politics of Islamic Revivalism: Diversity and Unity* (Bloomington: Indiana University Press, 1988), 3.

93. Esposito, *The Islamic Threat*, 10.

94. Ibid., 11.

95. Ibid., 12.

96. Shireen T. Hunter, *The Politics of Islamic Revivalism: Diversity and Unity* (Bloomington: Indiana University Press, 1988), x.

97. Moghadam, *Modernizing Women*, 147.

98. Interview, Beirut, Lebanon, June 1993.

99. Stowasser, "Liberated Equal or Protected Dependent?" 277.

100. Moghadam, *Modernizing Women*, 148.

101. Hassan al-Banna, "The Credo of the Muslim Brotherhood," in Anouar Abdel-Malek, ed., *Contemporary Arab Political Thought* (London: Zed, 1983), 46.

102. Cooke, *Women Claim Islam*, 88.

103. Carolyn Fluehr-Lobban, "The Political Mobilization of Women in the Arab World," in Jane I. Smith, ed., *Women in Contemporary Muslim Societies* (London: Associated University Presses, 1980), 236.

104. Tarek Heggy, *The Arab Cocoon: Progress and Modernity in Arab Societies* (London: Valentine Mitchell, 2010), 29.

105. Alastair Crooke, *Resistance: The Essence of the Islamist Revolution* (London: Pluto, 2009), 29.

106. Armando Salvatore, "Tradition and Modernity Within Islamic Civilization and the West," in Muhammad Khalid Masud, Armando Salvatore, and Martin van Bruinessen, eds., *Islam and Modernity: Key Issues and Debates* (Edinburgh: Edinburgh University Press, 2009), 14.

107. Jillian Schwedler, "Studying Political Islam, *International Journal of Middle East Studies* 43, no. 1 (February 2011): 137.

108. Crooke, *Resistance*, 26.

109. Ibid., 28.

110. Ibid., 178.

111. Khaled Abou El Fadl, "Islam and the Theology of Power," *Middle East Report* 221 (Winter 2001), http://www.merip.org/mer/mer221/221_abu_el_fadl .html.

112. John L. Esposito, "Modernizing Islam and Re-Islamization in Global Perspective," in John L. Esposito and Francois Burgat, eds., *Modernizing Islam: Religion in the Public Sphere in Europe and the Middle East* (London: Hurst, 2003), 3.

113. Bjorn Olav Utvik, "The Modernizing Force of Islam," in John L. Esposito and Francois Burgat, eds., *Modernizing Islam: Religion in the Public Sphere in Europe and the Middle East* (London: Hurst, 2003), 49.

114. Interview, Sana'a, Yemen, February 15, 2010.

115. Lara Deeb, *An Enchanted Modern: Gender and Public Piety in Shi'i Lebanon* (Princeton, NJ: Princeton University Press, 2006), 33.

116. Saba Mahmood, "Feminist Theory, Agency, and the Liberatory Subject," in Fereshteh Nouraie-Simone, ed., *On Shifting Ground: Muslim Women in the Global Era* (New York: Feminist Press at the City University of New York, 2005), 111.

117. John L. Esposito, "Islam and Civil Society," in John L. Esposito and Francois Burgat, eds., *Modernizing Islam: Religion in the Public Sphere in Europe and the Middle East* (London: Hurst, 2003), 69. See also Samuel P. Huntington, *The Clash of Civilizations and the Remaking of the World Order* (New York: Touchstone, 1997).

118. Katerina Dalacoura, *Islamist Terrorism and Democracy in the Middle East* (Cambridge: Cambridge University Press, 2011), 94–95.

119. Shmuel Bar, "The Religious Sources of Islamic Terrorism: What the Fatwas Say," *Policy Review* (June–July 2004), Hoover Institution, Stanford University, http://www.hoover.org/publications/policy-review/article/6475, accessed October 6, 2009.

120. Deniz Kandiyoti, "Contemporary Feminist Scholarship and Middle East Studies," in Deniz Kandiyoti, ed., *Gendering the Middle East* (London: I. B. Tauris, 1996), 9.

121. Personal interview, Amman, Jordan, March 11, 2011.

3

Expressions of Resistance:
Women and the Arab Spring

All of us were there, throwing stones, moving dead bodies.
We did everything. There was no difference between men
and women.[1]

At the end of 2010, Mohammad Bouazizi, an impoverished
Tunisian vegetable seller driven to despair by the actions of local police, set
himself alight. Although he himself did not live to see it, his desperate
action would have far-reaching repercussions. Within days, the people of
Tunisia had taken to the streets to demand the overthrow of their autocratic
president, Zine El-Abidine Ben Ali. The Tunisian uprising was swiftly followed by similar actions in Egypt, Yemen, Libya, and Syria. This extraordinary outpouring, dubbed the "Arab spring," took most people inside and
outside the region by surprise. What was also surprising to many was the
wholehearted involvement in the various revolutions of large numbers of
Arab women. For example, women in their hundreds took to the streets to
express their desire for change, used social networking sites to keep the
momentum going, and helped enormously both in charity and medical
needs. When the protests turned into violent confrontations, women put
their lives at risk and defied social norms to continue the struggle. In the
case of Libya, we could argue, women were the initiators of the revolution
when, on February 15, 2011, a group of women protested in front of the
security building in Benghazi against the executions of their sons and husbands in Ben Salim prison.[2] Their actions throw into doubt conventional
images of the "veiled, homebound, uneducated women who need help to
take the first steps towards emancipation."[3] It seemed that, far from being
"homebound" or "uneducated," Arab women in 2011 were capable of providing a convincing example of heroic activism. Their activism was so convincing, in fact, that the US government decided to present Libyan activist

57

Hana al-Habashi with an award that named her one of the ten most courageous women in the world that year.[4] This raises the question of whether, in
the longer term, their participation will translate into enhanced political
power.

Although we cannot hope to fully answer this question at such an early
stage, we attempt in this chapter to contextualize and analyze the recent
revolutionary uprisings in the Arab world (1) through the lens of the rich
and diverse tradition of women's activism; (2) by situating their activism
within the debate on "modernity"; and (3) from the perspective of violent
conflict, which places constraints on women's involvement but can also
create an empowering environment. Novel as women's appearance on the
streets was to some outside observers, their activism is far from new. As
long ago as the late nineteenth and early twentieth centuries, for example,
Egyptian and Palestinian women could be seen protesting with men against
British rule. Similarly Iraqi women were active in the demonstrations that
opposed British control and policies in their country. During one of those
demonstrations, a woman named Zakia Shweliya was shot and killed by the
police, and two others, Souad Khairy and Amida Misri, were arrested and
imprisoned.[5] In the 1950s and 1960s, women in Algeria struggled alongside
men to end the French occupation of their country. More recently, women
in Kuwait fought a battle throughout the 1990s and into the early twenty-
first century to win the right to vote and stand for election. The same thing
can be said of women in Saudi Arabia who, after a long struggle, have
recently managed to gain some political rights (initiated by the king) that
were welcomed by all women's rights observers. All across the Arab world,
women have participated in liberation struggles, civil society organizations,
and other forms of engagement, including feminist activism. By these
actions and their presence in the various Arab revolutions, women are defying "their stereotypes as victims of oppressive patriarchies."[6] They are stak-
ing their claim as citizens in the rapidly evolving democratic experiments
in the Arab world. However, "democracy" is a contested term, and progress
toward democracy, as Marina Ottaway notes,

> depends on the emergence of countervailing forces and organized groups that
> the government cannot ignore and that have to be accommodated in the polit-
> ical system. Simply including women in a hollow political process does noth-
> ing to create such countervailing forces. This does not mean that the promotion
> of equal rights for women has to wait until countervailing forces emerge or
> political institutions that curb the excessive power of the executive are put in
> place. Certainly, the two battles can be waged simultaneously. There should
> be no illusion, however, either that promoting women's rights will lead to
> democracy or that the emergence of institutions of checks and balances will
> automatically solve the problem of equality for women.[7]

One should also be careful not to essentialize Arab women. Their experiences vary widely across the region. In Tunisia, for example, women have been "in the vanguard of protest movements and social change since the drive to gain independence from France of the late 1940s."[8] Government policy since the attainment of independence in 1956 "has prioritized women's emancipation and integration into the economy, and the constitution and civil code have reflected and reinforced that position."[9] Against this background, civil society "played a significant role in laying the ground for the success of state feminism."[10] The same can be said of women in Iraq before the 2003 invasion: they enjoyed the benefit of state feminism, especially under the 1970 constitution and law number 71 (1987), in terms of personal rights and their contribution to the workforce. Yemeni women, although more "constrained by patriarchal social structures and limited in their earning capacities" than those in Tunisia and Iraq (before the invasion), at least play "a token role in contemporary political and economic life," unlike neighboring Saudi Arabia, where women, despite recent improvements, continue to experience significant restrictions on their rights and movement.[11] Nonetheless, throughout the region, women tend to lag significantly behind men in terms of literacy, participation in the workforce, and presence in the political sphere, and there is no doubt that by "failing to improve the status of women, the region is vastly under-utilizing its available human capital and lags behind other regions in competitiveness."[12] Women's exclusion has been defined as a form of gender-based violence.

As we stress throughout this book, women's roles and visibility vary from state to state, but the outcome is often the same: a lack of women in national parliaments and governments, an absence of the female voice in affairs of state.[13] For instance, women in Egypt comprise 60 percent of the population, but their representation in parliament during the Mubarak years was very modest, at only sixty-five female members. After the revolution, female membership is even weaker, at nine members only.[14] In Yemen, according to activist and Nobel Peace Prize winner Tawakkol Karman, women's lack of participation in political life makes it easy to abuse them. If women are not permitted to participate in public life, she remarked, they will suffer violence; a negative public image of women has been created, and therefore, when women become leaders, they have no positive role models. In her view, a more positive role model has been that of the women participating in sit-ins and street demonstrations: "many people have been amazed to see this."[15] Karman is correct about the importance of positive female role models; she herself provided an inspiring example of female activism by camping out in the center of the Yemeni capital Sana'a in 2011 to call for the overthrow of the country's president, Ali Abdullah Saleh. In response, the president "scolded women for 'inappropriately' mixing in public with men at the huge demonstrations then being staged."[16] As a result of comments like these, many women, in Yemen and elsewhere, have been nervous about appearing in the public space for fear of social disapproval or even physical violence. Although the constitutions of many Arab states have enshrined gender equality, the reality is frequently very different; cultural attitudes encourage female modesty and dependence. In this regard, one can refer to an incident that took place during a public celebratory meeting when the head of the transitional council, Abdul al-Jaleel, insisted that the presenter who was a woman should wear a scarf before she could initiate the program.[17] In some cases, women are verbally and physically abused by men if they venture into public space. For example, these days one can easily hear in the streets of some Arab capitals young men reproaching women for being in public but not dressed modestly. "What have you done with yourself?" shouted one young man at a young girl "un-Islamically dressed" while walking down Sharif Street in Cairo.[18] During the 2011 protests in Syria, a young woman in Damascus "said that men were afraid for the safety of their women. 'Since the start there has been live fire and men are afraid their mothers and sisters may be injured,' she said. She added that a lot of protests came out of the mosques, which are still largely male preserves. 'Many younger women are going out . . . but I think some women don't yet realize how crucial their participation is.'"[19] Even in "normal" times, the political domain is considered to be "not a safe and secure place for women's participation."[20] In the "abnormal" times of revolution, civil unrest, or foreign occupation, women are even less likely to claim a public role.

Women's Activism in the Arab World

There is argument to be made that, on the one hand, many Arab women have long felt entitled to participate in active resistance to various forms of oppression and, on the other, that their efforts have been supported by Islam as a tool of activism, which has provided respectability and motivation. The experiences of women in Yemen provide an illuminating example. Yemen "has a complex social structure based on ascribed status, which affects women more than men in daily life."[21] Women suffer from greater illiteracy and less mobility than men. Since the unification of north and south Yemen in 1990, the country has experienced various forms of violence and insecurity, which has inevitably affected women's position in the society; there have also been moves toward a more conservative version of Islam. Women complain of violence in their daily lives, for example, the imposition of marriage partners and prevention of education. According to Nabila in

Sana'a, some men use Islam to violate women's rights, because of their lack of knowledge about the religion rather than religion itself.[22] Hind added that women are brought up to believe men have the final word and that is why they accept what their fathers and husbands say.[23] However, Fawzia argued that, although there is "a threat of Talibanization" in Yemen, some of the Islamist groups recognize that women play an important role and, therefore, they try to use women: a "pro-women discourse has emerged," she suggested, "that does not conflict with the ideology of these groups." There is resistance to perceived western hegemony: most Yemenis do not welcome the imposition of western values. Activist women are aware of this and frame their demands within an Islamic discourse. As a result, women are becoming more prominent in the Yemeni Islamist party Islah and are fighting for greater representation in the decisionmaking process.[24] The pro-women Islamic discourse is being played out, as well, elsewhere. As we see in subsequent chapters, female supporters of the resistance movements interviewed for the three case studies are using the discourse of Islam to resist not only perceived western hegemony but also the policies of the occupation forces in their countries.

This kind of activism, within the bounds of Islamic propriety, has been defined as a form of feminism. The new "Islamic feminists" are "collapsing the opposition between modernity and Islam, secular and Islamic feminism, and feminism and cultural authenticity."[25] Azza Karam suggests that "there are diverse forms of feminism and multiple expressions for the activism advocated, which correspond to the types of oppression women perceive in different parts of the world."[26] Particularly appropriate are "postmodern conceptualizations of feminism," which adopt theoretical approaches "attuned to the cultural specificity of different societies and periods and to that of different groups within societies and periods."[27] Although we are sensitive to "cultural specificity" and unwilling to make too broad of a generalization, we also recognize that many Arab women have found an expression for their activism through Islam. In addition, although the current revolutionary movements are not explicitly "Islamic" in character but rather more broadly reformist, many women have gained experience and self-confidence through previous organizing within an Islamic framework. This, we argue, as in the Yemeni example, is a form of resistance. Clearly, there is a conflict between the growing confidence and commitment of large numbers of Arab women, who want to see change in their societies and have been empowered by Islamic activism to pursue such change, and the various traditions, cultural norms, and prohibitions that prevent women in some Arab states from playing a more active role. We should also not be too hasty in drawing conclusions. The Arab revolutions are ongoing, and the outcomes in the various states are likely to be uneven.

The debate about women in Arab-Muslim society, as we argue, is inextricably bound up with contested notions of modernity. Until 2011, there had been a tendency to regard the Arabs as "the quintessential Other, lagging behind modernity and its countless rewards."[28] Since the 1980s, the cultural imperialism of the west has provoked a reaction across the Muslim world, broadly termed "Islamic resurgence" or "revival," elements of which are addressing questions of what constitutes a modern society that does not embrace the dubious values of the west. As long ago as the early twentieth century, Egyptian thinker Muhammad Abduh argued that "Islam, properly understood, is adequately suited to modern needs."[29] But proper understandings of Islam and of "modern needs" are subjects of intense debate. It is not easy to detach the Arab world's experiences of European colonialism from notions of natural or indigenous development. How readily did the new indigenous elites embrace the authoritarian model bequeathed to them by colonialism? To what extent did foreign interference distort an otherwise modernizing Islamic model? Is it even possible to argue that this model of Islamic resistance has been appropriated by some women to participate in the Arab revolutions of 2011?

In the context of our discussion of Islam and resistance, two versions of modernity may be considered in relation to women, the first based on a generalized overview, originally set out in the 2002 *Arab Human Development Report*, which argued that "the deficit in women's empowerment was not simply a problem of justice and equity, but a major cause of the Arab world's backwardness"[30]; and another model, which Lara Deeb describes as the "pious modern in contrast to notions of modern-ness as involving secularization and women's 'emancipation.'"[31] Although these versions may appear to conflict, they are both partially responsible for Arab women's current ambiguous status: in formal terms, women tend to be excluded from the public sphere, but their participation in an increasingly popular "Islamic discourse," as Fawzia in Yemen observed, has provided a legitimate space for female participation. In the most optimistic scenario, the revolutions of 2011 will create a synthesis, thus releasing women's potential and moving Arab societies in a more genuinely egalitarian direction.

The question of women's agency is a key factor, of course, and there are a number of interesting recent studies that describe how some women in the Arab world are taking matters into their own hands: Connie Caroe Christiansen's work on young Muslim women in Morocco, Saba Mahmood's investigation of the women's mosque movement in Cairo, Lara Deeb's fascinating research on pious Shiite women and modernity in Lebanon, a study by Souhayr Belhassen of Islamist women in Tunisia, and the current research by Elisabeth Bergner on Islamic women in Syria.[32] These accounts of women's activism and subjectivity within the framework of religion challenge the western stereotype of the Muslim woman as oppressed and disempowered. They also raise the question of whether this new visibility extends to acts of Islamic resistance, including violence against the enemy and oneself, which we discuss more fully in subsequent chapters.

Arab Women and Violent Conflict

On March 9, fed up with the slow pace of reform, protesters returned to Tahrir Square to restate their calls for freedom, justice and equality. The army broke up the demonstration and arrested scores of demonstrators, including at least 18 women. While held they were beaten, threatened with charges of prostitution and forced to submit to "virginity checks." At first the army denied that the checks had taken place. In May, however, a senior general admitted it had been done so that the women would not later claim that they had been raped by soldiers. "The girls who were detained were not like your daughter or mine," he explained. "These were girls who had camped out in tents with male protesters in Tahrir Square."[33]

Women's participation in the revolutionary uprisings of 2011, which have sometimes included significant amounts of violence, raises a number of questions within the wider debate on women and conflict. Through their involvement in war, women very often become the victims of war, as the quotation above vividly illustrates. A "patriarchal brotherhood," as S. Zajovic observes, "demonstrates its 'male strength' through war," and this sometimes includes the sexual assault of women.[34] There are parallels between "constructions of masculinity, patriotism and violence" and constructions of women as "other."[35] In any discussion of the effects of violence against women in the context of conflict, there are three relevant factors to consider: (1) the "ideology of women's essential difference from men, of women as peacekeepers and homemakers"[36]; (2) the additional burden placed on women by the practice of domestic and other forms of intimate violence; and (3) cultural considerations such as traditional and religious practices. Although "women and girls share experiences with men and boys during armed conflict, the culture of violence and discrimination against women and girls that exists during peace times is often exacerbated during conflict and negatively affects women's ability to participate in peace processes and ultimately inhibits the attainment of lasting peace."[37]

This dismissal of women despite their participation in conflict can already be observed in some of the scenarios emerging from the Arab spring in which, despite a commitment to revolutionary change, some of the old patriarchal attitudes persist. For example, women in all the countries where changes took place have been deliberately marginalized from the political process: "I risked my life and my family to liberate Libya, but there has been no wide involvement of women in the political process as we were promised," says Hana al-Habashi.[38] What complicates the situation in Libya is the lack of civil institutions to protect and advance women's rights; tribal customs still dominate. The same has happened in other Arab spring countries such as Egypt (mentioned earlier) and Yemen, where 80 percent of women feel that their lives have worsened despite their participation in the revolution and the promise of a larger role in the public arena.[39] Similarly, in Tunisia, a debate continues about section 28 of the new constitution, which concerns citizenship and the relationship between men and women, that is, whether a woman is equal to a man or complements him.[40] Although the acknowledgment that "gender perspectives" can no longer be disregarded is a welcome one, violent conflict continues to discourage active female participation. We have been able to observe this phenomenon in the Arab uprisings: on the one hand, excessive violence has caused many women to retreat from the public sphere for their own safety, as in Syria and Libya; and, on the other hand, violence has occasionally been directed at women, in terms of bodily harm or damage to reputation, as the Egyptian general's comment implies. Our mention of these events may give the impression that women in predominantly Muslim societies are more victimized and marginalized than women caught up in conflict elsewhere, but that is not our intent; on the contrary, we seek to identify links and commonalities between the engagement of women in the current Arab revolutions, which we define as "conflict zones," and the experiences of women who choose or are forced to take part in civil wars, anticolonial struggles, and national liberation movements all over the world.

At the same time, women's own attitudes toward their problematic presence in conflict and men's reluctance to recognize that presence are changing. In the wake of the Tunisian revolution, Khadija Cherif, a university professor, remarked that the "women's role has been huge, not just in the revolution, but for years before it. . . . That role must now be recognized through gender equality on the political landscape."[41] Such sentiments have been expressed before. In the wake of the Algerian war of independence, for example, in which women played a significant and heroic role in the violent struggle to end French control, they were forced back into their homes, regarded as little more than passive symbols of a triumphant Arab Algerian nation. The same pattern occurred in Iraq in the aftermath of the Iran-Iraq War: women played a crucial role in keeping the country functioning properly while men were in the war zone, but when the conflict ended, they were encouraged to go back home and allow men to take their jobs. It is unlikely that Tunisian women will suffer a similar fate. Following the first postrevolution election, their rights are being enshrined in legislation.

The marginalization of women from both the waging of conflict and the construction of peace can be explained by a number of factors: (1) the generally brutal nature of conflict and the motivating characteristics of nationalist struggle; (2) traditional gender hierarchies, which tend to exclude women from decisionmaking; (3) religious constructs that place barriers in the way of female participation; (4) facts on the ground, such as the protection of children, that often make the involvement of women impractical; and (5) women themselves, who very often do not help or vote for each other. When women are active in politics, very often they advocate the interests of their party rather than women's interests as such. Women's absence is also a result of constructions of masculinity and femininity in certain societies and, in particular, results from the actions taken by "those institutions which are crucially responsible for the production of masculine identity."[42] Some of the women and men in these societies believe that biological difference plays a role in the construction of identity, and it is certainly the case that "life-damaging gender difference[s] must be challenged by addressing the culture of masculinity that sustains them. How men and women behave is socially shaped. Popular understandings of masculine characteristics play up biology. Testosterone, the male hormone, the 'metaphor of manhood,' is portrayed as driving men inexorably toward aggressive behaviour."[43] In the specific case of the Middle East, Julie Peteet argues that Arab masculinity "is acquired, verified and played out in the brave deed, in risk-taking, and in expressions of fearlessness and assertiveness."[44] To be a real man "is to be ready to fight and, ultimately, to kill and to die."[45] For example, as we will argue, one of the objectives of modern Palestinian guerrilla action was "to revitalize Palestinian identity,"[46] which suggests a link between identity and militancy. This link is being played out in the Arab revolutionary movements as well.

Largely excluded from playing a military role, most Arab women have traditionally had little option but to internalize the conventions of Arab-Muslim society and to operate within its parameters. They have tended to focus on what are generally regarded as "smaller" concerns, such as home, family, and the preservation of society. Although these provided a degree of protection and permitted some women to engage in certain previously unfamiliar activities, they still tended to restrict most women's freedom to maneuver and reinforced existing gender hierarchies. As a result, as men sought to prove their manhood through participation in war, women usually remained on the sidelines as grieving widows, the mothers of martyrs, or the innocent victims of a merciless enemy. In short, men's and women's expectations, and also the positions they occupied, tended to be asymmetrical. Although it may be the case that the majority of Arab women have been constrained by violence and traditional practices from playing a significant role in either the waging of conflict or in the postconflict phase, there is also an argument to be made in the opposite direction. First, women's actual experiences throw such claims into question—they have been involved at all stages, from civil society organizing to military combat. Second, the revolutions of 2011 have presented women with more explicit opportunities for nontraditional forms of behavior. Evidence reveals that many of these women were not merely victims or helpless bystanders but also agents. In an environment of upheaval and uncertainty, many found appropriate strategies to counter the pressures of conflict and to survive. The evidence of their constructive involvement casts doubt both on allegedly "male" modes of conflict resolution and the stale image of the Arab Muslim woman as a silenced, oppressed being. It leads us to conclude that the voices and activities of women may be capable of contributing to more durable solutions to the current crises in the Middle East. We explore this argument in greater depth in Chapters 4–6.

New Challenges to Old Patterns

> There is "a strong misogynist streak in Arab society: a kind of fear and dislike [of women] existing alongside respect and admiration."[47]

The various scenarios being played out in the countries of the Arab spring highlight constructions of masculinity and femininity. Although men "are taught to have a stake in the military's essence—combat"—as a validation of their own male "essence" and tend to control the policies that lead to war or civil unrest, as well as the armies and weapons that make wars, women are more likely to be associated with peace, harmony, and domesticity.[48] Akbar Ahmed has pointed out that it "is no coincidence that the *dramatis personae* on the world stage after September 11 are mainly male."[49] He suggests that "the dangerously ambiguous notion of honor—and the even more dangerous idea of the loss of honor—propels men to violence."[50] But one could argue that the male practice of war making and even glorification of war and the celebration of heroism are regarded by many as problematic and that the linkage of men with war and women with peace is somewhat simplistic. For example, Palestinians have not made a direct linkage between war-making activities and manhood. Rather, "Palestinian masculinity references abilities to protect, defend and sustain home and family, whether this protection demands militancy or social astuteness. . . . In fact, among Palestinians, the space of combat and violence was not defined as exclusively male."[51] On the other hand, as Yezid Sayigh points out, the system of political management developed by the Palestinian leadership was "male-dominated, in many ways patriarchal."[52] This style of managing public affairs can be observed throughout the Arab world.

To be in a position to "resist" war or oppression or military occupation is to possess not simply courage but the luxury of making choices. For many Arab women—and very often men too—such choices have not previously been available. The assumption that women are absent from the battlefield also ignores the more complex realities of modern conflict in particular societies and the extension of the "battlefield" into all areas of life, which has meant that resistance is no longer a "choice" or a "luxury," and women are finding ways to respond, and they are doing so in ways that both challenge and embrace tradition. One method of resistance involves dress. Although the Islamic headscarf is associated "with passivity, submissiveness, and segregation," among the new generation of Arab women strugglers, "the majority choose to wear the hijab. Urbanized and educated, they are no less confident or charismatic than their unveiled sisters. They are an expression of the complex interplay of Muslim culture, with processes of modernization and globalization being the hallmark of contemporary Arab society."[53] Their decision highlights the Islamic framework in which their struggles have been unfolding and the confidence it has bestowed on many women.

One of the consequences of war is the destruction of the familiar. If old attitudes disappear in the process, that might indicate the possibility of a radical reappraisal of women's roles. In practice, however, wars and revolutions are more likely to produce another version of the old order, although under a new leader or a revised set of rules. For women, therefore, violence is nearly always solely destructive since it is rarely capable of transforming their lives. Nonetheless, the Arab revolutions of 2011, in the early stages at least, seemed to offer a tantalizing possibility of genuine change. Not only are they "shaking the structure of tyranny to the core," they are also "shattering many of the myths about the Arab region that have been accumulating for decades. Topping the list of dominant myths are those of Arab women as caged in, silenced and invisible."[54] This phase of Arab women's activism can be conceptualized in terms of resistance; many women have been empowered by the nontraditional opportunities presented by the 2011 revolutions, even if they were not overtly Islamic revolutions. At the same time, elements of conservatism remain. Even if women's role may indeed be "inscribing a new feminism," the habit of sexualizing female activism is hard to shake off. According to one Egyptian woman, "the men were keen for me to be here when we were demanding that Mubarak should go. But now he has gone, they want me to go home."[55] When the Egyptian parliamentary elections began in November 2011, women were notable by their absence; faced "with the very real possibility of an almost entirely male parliament, many Egyptians are wondering: Were women left behind by the Revolution?"[56] In Libya, too, they "smuggled bullets in handbags, tended wounded fighters, cooked meals for frontline units, sold their jewellery to buy combat jeeps and sewed the flags that fly in liberated cities. But with the overthrow of Muammar Gaddafi almost complete, many Libyan women are asking whether it's their revolution too."[57] It is still too early to claim with any certainty that the revolutions have been "anti-women" or "pro-women"; they contain elements of both. The danger may be an overreliance on familiar methods of control and the habit, in times of insecurity, to blame "unruly" women.

In order to gain a clearer understanding of Arab women's participation in violent conflict and the effects it has on their rights and entitlements, we now turn to three case studies of situations in which women have practiced active resistance against oppression and occupation. Iraqi, Lebanese Shiite, and Palestinian women have struggled alongside men against the violence in their countries in the late twentieth and early twenty-first centuries, and they have relied on Islam as a tool of protection and empowerment.

Notes

1. Egyptian activist Asmaa Mahfouz, quoted in the *Economist*, "Now Is the Time: Women and the Arab Awakening," October 15, 2011.
2. Al Jazeera Arabic, May 12, 2012.
3. Marina Ottaway, "The Limits of Women's Rights," in Thomas Carothers and Marina Ottaway, eds., *Uncharted Journey: Promoting Democracy in the Middle East* (Washington, DC: Carnegie Endowment for International Peace, 2005).
4. Al Jazeera Arabic, May 12, 2012.
5. Haifa Zangana, *City of Widows: An Iraqi Woman's Account of War and Resistance* (New York: Seven Stories Press, 2007), 36.
6. *Economist*, "Now Is the Time."
7. Marina Ottaway, "Women's Rights and Democracy in the Arab World," Carnegie Papers, No. 42 (Washington, DC: Carnegie Endowment for International Peace, February 2004), 7.
8. Juan Cole and Shahin Cole, "An Arab Spring for Women," *Nation*, April 26, 2011.
9. Valentine M. Moghadam, *Modernizing Women: Gender and Social Change in the Middle East*, 3rd ed. (Boulder: Lynne Rienner, 2013), 44.
10. Nicola Pratt, *Democracy and Authoritarianism in the Arab World* (Boulder, CO: Lynne Rienner, 2007), 56.
11. Sheila Carapico, "Women and Public Participation in Yemen," in Suha Sabbagh, ed., *Arab Women: Between Defiance and Restraint* (New York: Olive Branch, 1996), 62.
12. Dona J. Stewart, *The Middle East Today: Political, Geographical and Cultural Perspectives* (London: Routledge, 2009), 147.
13. According to statistics compiled by the Inter-Parliamentary Union, the representation of women in national parliaments in the Arab states, at 10.5 percent, is the lowest in the world.

14. News Night, February 13, 2012.

15. Interview, Sana'a, Yemen, February 17, 2010.

16. Cole and Cole, "An Arab Spring for Women."

17. Al Jazeera, August 20, 2012.

18. Research work, Cairo, June 2012.

19. Xan Rice, Katherine Marsh, Tom Finn, Harriet Sherwood, Angelique Christafis, and Robert Booth, "Women Have Emerged as Key Players in the Arab Spring," *Guardian*, April 22, 2011.

20. UNIFEM Report.

21. Helen Lackner, "Women and Development in the Republic of Yemen," in Nabil F. Khoury and Valentine M. Moghadam, eds., *Gender and Development in the Arab World* (London: Zed, 1995), 76.

22. Interview, Sana'a, Yemen, February 20, 2010.

23. Interview, Sana'a, Yemen, February 20, 2010.

24. Interview, Sana'a, Yemen, February 21, 2010.

25. Zohreh T. Sullivan, "Eluding the Feminist, Overthrowing the Modern? Transformation in Twentieth-Century Iran," in Lila Abu-Lughod, ed., *Remaking Women: Feminism and Modernity in the Middle East* (Princeton, NJ: Princeton University Press, 1998), 236.

26. Azza M. Karam, *Women, Islamisms, and the State: Contemporary Feminisms in Egypt* (Basingstoke: Macmillan, 1998), 8.

27. Linda J. Nicholson and Nancy Fraser, "Social Criticism Without Philosophy: An Encounter Between Feminism and Postmodernism," in Linda J. Nicholson, ed., *Feminism/Postmodernism* (London: Routledge, 1990), 34.

28. Jean-Pierre Filiu, *The Arab Revolution: Ten Lessons from the Democratic Uprising* (London: Hurst, 2011), 5.

29. William Shepard, "The Diversity of Islamic Thought: Towards a Typology," in Suha Taji-Farouki and Basheer M. Nafa, eds., *Islamic Thought in the Twentieth Century* (London: I. B. Tauris, 2004), 70.

30. Marina Ottaway, "The Limits of Women's Rights," in Thomas Carothers and Marina Ottaway, eds., *Uncharted Journey: Promoting Democracy in the Middle East* (Washington, DC: Carnegie Endowment for International Peace, 2005), 115.

31. Lara Deeb, *An Enchanted Modern: Gender and Public Piety in Shi'i Lebanon* (Princeton, NJ: Princeton University Press, 2006), 32.

32. Connie Carøe Christiansen, "Women's Islamic Activism: Between Self-Practice and Social Reform Efforts," in John L. Esposito and Francois Burgat, eds., *Modernizing Islam: Religion in the Public Sphere in Europe and the Middle East* (London: Hurst, 2003); Saba Mahmood, *Politics of Piety: The Islamic Revival and the Feminist Subject* (Princeton, NJ: Princeton University Press, 2005); Deeb, *An Enchanted Modern*; Elisabeth Bergner, "Post-Islamist Revivalism: Syrian Women and the Da'wa Movement" (unpublished); Souhayr Belhassen, "Femmes tunisiennes islamiste," *Annuaire de l'Afrique du Nord* (Paris: Editions CNRS, 1981), 77–84, quoted in Salwa Ismail, *Rethinking Islamist Politics: Culture, the State, and Islamism* (London: I. B. Tauris, 2006), 143.

33. *Economist*, "Now Is the Time."

34. S. Zajovic, "Cleansing," unpublished paper, Women in Black, Belgrade, 1993.

35. Liz Kelly, "Wars Against Women: Sexual Violence, Sexual Politics, and the Militarised State," in Susie Jacobs, Ruth Jacobson, and Jennifer Marchbank, eds., *States of Conflict: Gender, Violence, and Resistance* (London: Zed, 2000), 53.

36. Lyne Segal, *Is the Future Female? Troubled Thoughts on Contemporary Feminism* (London: Virago, 1987), 175.

37. United Nations, *Women, Peace, and Security: Study Submitted to the Secretary-General Pursuant to Security Council Resolution 1325 (2000)*, New York, 2002.

38. Al Jazeera, May 12, 2012.

39. Al Jazeera, September 24, 2012.

40. Al Jazeera, August 13, 2012.

41. Rice et al., "Women Have Emerged as Key Players in the Arab Spring."

42. Deniz Kandiyoti, "The Paradoxes of Masculinity: Some Thoughts on Segregated Societies," in A. Cornwall and N. Lindesfarme, eds., *Dislocating Masculinity: Comparative Ethnographies* (London: Routledge, 1994), 19.

43. Cynthia Cockburn and Ann Oakley, "The Culture of Masculinity Costs All Too Much to Ignore," *Guardian*, November 25, 2011.

44. Julie Peteet, "Male Gender and Rituals of Resistance in the Palestinian Intifada: A Cultural Politics of Violence," in Mai Ghoussoub and Emma Sinclair-Webb, eds., *Imagined Masculinities: Male Identity and Culture in the Modern Middle East* (London: Saqi, 2000), 107.

45. Cynthia Cockburn, "The Gendered Dynamics of Armed Conflict and Political Violence," in Caroline O. N. Moser and Fiona C. Clark, eds., *Victims, Perpetrators, or Actors? Gender, Armed Conflict, and Political Violence* (London: Zed, 2001), 20.

46. Rex Brynen, "PLO Policy in Lebanon: Legacies and Lessons," *Journal of Palestine Studies* 18, no. 2 (Winter 1989): 58.

47. Edward W. Said, in a conversation with Salman Rushdie on Palestinian identity in 1986, *The Politics of Dispossession: The Struggle for Palestinian Self-Determination, 1969–1994* (London: Vintage, 1995), 120.

48. Cynthia Enloe, *Does Khaki Become You? The Militarization of Women's Lives* (London: Pandora, 1988 [1983]), 15.

49. Akbar S. Ahmed, *Islam Under Siege: Living Dangerously in a Post-Honor World* (Cambridge: Polity, 2003), 16.

50. Ibid., 14–15.

51. Julie Peteet, "Icons and Militants: Mothering in the Danger Zone," in Therese Sabiba, Carolyn Allen, and Judith A. Howard, eds., *Gender, Politics, and Islam* (Chicago: University of Chicago Press, 2002), 137.

52. Yezid Sayigh, "War as Leveler, War as Midwife: Palestinian Political Institutions, Nationalism, and Society Since 1948," in Steven Heydemann, ed., *War, Institutions, and Social Change in the Middle East* (Berkeley: University of California Press, 2000), 216.

53. Soumaya Ghannoushi, "Rebellion: Smashing Stereotypes of Arab Women," Al Jazeera, April 25, 2011, http://english.aljazeera.net/indepth/opinion/2011/04/201142412303319807.html, accessed October 18, 2011.

54. Ibid.

55. Quoted by Catherine Ashton, "Women Are Essential to Democracy," *Guardian*, April 23, 2011.

56. Posted by Mara Revkin, "Has Egypt's Revolution Left Women Behind?" December 8, 2011.

57. *Guardian*, September 17, 2011.

4

Islam and Revolution:
Shiite Women in Lebanon

In what has been described as a "month of madness," in July–August 2006,[1] the Israeli army launched a devastating attack on Lebanon, killing over 1,000 civilians, displacing nearly 1 million from their homes, and flattening entire villages and neighborhoods.[2] The Islamic resistance movement Hizbullah responded by firing missiles into northern Israel, causing widespread panic. The outcome of the conflagration, although inconclusive, was perceived by many Arabs and Muslims as a victory for Hizbullah, thus transforming it into one of the most popular organizations in the Arab world, and bolstering its already formidable reputation for ending the Israeli occupation of southern Lebanon in May 2000. But members of Hizbullah are also controversial, regarded by some as "heroic liberators" and by others as "terrorists." Since Lebanese citizens identify themselves primarily through sectarianism and space does not permit a thorough analysis of all shades of experience, we have chosen to focus on Shiite women as a way of understanding women's experiences of violent conflict and resistance in Lebanon.[3] Most women—and men too—were undoubtedly victims of the Lebanese civil war and the Israeli invasion and occupation of Lebanon, but they also played other roles. It is on the Shiite women of Lebanon, their experiences of violence, and their strategies for survival that we concentrate in this chapter.

Have women merely "survived" the horrors of war? Or has their experience incorporated a deeper process of empowerment? Shiite women in Lebanon are affected by a number of factors that impinge upon their lives directly or indirectly. Their religion—the minority Shia branch of Islam—circumscribes their behavior in specific ways. In addition, the adversity that frames their lives, caused by intercommunal violence and foreign invasion, has given some of them an opportunity to engage in nontraditional activities. Finally, the presence of "revivalist" or "fundamentalist" Islamic movements in their midst has led some women to reappraise their lives and to make what could be called "revolutionary" choices.

One could argue that the masculine character of the Lebanese war, described by one writer as "this excess of maleness that had taken hold of my city," contributed to a reordering of gender relations.[4] According to this view, long-term violence combined with a renewed and triumphant commitment to sectarian identities has created stark divisions between the sexes. It seems to be the case that, in Lebanon, some men have experienced the possibility of changing their society by their own endeavors, that is, by fighting, hurting others, and being prepared to sacrifice their lives. In the end, the all-or-nothing bid for power failed for all the political and military factions involved, and the people were forced to consider alternative routes, such as compromise, social pacts, a balance of power, and accommodation. More than twenty years after the formal end of the civil war, they are still struggling to create a more equitable political system, and it remains to be seen how successful their efforts will be. Shiites have become increasingly central players in the Lebanese power game. Shiite nationalism in Lebanon was forged under conditions of defiance and adversity. Perceiving themselves as a disadvantaged minority within their own country, Shiites turned to nationalist agitation in order to enhance their position in Lebanese society. In response to Israeli aggression in Lebanon, Shiite nationalism developed particular modes of heroism, as demonstrated in the 2006 "war."

We need to determine, from the perspective of the definitions of resistance articulated in this volume, whether the revolutionary element of Shiism has had a notably liberating effect on Lebanese Shiite women, many of whom claim to identify with their communal resistance movement. Huda, for example, a twenty-three-year-old university student in Beirut, asserted that the Islamic resistance is the "blood that runs in our veins," and others expressed similar sentiments.[5] But how heartfelt is their support? Do they really feel part of "an Islamist community that functions as an experimental model of how a just, equitable and compassionate community of Muslims might still function in a state, Lebanon, that is dominated by western values" and also continues to be framed by strong patriarchal values?[6] Or does their loyalty stem from insecurity or even gratitude? In order to answer these questions, we will contextualize the discussion within a broader understanding of how the Shiites developed their own distinctive brand of resistance, the effect this had on other Lebanese communities, and the obstacles faced by Lebanese women as a group and Shiite women as a subgroup.

We explore in this chapter the theme of how women and men cope with the violence and insecurity of war. For some of the men who fought in the civil war, defeat may have felt humiliating. It removed both meanings and objectives and left an empty space. In the absence of war, there were few opportunities to exercise power and no one left to impress. Having failed to conquer each other, these men must now be content with controlling the "small society" of the family, and within such a determinedly masculine culture, women have little choice but to submit. This is very much in line with women's historical experiences of rulers who associate social order with ever-tighter controls over women. But how do women fit into this scenario of disappointment? Does it apply in the case of Lebanese Shiite women? The evidence revealed by this research casts doubt on the argument that masculine values have triumphed; it suggests, on the contrary, that any "reordering of gender relations" is capable of benefiting women as much as men.

The second theme revolves around the relationship between resurgent Islam and the Lebanese Shiite community. The community has traveled from a position of political marginality and irrelevance in the early days of national independence to its present, more assertive role in the postwar reconstruction of the country during the 1990s and beyond. It has done so by a skillful mixture of force, social programs, and religious piety. Out of their roots as an oppositional movement of the oppressed, the Shiites have created an ideology of resistance and dignity that has served to empower both men and women. But have women been able to derive sufficient benefits from the Islamist vision to compensate for the suffering they have endured as a result of war and occupation? Our research suggests that the black-and white picture of Islamist politics solely as a man's world is far from accurate.

For the Lebanese Shiites, resistance principally involves resisting Israeli aggression against Lebanon and against Muslims in general. Because Israel is defined as a puppet of the United States, the Lebanese see themselves as resisting western hegemonic practices. Women are aware that their own resistance also includes an articulation of their rights and entitlements as women. Even though they have not been able to avoid the violent struggles that have beset their country since the 1970s, including the civil war (1975–1990) and the Israeli occupation of part of their land (1978–2000), they have tended to do so in ways that at first glance seem relatively traditional and uncontroversial. Their scope for maneuvering has been influenced by the growth of militant Islamist groups, a trend that has significantly affected some women, who claim not only to be empowered by it but also to see it as providing a model for a compassionate community of Muslims. They envisage, in other words, an alternative non-western version of modernity, one that respects and enhances indigenous traditions. One should stress, however, that not all Shiite women share these views. Some express disapproval over the confrontational tactics of Islamist parties and would prefer to create a future less defined by sectarian identities; at the same time, they acknowledge the ties of tradition that bind them to family and village. As discussed in Chapter 1, the mechanics of resistance are clear: It is deliberate and self-conscious. Its intention is to repel the invader but also to refuse the hegemonic project of the west.

Although Lebanese sovereignty is not in question, negotiations continue over future political arrangements for the state, especially in the wake of the assassination of former prime minister Rafiq Hariri in 2005. To date, these arrangements have tended to exclude women. The majority of politicians from all confessions are men who have attained status within their communities, and there are few female members of parliament. Hizbullah holds several seats in the national parliament, none of which are occupied by women, although, according to Deputy Secretary-General of Hizbullah Na'im Kassim, there is no reason why a woman, even a Hizbullah woman, should not become a member of parliament.[7] Lebanese women's experiences contrast with those of Iraqi and Palestinian women, who have been participating in their national parliaments for some time. The interesting question, in the context of this book, is what constitutes modernity for Lebanese Shiite women; in this chapter we seek to ascertain the diverse roles played by women, as subjects, in the Islamist "revolution" in Lebanon. We argue that their experiences of resistance have given them a kind of power within the confines of their community and that this is likely to translate into a more inclusive environment for women's participation in the future.

War and Violence in Lebanon

Although small, Lebanon, politically speaking, is a country of enormous diversity and even greater complexity. It is an artificial creation, a remnant of colonial politicking, traditionally part of a larger entity (the Ottoman Empire, Greater Syria, the French Mandate). Its diversity may be regarded as a source of strength, but it did contribute to the weakening of Lebanese civil and political life in the latter part of the twentieth century. Modern Lebanon became the site of competition between mutually exclusive and frequently antagonistic groups. The state, the result of an unwritten National Pact between Christians and Muslims, seemed incapable either of creating an all-encompassing "Lebanese" identity or of satisfying the aspirations of all its citizens.[8] "The principle of fixed proportional sectarian representation, known in Lebanon as confessionalism, applied not only to the highest offices but also extended throughout the political system.[9] The situation was further exacerbated by the presence of large numbers of Palestinian refugees, who arrived in Lebanon after 1948, the various invasions and occupation by Israel, and the interference—some would say "constructive support"—of neighboring Syria.

The lack of a clear Lebanese identity was a stumbling block from the beginning. Ghassan Salame suggests that the rise of the modern state "represents a real challenge to the individual, a challenge to his feeling of belonging to a group and to the security of having a defined place within it."[10] Some Lebanese, he believes, "have felt that they were alien to the Lebanese identity and that this was imposed on them by external powers. . . . Most of the Muslims before 1943 and some Maronites after 1975 think . . . that . . . their attachment to Lebanon is not 'primordial,' is not 'given,' and could consequently be negotiated or even radically repudiated."[11]

As a result of its historical development, Lebanon has had to contend with the problem of sectarian spaces. With an increase in urbanization in the mid-nineteenth century, "Beirut began to assume some of the features associated with confessional segregation."[12] These divisions became entrenched. By the 1930s, the neighborhoods of Beirut had become "the scene of violent clashes between Christian and Muslim gangs, one side brandishing the banner of Lebanism, the other of Arabism."[13] With the arrival of the Palestinian refugees in 1948 and the beginnings of Israeli incursions into the south of the country, there was a movement of displaced people, mainly Palestinians and Lebanese Shiites, to Beirut. The so-called misery belt started to grow on the fringes of the city, contributing to what Samir Khalaf describes as a "burgeoning geography of fear."[14]

The civil war, which started in 1975 and continued for over fifteen years in a bewildering variety of guises and degrees of intensity, is regarded with incomprehension by most people outside Lebanon, and even by many within the country. It has been described as an "explosion of anger, hatred, and fear that penetrated every corner of people's lives,"[15] an "orgy of violence and death."[16] The war was an event so terrible and so utterly and randomly destructive that few seemed able to make sense of it. What they did know was that *danger* engulfed the whole society as the conflict invaded areas of life hitherto regarded as safe, comfortable, and private: "No space could provide shelter against the ubiquity of danger. There was no longer any difference between the experiences of the home and the street."[17] The violence in Lebanon

> was not only relentless, protracted and futile. It also assumed, particularly during the last interludes of civil strife, even more pathological forms: it became random, diffused, and displaced. Unlike other comparable encounters with civil strife, which are often swift and localized and where much of the popu-

lation could remain sheltered from its cruelties, the Lebanese experience has been much more overwhelming and homogenizing. The savagery of violence was also compounded by its indiscriminate, random and reckless character. Hence there is hardly a Lebanese today who could be exempt from some of its atrocities, either directly or vicariously as a mediated experience. Virtually no area of the country has been spared the ravages of war.[18]

Or, as Mai Ghoussoub reflects: "I needed to cross thousands of miles . . . to realise how terribly cruel our cruelty was."[19]

As the conflict proceeded and one atrocity succeeded another, order and any semblance of civil society gradually disappeared. Eventually a situation of anarchy prevailed, in which individuals joined militias, sought the protection of armed groups, locked themselves away in rooms, or left the country altogether. The lone sniper became a figure of romance and heroism to many. Yet, according to Miriam Cooke, "this was not a war of suicide, but a war of survival."[20]

Women's Identity and Resistance

Almost everyone in Lebanon suffered as a result of the war, but it is likely that women suffered more than men. The issue of space, in the sense of male-controlled space or the violation of safe places, is significant here. As war is traditionally—and in most cases exclusively—a male arena, one would assume that women were, on the whole, excluded from it. However, as the violence penetrated many aspects of Lebanese life, women could not avoid being dragged in, whether as accidental victims or willing participants. Roula, a thirty-seven-year-old computer technician in Nabatiyyeh, recalled that, during the Israeli occupation, Israeli snipers used to fire at them every morning as they went to school. It was difficult to travel from her village to Nabatiyyeh, she said, "a bad story every minute"; they even saw blood and intestines in the street.[21] The assumption of female exclusion is, therefore, inaccurate.

Until the 1960s, political "bosses (*zu'ama*) from a handful of powerful families dominated Shi'i politics . . . and maintained their control through extensive patronage networks."[22] Evelyne Accad argues that

> Arab society in general, and Lebanese in particular, has always had pride in the za'im (leader, chief, hero). The za'im is the macho man par excellence. Not only does he embody all the usual masculine values of conquest, domination, competition, fighting, boasting, etc., but also that of *shatara* (cleverness). . . . Za'im and shatara are concepts much valued in tribal society. The Lebanese war has transformed the za'im into the askari (man with the gun, militiaman).[23]

There is a suggestion, supported from evidence from conflict situations elsewhere, that this traditional respect for masculine values was reinforced during the war, adding respectability to men's behavior and consequently belittling traditional "feminine values." But one should question such suppositions; the idea of "masculine values" is fluid and fails to take into account the actions and attitudes of the majority of Lebanese men, who neither chose to join militias nor supported the anarchic environment of war. Interviews conducted in Lebanon revealed the existence of strictly observed gender boundaries that started to dissolve in the face of multiple forms of war and violence.

Many women described what they did and what happened to them during the war. A senior civil servant spoke about working

> with the Higher Relief Committee to provide for displaced people all over Lebanon. I moved between east and west and was exposed to harassment from the militias. I was exposed to bombs. I was arrested for a few hours. But I continued to believe in the unity of Lebanon. The unity of the family was the main support to the unity of the country. It made people able to face war.[24]

The "unity of the family," as she said, provided an impetus for women's empowerment. Safiyya, a Lebanese academic, observed that very often, "women were alone with their children; they were forced to take responsibility and, therefore, became more powerful."[25] This feeling of becoming "more powerful" was frequently mentioned during interviews with Lebanese Shiite women. Maha, who worked as a volunteer during the war, said, "Before, no one could imagine they could survive and bear such a war. But there is something dormant in every person and this comes out when it is needed."[26] Wafa in Beirut recalled that her organization gave aid and food and helped families during the war; after the war, it tried to help women psychologically by holding workshops and working with families and in schools. Women "need help to realize their potential," she said; "a woman is in charge of her family and she tends to forget herself and her own needs."[27] These accounts give us a fascinating insight into the fluidity of gender boundaries and the growth of female agency.

During the war, it was not just men who carried weapons and women who supported them. In some cases, women too resorted to acts of direct violence: In 1988, a woman shot and gravely wounded South Lebanon Army (SLA) leader Antoine Lahd. On April 9, 1985, sixteen-year-old Sana Yusuf Muhaydali targeted a group of Israeli soldiers on the road between Batar and Jazeen in southern Lebanon. She "broke through the ranks of the enemy in a car loaded with 200 kilograms of high explosives. The operation led to large numbers of casualties among the enemy—about 50 killed and injured and the grounding of a number of heavy vehicles."[28] There are less spectacular examples. Umm Abbas in Sidon described how, during the occupation, she attempted to plant a bomb at an Israeli checkpoint; she was not successful but insisted she would do it again if she got the opportunity.[29] However, this sort of direct action is rare among Shiite women. They are more likely to support the male fighters and are praised for giving birth to sons. As Sahar in Baalbek remarked, Shiites "honour the mothers who brought up individuals with the motivation to resist. Islam gave women this power, and now mothers pass on the power to their sons to resist."[30] On the whole, there appears to be no discernible tension between, on the one hand, "becoming more powerful" and gaining the courage to resist and, on the other, taking pride in sustaining traditional roles of motherhood and support.

A "Stigmatized Identity"

> *Within Lebanon, public piety is linked to a general performance of religious identity. . . . For Shi'i Lebanese in particular, this involved embracing and reclaiming what was once—and still is to a certain extent—a stigmatized identity.*[31]

It is clear that the women who remained in southern Lebanon throughout the Israeli occupation faced the most challenging and painful situation. Many of the young men were forced to flee the area for their own safety, whereas women had little choice but to stay. The occupation began in 1978 when Israel entered Lebanon to curb the activities of the Palestinian resistance along its northern border. Although the Israelis eventually withdrew from most of the country, they retained control of a narrow strip of land, extending approximately 20 kilometers (12 miles) into Lebanese territory, enforced by a local proxy, the Christian-led SLA. This was a period of considerable anguish for local villagers, who are mostly Shiite. In response to the determined resistance of Hizbullah in the form of guerrilla warfare following a second Israeli invasion in 1982, the occupation ended in May 2000.

In the highly unstable environment of southern Lebanon since the late 1970s, any attempt to create a better society must have been uneven and circumscribed by various imperatives, such as survival, resistance, and the control of fear. Under such conditions, it is likely that leaders sought relatively straightforward options that relied on the primordial sentiments of the mass of the population. By appealing to Islamic belief, political groups were able to mobilize the community. Local people united in their determination to defend themselves against the invaders. Their resistance was facilitated by the shared values of Islam and exacerbated by poverty and alienation. The Shiite resistance against Israeli aggression in the south from the late 1970s on encouraged an environment of communal solidarity for women as well as men. Shiite political parties used the occupation to mobilize the masses, and to this end, Islam became a powerful weapon of resistance.

Umm Bassam, who lives in the southern Lebanese town of Bint Jbeil, occupied by Israel until 2000, said that her

> impression of the Israelis is of a relationship between subjected and oppressors. Some people, including women, were arrested, especially in the period before the liberation. People felt they were not free psychologically. Women were not able to practice their rights. Everything was restricted, for example hospital treatment. There were many physical restrictions. I was unable to see my brothers for two years. We weren't able to be together as a family during feasts. The whole occupation was bad, but the worst part was just before the liberation. The occupiers did anything they wanted. People had no choice but to cope with this reality. Our only outlet was to talk to each other, but people could only do this if they trusted each other—there were many spies.[32]

Others described this period as "living in terror." Umm Rafiq, a married teacher in Bint Jbeil, said, "We were worried about our families and our children. We were worried that the Israeli army would come to take our children." She added that

> most of the people under occupation lost their rights and lost their freedom of movement and freedom of speech. Israel liked to exercise arbitrary power, such as ordering people to leave their homes, preventing them from going to Beirut. They had to pay money all the time or give up their sons. The only alternative was for people to send their sons away.[33]

As these accounts make clear, women in southern Lebanon experienced the Israeli invasions and occupation as repressive and humiliating. The response of many was to seek consolation in the familiar as a form of resistance, expressed as a determination to withstand adversity. There is a strong element of opposition in Lebanese Shiite practice, and local people were able to draw upon these traditions. Shiite society subscribes to the belief that man

> is a slave of his basic urges and woman is a captive of her love. What causes man to stumble and lose his footing is his basic motivational urges. According to psychologists, woman has more patience and endurance in the control of her passions. However, that which imbalances woman and enslaves her is the sweet voice of affection, sincerity, fidelity and love from man.[34]

Thus, although women and men are regarded as equal in religious terms, "woman is a human being with particular conditions, and man is a human being with other conditions. Man and woman are equal in their being human, but they are two kinds of human being with two kinds of character- istics and two kinds of psychology. . . . Nature had a purpose in these two different conditions."[35] Men and women, in other words, are designed to occupy different "spaces" in the world. Yet, although their functions and their "societies" differ, both deserve equal respect.

Many of the women interviewed stressed the equality of men and women in Islam. These women were knowledgeable about their religion and eager to promote its positive qualities. As Hizbullah member Umm Ghassan remarked, "Islam gave women a very strong role in society. First, they have to learn, to acquire more knowledge. Then, they are allowed to work in the society, to be leaders, to have political views, to participate in every way."[36] This supports the assertion by Sayyid Hasan Nasrallah, secretary-general of Hizbullah, that there is nothing to prevent women from assuming leadership positions.[37] Nabila, who spoke on behalf of the other Shiite party Amal, agreed, saying, "Islam stresses the freedom of all human beings, and this freedom is not in conflict with the freedom of the commu- nity. But it is not a freedom for a woman to do whatever she likes. She must respect her community and herself."[38]

The writings of the late Iranian scholar Ayatollah Murtada Mutahhari on the rights of women in Islam are much respected in the Lebanese Shiite community. He formulated a theory that argues for seeing women's rights in a new light. By illustrating, as he saw it, the flawed and ethnocentric rea- soning behind western philosophy and feminism and the weaknesses of the Universal Declaration of Human Rights, Mutahhari sought to prove that an alternative Islamic model exists. He argued, "despite the fact that Islam acquainted woman with her human rights, gave her individuality, freedom and independence, it never induced her to revolt and mutiny against, or be cynical towards the male sex."[39] This statement echoes Hizbullah's argu- ment that there are "huge differences between the western and the Islamic universal view. In western thought, politics and governance are regarded as 'ends.' In Islam, however, it is quite the opposite: it is politics which is at the service of spreading human values and ethics."[40]

Lebanese Shiite women frequently refer to the heroic female figures of Shiite history. For example, the Prophet Muhammad's first wife, Khadijah, is celebrated as being both the first to embrace the new religion and a pillar of strength and reassurance to the Prophet until her death. Muhammad's daughter, Fatima, who was married to Ali, the first Shiite imam, is also held in great esteem as the archetypal good wife and mother and an exemplary role model for all Muslim women. Fatima's daughter, Zaynab, who fought alongside her brother, Husayn, on the battlefield at Karbala, is regarded as the prime example of female behavior during times of war: there should be a balance between the instinctive defense of one's country and the appropriate modesty of one's sex. Legends of her activities "provide an image of the ideal Muslim woman as an assertive, tough, daring, knowledgeable, brave revolutionary fighter."[41] In particular, consistent "with their expected role as mothers of martyrs," Shiite women frequently point to "Zaynab's strength of mind and ability to endure the loss of all the men in her family."[42] According to Nasrallah, "Israel has always tried to panic people, to make them flee. But women—wives, daughters, etc.—had a central role, to fix people in their places. This is like the historical example."[43] This determination "to fix people in their places" lies at the heart of the resistance project.

Lebanese women's writing in response to the war illuminates the growing imperative not to leave their villages, which allows us to view these traumatic events in a different way. During the period before the Israeli invasion in 1982, women such as novelist Emily Nasrallah, who is originally from Kfeir in southern Lebanon, "wrote progressively of their staying in Lebanon and waiting as first 'Doing Nothing,' then as 'Survival' and finally as 'Resistance.' With time, they described this staying in Lebanon, which had originally been unthinking, as though it were a need."[44] Our research, which is based on eyewitness accounts, confirms that to begin with, Shiite women kept out of the way and tried to survive the conflict as best they could; as hostilities intensified, resistance became a matter of honor for women in the South, and eventually, many felt they had no choice but to become active in the struggle against Israel. This scenario equates to Scott's notion of "everyday acts of resistance": they may not appear particularly heroic, but taken as a whole, they represent a movement of refusal.[45]

When it comes to the violence of war, opinions are again divided on its impact on women. According to Majida, a university professor, "The resistance movement was very empowering for women. Lebanese women identify with men and, therefore, have pride in the resistance."[46] Safiyya agreed that "war did not increase violence against women. On the contrary, it gave them a sort of power."[47] Part of the explanation for women's feelings of empowerment can be attributed to the fact that they have survived. Lamia, a journalist in Beirut, was also of the opinion that the resistance is empowering for women. In southern Lebanon, she said,

> most of the women are Shi'a and it is normal that the effect of the resistance is positive on these women; they have sons and other family members in the resistance; they accept the resistance. Their role is support, emotionally. Women are ready to give their sons and their husbands to the resistance; they think this is the solution to the problem with Israel.[48]

Similarly, Umm Fawaz, who lives in the village of Ayta Shaib on the Lebanese-Israeli border, which was badly damaged during the 2006 war, asserted that she "gives her soul for the resistance." Before the May 2000 liberation, she said, she lived in the village while her sons lived in Beirut, but now they are all together. For that, she said, "we have to thank the resistance. No one has helped us except for the resistance."[49]

Much has changed for Shiite women in Lebanon over the past decades. They are now better educated, frequently attend university, have jobs, and bear fewer children. Many women in al-Dahiya (the southern suburbs of Beirut) "have achieved higher levels of education than ever before and have begun to play a vocal and visible role in spaces that have been historically marked as male."[50] For example, Huda, the college student in Beirut, is engaged to an engineer. She said that although she sought her parents' approval, it was her own decision what to study and whom to marry.[51] When we met the residents of al-Dahiya and southern Lebanon, we realized that they are experiencing a religious resurgence, which expresses itself in dress and behavior. In Lebanon, as in Iran, these choices must be recognized as authentic expressions of empowerment, as ways of shaking off western-style modernization.

Musa al-Sadr and the Amal Movement

South Lebanon, a flowering, rolling land punctuated by deep valleys and rocky hills, has always felt forgotten.[52]

In the first half of the twentieth century, the Lebanese Shiite community "languished under the domination" of the *zu'ama*, "whose political power stemmed from land wealth and the political ineffectualness of their clientele."[53] These men had little interest in championing the concerns of a rural, peasant-based population. However, the Shiites were also experiencing "wide-ranging economic change and social disruption."[54] As a result of "changing agricultural patterns, increased access to the media, improved internal transportation networks, internal and external migration, and a deteriorating security environment, traditional political leaders became less capable of meeting the escalating needs and demands of their constituents."[55] The Shiites, in other words, were ripe for social mobilization.

Much of the credit for the early politicization of the Shiites must be given to the Iranian-born cleric Musa al-Sadr, who founded Harakat al-Mahrumin (Movement of the Deprived or Disinherited). Al-Sadr began his work in southern Lebanon in the early 1960s by seeking to improve the marginalized, impoverished status of the local Shiite population. He approached this in two ways: by trying to persuade the central Lebanese government to devote more resources to the south of the country and by founding local institutions for the welfare and betterment of the Shiites. To this end, he was able to use "the revolutionary idioms of the sixties" to change perceptions of religious authority and to advance the interests of his community.[56] He attempted to operate within Lebanon's complex confessional system and "to tackle the immense social needs of his community by filling the role left vacant by the state and the politicians."[57] Although he promised to struggle "until the security needs and social grievances of the deprived . . . were satisfactorily addressed by the government,"[58] it soon became apparent to him that the Shiite problem "had to do with deprivation and degrading physical conditions, the lack of spiritual and cultural guidance, and the socio-political reality of being a part and yet not full participants in a country."[59] Gradually, he began to adopt a more militant stance. By all accounts, al-Sadr was a charismatic and widely revered figure, and although he mysteriously disappeared in 1978 during a visit to Libya, "his aura still resonates in almost mythic proportions."[60] In the words of one biographer, he was "a man with his own style and a man who knew how to get and hold attention."[61] The original social protest movement on behalf of the powerless and largely ignored Shiite community of southern Lebanon turned to violence when its demands for justice and a larger share of the communal pie were ignored. The Amal movement (*harakat amal*), which later participated as a Shiite militia in the civil war, was created in 1974.

The towns and villages of southern Lebanon are inhabited largely, although not exclusively, by Shiite Muslims. This has meant that the Shiites have been on the front lines of a war between the Palestinian *fida'yin* (fighters) and the Israeli army.[62] Both sides in this low-intensity conflict have inadvertently or deliberately targeted the civilian population in southern Lebanon. The local Shiite community, therefore, more than anyone, suffered from the ongoing border scuffles, their villages becoming war zones. In the beginning, the villagers of southern Lebanon were sympathetic to Palestinian calls for justice and return. However, whenever a Palestinian military operation took place against Israel, the Israelis would retaliate by attacking Lebanese villages. As a result, countless innocent Lebanese civilians were killed and wounded, and, slowly, sympathy changed to anger.

Even among sections of the Shiite community, Amal's reputation is far from spotless. The movement has been accused of selling out, being hypocritical, and seeking power for its own sake. At best, it exploited the anti-Palestinian climate "to mobilize the disenchanted Shiites along chauvinist Lebanese and sectarian Shiite lines."[63] In response, the ideologically more extreme Islamic Amal movement was founded in the early 1980s by Husain Musawi. While the other rival Shiite organization, Hizbullah, insisted that violent resistance was the only way to end the Israeli occupation, Amal decided to place its faith and its energy in the removal of Israel by negotiation rather than armed struggle. Since the end of the civil war, the Amal militia has transformed itself into a political party. Now led by Nabih Berri, it has gained parliamentary seats in general elections since 1992, and Berri continues to serve as speaker of the Lebanese Chamber of Deputies.

Since many Shiites were drawn to the seemingly more wholehearted ideology of Hizbullah, Amal has lost some of its support. A number of the defectors, including women interviewed for this book, are of the opinion that they would have continued to support Amal had it remained true to the teachings of Musa al-Sadr. As it is, they find its present, more pragmatic approach unconvincing. According to Umm Sadeq in Beirut, "If Imam al-Sadr was still here, there would be no need for Hizbullah. Since I was a child, I wanted Islam to rule all sides of my life; I did not find it in Amal."[64]

Amal Women and Violent Conflict

Al-Sadr's teachings were revolutionary in the sense that they applied as much to women as to men. He believed that girls were entitled to receive a comprehensive education, and he gave special attention to girls from poor backgrounds. Remembered as a pious and intelligent individual, al-Sadr possessed an uncompromising vision of Islam. For him, it meant the liberation through education and religious devotion of *all* individuals, male and female. However, despite al-Sadr's enlightened approach to women's rights, as in every other patriarchal society,

> Lebanese Shi'a politics was a man's world. The woman merely represented an additional vote which the male head of the household had at his disposal to support his candidate of choice. . . . The commitment to bringing women to the forefront of Lebanese social and political life was symbolic of the cleric's leadership as a whole. . . . The aim was to make public the role of the ordinary woman within the traditional mould, to involve her in a world that complemented the domestic private sphere in which she operated.[65]

As a result of the aggressive Israeli presence on their doorsteps, Shiite women have had no choice but to involve themselves in the violence. They have done this as both victims and agents, and some of them have acted under the banner of Amal. According to Randa Berri, wife of Nabih Berri,

> The war was a big shock for everyone, especially women. Before the war, women had not known what to do; they were used to moving in a small society and were never educated to be part of the nation or the larger society. In Lebanon, women were not educated about this responsibility—until the big shock came. Therefore, women learned a lot from this war, but at a very high price. This is what happens when a country does not support its population.

One cannot expect Lebanese women to read all this history or understand all this complexity, but it has become even more important after the war. Women had to pick up their education themselves. This is continuing, and it gets better every day. Women were very active during the war but could have been more so if they had known the truth before the war. Now women in general in Lebanon are trying harder to write a new history, so it is harder to judge women now, and they cannot be blamed for things that are out of their hands. Many are very intelligent, and now they have a chance.[66]

Other women support this view. In the words of Amira in Nabatiyya:

In the past, it was simpler for girls; they thought only of clothes and marriage but when the war came, the pain in their hearts made people think more deeply. They looked to the future and to education. One result of the war has been migration, whereby people see more of the world and get new ideas. Now most people want society to change; they want women to have more education. Islam stresses a girl must receive education and has the right to acquire knowledge. Many women now work outside the home.[67]

War has given women both suffering and opportunities. According to Hasana, who worked for Amal in southern Lebanon,

Women were active with the resistance. They carried ammunition under their clothes and kept watch at night. They sat in groups on hills or on the tops of buildings to look out for the Israelis and to warn the men. Women made fires out of tires and girls blocked off the street so that the Israelis could not enter until the men had escaped. Women also encouraged their children to confront Israel; they prepared them for war so that the children would not be afraid.[68]

Umm Mahmoud agreed that "the Israelis injured women, beat them, and killed them. Old women too found ways of confronting the Israelis; for example, an old woman was heating oil to cook, and she threw it at the Israeli soldiers. When someone is killed, this is a gift from God. We have no choice in death, and to be a martyr is a matter of pride in Islam."[69]

Most of the women interviewed referred to the centrality of Islam in their lives and stressed the link between religion and resistance. Umm Jamil explained the division between the sexes as follows:

The Quran speaks of the job of the man and the woman together; there is no separation between them and the Quran always addresses them both. The man is not superior; they are the same. But women and men are physically different; the woman is not as strong in her body. In the resistance movement, in the first place, it is up to men to confront Israel. Women's role is to bring ammunition, bring news, care for the men. It is a different role. A woman's job is to build a new society rather than to fight the enemy. But, in some cases, where the enemy is very near and there are not enough men, everyone—including women, children, and old people—must face the enemy.[70]

Many of the women interviewed, both in southern Lebanon and in Beirut, were eager to talk about al-Sadr and the principles of the Amal movement. According to Amira, the first principle is to believe in God in one's heart, the second is to draw good lessons from all experiences and practice them in one's life, the third is to remove the oppression of rich over poor in order to create a more equal society, and the fourth is to create good behavior between people.[71] In the words of Nabila, a representative of the Amal women's organization:

> Imam al-Sadr focused on women's role. He said he wished he could mobilize women to fight for the nation, to take up arms. This is the ideology of the Shi'a. True Islam gave woman her rights and a major role in society. Women's most sacred role is to enhance family links and establish a good family. Imam al-Sadr said that a woman can be in the government, can rule, but it is better if she raises the ruler.[72]

Her words chime with the views of others who make a distinction between the role of men as public figures and women as mothers and supporters, but there is no consensus on this subject, and many Shiite women agree with Nasrallah that there is nothing to prevent greater female participation in the future.

The village of Maarake in southern Lebanon used to be a center of Amal resistance during the Israeli occupation in the early 1980s. Zaynab Jaradi, widow of Amal leader Khalil Jaradi, who was murdered by the Israelis in 1984, talked about her husband's death and her present life. Khalil, she explained, was a religious man who defended his country as a matter of honor. In his dealings with the Israelis, he had developed powers that sounded almost magical: he could, it seems, appear and disappear at will. Although the Israelis had tried many times to capture him, they were always unsuccessful, and so, in exasperation, they placed a remote-controlled explosive device in a local *husainiya* (religious meeting place) where they knew the local leaders would gather to discuss future strategy. In what has been described as "the most notorious incident" during Israel's "iron-fist" policy in southern Lebanon, fifteen people—including Khalil Jaradi—were killed and over fifty injured.[73] Zaynab had also been involved in the resistance. She had worked as a nurse and had smuggled ammunition under her clothing. She proudly evoked the familiar image of the heroic mother, a baby in one hand and a gun in the other. According to the Quran, she said, it is a matter of pride to die for one's belief, but a woman's primary role is to wait for her husband to return from fighting the enemy and for God's will to be revealed. Nowadays, she is no longer involved with the resistance but teaches children instead.[74]

During the years of war, many women participated in the struggle. They regard it as a religious duty but explain that, according to the Quran, the tasks of men and women in war are different. In the words of one Amal woman, "Our weapons are our thoughts and words. We have first to understand where we are and where we stand before we carry arms. If we have to carry arms, then of course, we will; otherwise our role is primarily social and educational."[75] Women's first obligation is to defend their homes and children; in addition, they may perform support roles in the fighting. These, as Zaynab Jaradi explained, included the smuggling of food and weapons (pregnancy was a popular disguise); keeping watch for the enemy; and creating a diversion so that men could get away. Women have also had the task of explaining "to families and neighbors what was going on. We taught them how to face grave situations bravely. We offered them various services and ran special courses for mothers to teach them how to cope with the war situation. We also taught them religion and the place of women in Islam."[76]

In return, though, the women of southern Lebanon have suffered a variety of humiliations at the hands of the invading Israelis. Amira in Nabatiyya described how she started work when she was eighteen years old, helping people, especially the children of martyrs:

> My job was to protect the men from the Israelis, to hide them. I could not confront the Israelis with a gun, could not fight, so I encouraged people and organized meetings to discuss how best to confront Israel. It is important to have someone to encourage people. I made the men fighting Israel into heroes. One person alone cannot fight Israel, so my job was to make such a man a hero. If a family knows that their son is fighting Israel, they try to dissuade him, but my job was to persuade him that it is a good thing. I did not do this job because of personal needs but in the national interests and in the interests of the people. I worked with Amal.[77]

It is clear from their accounts that these women regard themselves, and are regarded, as an integral part of the resistance movement. In a war-centered society, it seems likely that the honor and the glory will lie with those who take up arms. They are the heroes, whereas those who support them are not usually remembered. We argue, however, that in contrast to Islamist movements in Egypt and Algeria that have made women more reserved, the Islamic revival in Lebanon has encouraged women to be active and outgoing.[78] Amal women claim that, as a result of the desperate conditions caused by war and occupation, together with their role in the resistance movement, there has been "a rebirth of the fundamental character of women," which suggests a reversion to the revered heroines of Shiite history.[79]

Some activists report that it became "quite normal" for Amal men to marry women who devoted all their time to the movement. Said one woman, "We never imagined that our men would reach this stage of understanding women's position—even in a hundred years."[80] Another felt that "our traditional life and women's confinement to the home didn't generate anything but injustice and a stupid acquiescence towards it." But after Musa al-Sadr began his work in southern Lebanon, "we started to raise our voices; as women we started forming groups in which women were educated and encouraged to rebel against our unfair conditions."[81] These women's testimonies support Randa Berri's assertion about Lebanese women "writing a new history."

Hizbullah: The Creation of a "Community of Resistance"

Hizbullah (*Hizb Allah*, "the party of God"), was founded in 1982 in response to two immediate crises: the large-scale invasion of Lebanon by Israel that took place in June of that year and the ongoing Israeli occupation of Lebanese territory, and the Amal movement's perceived departure from "the true path of Islam." At that time, many in the Shiite community, especially "among the young generation, who did not find in Amal a cogent response to their fervor and their desire to launch a *jihad* against Israel and bring about a change in the Beirut regime, left Amal and joined Hizballah."[82] Amal Saad-Ghorayeb describes Hizbullah as "the political and military outgrowth" of a broad cultural movement that incorporated various Islamic groups.[83] As the women's narratives reveal, many Lebanese had felt impotent in the face of Israeli strength; they were looking for a way to defend themselves that was both effective and appropriate in terms of their cultural values. Hizbullah's centers of support are located primarily in the southern suburbs of Beirut, in the Bekaa Valley, particularly the town of Baalbek, and in the Jabal Amil area in southern Lebanon.

Deriving its ideological inspiration from the political writings of Ayatollahs Ruhollah Khomeini and Muhammad Baqir al-Sadr,[84] Hizbullah declared

> frankly and clearly that we are a nation that fears only God and that does not accept tyranny, aggression, and humiliation. America and its allies and the Zionist entity that has usurped the sacred Islamic land of Palestine have engaged and continue to engage in constant aggression against us and are working constantly to humiliate us. Therefore, we are in a state of constant and escalating preparedness to repel the aggression and to defend our religion, existence and dignity.[85]

The group's rhetoric, rooted in the sacred and drawing on a warrior tradition, seemed to offer a kind of redemptive power. Hizbullah's objectives were set out in 1985 in an "Open Letter Addressed by Hizbullah to the Downtrodden in Lebanon and in the World." These included "Israel's final departure from Lebanon as a prelude to its final obliteration from existence"; the liberation of "venerable" Jerusalem; the expulsion of the United States, France, and their allies from Lebanon "and the termination of the influence of any imperialist power in the country"; and an opportunity for the Lebanese people "to determine their fate and to choose with full freedom the system of government they want, keeping in mind that we do not hide our commitment to the rule of Islam and that we urge them to choose the Islamic system that alone guarantees justice and dignity for all and prevents any new imperialist attempts to infiltrate our country."[86] Such boldness of vision and clarity of intent proved irresistible to large numbers of disaffected Shiites who had been inspired by the 1979 Iranian revolution, disappointed by Amal's move to participate in the Lebanese system, and infuriated by Israeli aggression against the Lebanese and Palestinians.

As a pan-Islamic movement, Hizbullah regards itself as "a part of the Islamic nation in the world."[87] It acknowledges a close allegiance to the leadership of the Islamic Republic of Iran and, in particular, the late Khomeini. In the words of Sayyid Ibrahim al-Amin, "We in Lebanon do not consider ourselves as separate from the revolution in Iran, especially on the question of Jerusalem. We consider ourselves—and pray to God that we will become—part of the army which the Imam wishes to create in order to liberate Jerusalem. We obey his orders because we do not believe in geography but in change."[88]

The question of "geography" is an interesting one. Former Hizbullah secretary-general Shaikh Subhi al-Tufayli has stated, "We do not consider ourselves a Lebanese party but an Islamic party."[89] Yet, as Lara Deeb suggests, "Iranian efforts to infuse the Lebanese Shi'a with a pan-Shi'i identity centered on Iran have run up against the Arab identity and increasing Lebanese nationalism of Hizbullah itself."[90] However, it is also a highly pragmatic party, and some have argued that shifts have occurred, first, from a pan-Islamic to a nationalist perspective, and second, from "Khomeini's doctrine of *Wilayat al-Faqih*[91] to a blend between Islamic concepts and notions of representation, popular will and political equality for all."[92] One commentator suggests that, since 1989, the party has entered a "new phase," which can be described as the phase of "political *jihad*."[93] Deeb argues that it has grown since the mid-1980s "from a militia dedicated to resisting the Israeli invasions and occupation of Lebanon, to a multifaceted organization that is both a legitimate political party and a vast social welfare network."[94] However, many Lebanese fear that Hizbullah may have overstretched itself when, at the end of 2006, supporters of the party set up a tent encampment in the center of Beirut to oppose the tribunal put in place to investigate the assassination of Hariri. This was followed by further provocation. In May 2008, what began as a cost-of-living strike turned violent and led to a three-day takeover of West Beirut by Hizbullah. In the ensuing military showdown, Hizbullah prevailed, demonstrating its ability to overpower any opponent. Outside its own constituency, some argued that "it is seen more than ever as a Shiite militia brutally defending its parochial interests rather than those of a self-proclaimed national resistance."[95]

At the same time, within the Shiite community, Hizbullah sees itself as building "communities of resistance,"[96] and our own observations indicate that this objective is widely shared and seen as being in line with Islamic moral principles. Most Hizbullah members continue to assert their primary identity as Muslim. For example, Secretary-General Nasrallah has argued that "just as the affiliation to Christianity, Communism or any other belief system does not conflict with one's Lebanese identity, Hizbu'llah's affiliation to Islam . . . does not undermine its 'Lebanese identity or patriotism.'"[97] Hizbullah's critics, particularly in the United States, Israel, and some western European countries, prefer to define it as a "terrorist" organization. In Israel, in the immediate aftermath of the September 11, 2001, attacks on the United States, the government positioned itself "to associate Israel with America's war on terrorism, thereby gaining further leverage against Israel's enemies."[98] Nonetheless, Hizbullah remains immensely popular in the Shiite community because, like Hamas in Palestine, it "uses resistance as a tool with which to control and direct the powerful feelings which occupation and humiliation have unleashed."[99] Its success lies in "creating a psychology of willpower; entrenching a culture of resistance and steadfastness within the community; [and] instilling the willingness to sacrifice on behalf of the community."[100] These achievements are firmly supported by many in its female constituency.

Hizbullah and Women

The resistance, from the start, appeared to accommodate and give a role to all members of the "struggling community." In its "Open Letter," Hizbullah states,

> Through their Islamic resistance, the strugglers—the women with rocks and boiling oil for their weapons, the children with their shouts and their bare fists for their weapons, the old men with their weak bodies and their thick sticks for their weapons, and the youth with their rifles and their firm and faithful will for their weapons—have all proven that if the nation is allowed to manage its affairs freely, it is capable of making miracles and changing the imaginary fates.[101]

Although many outsiders, particularly in the west, continue to associate the black-robed women of Hizbullah with powerlessness, the evidence produced by our research indicates that both Hizbullah's policies toward women and also the outlook of individual women who are associated with the party contradict this simplistic view. As "Hanan," a Lebanese academic, explains, "The resistance tries to empower women by recruiting them. It educates women through lectures. This is the legacy of Fatima; her progeny is their origin. Women are not despised in the discourse, so women feel strong."[102]

In general, the women of Hizbullah are confident of their roles, both in the family and in the larger society. They speak in positive terms of the achievements of Islam and the certainty of its eventual triumph. Their role in the struggle is equally clear-cut. In Islam, according to Umm Ghassan, there are two ways: either to kill the enemy or to die oneself. Men bear the primary responsibility for waging war, she said, but if the enemy enters one's country, women too may fight and, therefore, are able to become martyrs.[103] The concept of martyrdom is a crucial one in Shiite oppositional ideology and for Hizbullah. During the Iran-Iraq War, Ayatollah Khomeini is said to have given permission to women to undertake military activities although, afterward, they were expected to resume their domestic duties. In Lebanon, although they are "not permitted to take part in the physical aspect of the *jihad*," most Hizbullah women "pray that, should their fighting husbands die, they do so on the battlefield. To lose one's husband in a *jihad* brings a certain standing to a widow in society,"[104] as many of our interlocutors confirmed. Lebanese Shiite women see no contradiction in these roles; many were keen to stress their own key role in the defense of country and family. Nasrallah explained it this way:

> In line with the traditions and customs of Shi'a culture in Lebanon, there was an avoidance of military participation for women. The reasons for the non-participation of women were, first, there was no need as there were enough men to do the fighting; and, second, it was to keep women away from Israeli military retaliation; for the Israelis to harm women would be very cruel and, as far as the community is concerned, would lead to uncalculated reactions. Therefore, throughout all Islamic resistance movement operations, women did not take up arms. Even in martyrdom operations against Israel, it was just the young men.[105]

Following the devastating Israeli invasion of Lebanon in 1982, Hizbullah women, like those of Amal, performed a number of vital functions, the most important of which was to support their husbands and children and to inspire the men with strength and courage to fight the enemy. This activity is reminiscent of the early days of Islam and before, when women used to accompany their menfolk to the battlefield in order to urge them on with songs and inspirational words. Such images remain potent in the imagination of many Hizbullah supporters, both men and women, who were expected to undertake actions according to their capabilities. Women occasionally smuggled weapons under their voluminous garments, guessing—

often correctly—that the Israelis would be unlikely or unwilling to search a modestly dressed female. As Roula in Nabatiyya observed, "during the time of the Prophet, women used to be side by side with men; and, in the 2006 war, women were present too, providing emergency relief and food, and dealing with injuries."[106] Hizbullah member Umm Ghassan explained that, in 1982, women had a very important role in fighting Israel. They were not afraid and gave their husbands and sons the strength to go to war. Although women may acquire knowledge, she said, they must take a secondary role to men. They may help with weapons, nursing, and medical work, but if there are enough men, they should not take a direct part in the fighting.[107]

Julie Peteet has written about "mothering in the war zone" and how, in "protracted military conflict, with its attendant losses of life, women, in particular the mother of the martyr, symbolize life giving, or national generativity, loss, and sacrifice."[108] Umm Fouad in Nabatiyya explained that she supports the work of the man who goes for jihad; at home, she takes responsibility for her children, and she raises those strong men. Women can participate in war if necessary, she said: "they can join the defense of their country if the enemy enters. If there are no men available to fight or work, then the women will go; they are in harmony." She concluded that "the war has just begun; if Israel comes back to Lebanon, we will send our sons to fight."[109] Similarly, the mother of one of the first Lebanese suicide bombers, a seventeen-year-old youth who destroyed the Israeli military headquarters in Tyre in November 1982 with enormous loss of life, is reported to have expressed her profound happiness that her son had become a martyr; she wished all her sons would follow his example.

In the words of Nasrallah, "The fighter's strength and superiority does not stem from the type of weapon he carries inasmuch as it stems from his will . . . and his advance toward death."[110] According to one woman, "All southern women urged their children to join the Lebanese resistance and give their blood for the liberation of the land. Here, it is no longer the habit of women to mourn their dead children; instead they celebrate their death and hand their guns on to their younger brother or sister."[111]

But the reality may be more complicated. Although it is always painful to lose a beloved son, in Palestine, Iraq, and elsewhere, women are expected to put aside their private grief and, like the mothers described above, to celebrate the martyrdom of their children. The role of *umm shahid* (mother of the martyr) entitles individual women to honor and respect within the community for their sacrifice. These mothers "occupied a position in the order of national activism," but "one ranked as somehow less central than formal masculinist militancy."[112] Some of the women interviewed referred to the very real possibility of sacrifice; Roula in Nabatiyya, for instance, asserted that during the 2006 war, "all of us were in agreement with Nasrallah; we were ready to offer ourselves and our children as martyrs because we believe in him."[113] These female roles of support and sacrifice are constant motifs. They permit the male fighter and the male martyr to claim the lion's share of glory. This may be acceptable under the extraordinary conditions of resistance, when it is crucial to maintain group solidarity, yet—one could argue—it becomes more problematic when the violence is turned against fellow Lebanese, as in 2008. It is likely that Hizbullah supporters would claim such behavior is necessary to resist unwelcome western interference in Lebanon's affairs.

Yet many women claim they are far from excluded. Their experience of Islam is just as authentic as men's. They were also subjected to some of the same humiliations as men. Despite their avoidance of direct conflict, many women were arrested by Israel and detained in Khiam prison. According to Suhair, a former prisoner,

> Since I was a believer in Islam I decided to become active in the resistance. I gave up school when I was twelve or thirteen. During the Israeli invasion, we were forced to flee. I saw massacres, corpses, and bloodshed. After we returned to our home, Israeli soldiers used to attack our house and to submit us to inhumane acts. I began to fight back. Most of the people who witnessed such acts chose to take part in the resistance, although in a variety of ways. We started when we were young, boycotting Israeli products and refusing to pay taxes to the Israelis. Then I started to work on education, spreading the teaching of Islam and encouraging people not to have contact with the Israelis. I took part in social, not military activities, although I sometimes carried weapons for the fighters.[114]

Suhair described how she was arrested in 1990 for taking part in the Islamic resistance. All her life, she said, she witnessed attacks on Lebanon by the Israelis and eventually decided to fight back. From the first moment of her arrest, she related,

> I was subjected to torture. They covered my head with a sack and put me in the back of a car, which transported me to Khiam. They removed my clothes, handcuffed and blindfolded me, and started to question me in a rude way, insulting me and insulting Islam. They scalded my body with electrical wires. After being subjected to different tortures, I fell down, and they kicked me and made me bleed. Prisoners were given electric shocks in different parts of the body. When the weather was very cold, prisoners were taken outside, in the rain, and hot water was poured on them, then cold water. They were told to kneel down, and dirty water was thrown over them. All the torturers were men. The prisoners were moved around, often kept in isolation, given food while they were tied up, as if they were dogs. The women prisoners were threatened with rape; family members were threatened too, but they did not rape anyone.[115]

Several former prisoners referred, either directly or obliquely, to rape, but always as a threat, as in Suhair's narrative, and never a reality. Although sexual violation would be regarded as deeply shameful and few would be prepared to discuss it, survival of inhumane conditions and the presentation of the enemy in a negative light are matters of pride. This means either that rape really did not occur or that there is a conspiracy of silence among former prisoners in order to protect the integrity of the resistance. These memories of imprisonment, like the 2008 takeover of West Beirut, threaten the image of the resistance as a moral community.

Many women lost their husbands. Ghada, the widow of a martyr, described the death of her husband. She said she believes that "when God chooses a martyr, it is because of their good characteristics. My husband was very devoted to his country." His devotion inspired him to participate in military operations as a member of the Islamic resistance movement. On the day before his death, she said,

> he left the house. I took my children and visited a neighbor. I felt uncomfortable but did not know why. When I returned home with the children, I watched the television and heard news of a military operation against enemy positions. It showed images of the Islamic resistance. My mother-in-law saw an image of her son: he was lying there, partly naked; the Israelis were poking him with a stick.

Her husband's body was kept by the Israelis for nine years and eventually released in an exchange of human remains.[116]

Female members of Hizbullah are well aware that many changes have occurred since the 1970s. Before the war, they argue, Lebanese society was strongly influenced by Europe and the United States and was following a particular path toward modernization. The Shiite community, as a disadvantaged group, lacked cohesion and organization, but that changed because of Musa al-Sadr, who galvanized the Shiites into action. Their response was militaristic but also involved a return to religion. Young people started to reclaim their religion and, as a result, discovered new confidence. But religion, in the opinion of several interviewees, is not simply praying and fasting; it structures one's entire life politically, socially, and economically. The return to religion, for many young women, was also an act of rebellion. Their mothers had become secularized and, in many cases, were shocked at the resurgent religiosity displayed by their children. One hears stories of parental disapproval and dismay when teenage daughters suddenly decided to adopt the full Iranian-style *chador*. This would appear to be a revolution that women have chosen for themselves.

Even though Israel has withdrawn from Lebanese territory, many people fear that the Israelis could return or attack at any time. Inevitably, the years of war and struggle have taken a toll on all the Lebanese who lived

through that time, whether they stayed in their villages or fled to supposedly safer places. Some women reported stress-related illnesses; others
have long-term disabilities. Women are apprehensive about the future; they
worry about their children's well-being. It is clear that women are significantly underrepresented in political and governmental positions, and one
gets the feeling that many people still believe that "women are not yet
ready" or that affairs of state should be handled by men.

But Lebanese Shiite women have also developed important strengths.
Heightened feelings of piety may be observed among women with an affiliation to political Islamist groups. They are convinced that their belief in
Islam has allowed them to triumph over the enemy, and therefore it is the
correct path. Another source of empowerment is the centrality of martyrdom. Many Hizbullah women have a male relative who was martyred by
the Israelis, and their sacrifice allows them to occupy a place of honor
within the society. Most women demonstrate feelings of pride in the Islamic
resistance; they are proud that it remained steadfast and courageous and, in
the end, was triumphant.

In postwar Lebanon, Hizbullah is engaging in a process of reform
through Islamic rather than western notions of modernization, and women
are included in this project. Nasrallah stated the position very clearly:

> After the war, Lebanon engaged in reconstruction. It needs psychological and
> educational rehabilitation to keep the country out of future civil war. Woman
> has a large role [to play] in this regard. The psychological and educational im-
> pact of women is larger than men, especially in Lebanon. Hizbullah works on
> encouraging this plan and trying to convince others who are hesitant. Women
> themselves need encouragement; it is not enough just to open the door. Women
> must be prepared to advance and take the initiative.[117]

Umm Rafiq in Bint Jboil echoed his sentiments: "Women's opportunities
increased after liberation," she said. "Women should take more of a role in
the political development of the country."[118]

The War Between Israel and Hizbullah, 2006

In July 2006, after Hizbullah seized two Israeli soldiers on the Lebanese-
Israeli border, Israeli forces invaded Lebanon. During thirty-four days of
intense bombardment, approximately 1,300 Lebanese, the majority of them
civilians, lost their lives, and many more were injured or saw their homes
destroyed or badly damaged as Israel attempted to create a "killing box" in
southern Lebanon "where Hezbollah could be destroyed in detail by bombing and shelling."[119] In response, Hizbullah successfully "provided the
model for the evolution of asymmetrical warfare applied strategically over

a wide area."[120] As Rashid Khalidi observes, if "the American and Israeli governments do not shift their worldviews away from the empty bombast about terrorism, which leads to an excessive reliance on the use of force, and toward resolving the deeper issues through diplomacy, they risk stumbling into a major conflagration."[121]

The tactics of Hizbullah, before, during, and after the 2006 war should be considered from three distinct perspectives: that of the international community, that of the population of Lebanon, and that of Hizbullah's own community. Even though the expectation of Israel and its international supporters, in particular the United States, was that Hizbullah "somehow could be expunged from Lebanon," most Lebanese observers acknowledge that this is simply not realistic.[122] From its image as the "Islamic resistance," feared or derided by non-Shiite Lebanese, Hizbullah was transformed into the "national resistance" during the 2006 assault. The Shiite community in southern Lebanon regards the group as "the only viable possibility for protecting their villages and homes and livelihoods from Israeli attack."[123] But there have been criticisms, even among the Shiites, about the tactics employed by Hizbullah. Hanan, a Beirut intellectual, reported that her friends and family were "devastated" by the 2006 invasion; they felt "cheated" by the resistance. In her view, some of the women directly affected by the conflict are hiding their true feelings. The loss of home, the place where they raised their children, is likely to make women feel depressed, she said; it is "like losing their identity."[124]

But others disagreed. Many of the women interviewed related their experiences of the 2006 war. Huda, for example, said she had "many bad experiences"; she lives in the al-Dahiya area of Beirut and recalled that there were frequent bombings near her home; she and her family had to keep moving.[125] Umm Fadi, who has seven children and lives in Ayta Shaib village on the Lebanese-Israeli border, said that she spent the first two weeks of the war in her village. One of her sons was wounded, and her house was bombed. The resistance, she said, helped them to leave the village; they went to the next village, and, when the war stopped, they returned. There was only one room of the house left to live in.[126]

The town of Bint Jbeil, near the Israeli border, was declared by the Israelis to be a "Hizbullah stronghold" and thus was heavily bombarded. Abu Hasan, who is eighty years old and whose wife is bedridden, described how he, his wife, and his daughter spent thirty-three days in one of the bedrooms of their home; every second, he recalled, the city was hit by missiles or bombs. It was thirty-three days without sleep. Part of their house was hit at the front. They boiled water to cook and wash. The dust from the bombs, he said, was the worst thing. Afterward, he had to spend fifteen days in the hospital. His wife could not move. They were not aware of the cease-fire that enabled many people to leave the town, so they were forced to stay. They prayed all the time not to die. He said that "it was a miracle to survive."[127] Fawzia, a twenty-nine-year-old computer technician, recalled that her grandfather was killed on the first day of the Israeli invasion in 1978. In the 2006 war, she and her family stayed in the bottom of their house for ten days. There was bombing all around, she said, but eventually "we took a chance and managed to get out." She added, "Whatever happened to us, we still support the resistance and do not blame them."[128] Umm Wissam, also in Bint Jbeil, stayed in the town for twenty-one days; her house was destroyed, and two of her sons, aged twenty-three and thirty-one, who were working with the resistance, were killed. She feels that Hizbullah "gives everything to the people; it protects them, whereas the Lebanese state is unable to do anything against Israel."[129] In Baalbek, Umm Nabil, who is eighty-four years old and illiterate, recalled that her son did not feel scared of the Israelis; he stood on the balcony and watched as they bombed the hospital while she stayed in the house, sometimes watching and sometimes hiding. The narratives of these "ordinary" people provide an insight into circumscribed lives that might, at any moment, be violently interrupted. Many feel that, without the resistance, they would be victimized by expansionist Israeli policies. They have been demonized as "violent extremists," as "terrorists," and yet they are the ones, they claim, who have been terrorized. Although some may be critical about the rhetoric of Hizbullah, many others claim they have been empowered.

Conclusion

A potent image is that of tender plants in inhospitable places. Against the odds, they survive and even flourish, and this could be said too of the women who fought Israeli aggression in the south of Lebanon—and won. Their determination to survive is impressive. They have endured torture, imprisonment, the threat and reality of rape, the killing and terrorizing of their children, and the destruction of their homes and villages, an Israeli act of collective punishment intended to flush out the fighters. In order to intimidate local communities, the Israelis invaded the private space of women, who say that the preservation and strengthening of their faith has been essential as a means of resisting such violations. It has helped them to face the enemy boldly and to bring their children up to do the same. Although women's lives and the nature of the Islamic resistance have changed since the 1980s, the war of 2006 illustrated again to southern populations the necessity of the resistance, both as a form of protection and as a method of dignity and assertion in their lives.

Notes

1. Lakhdar Brahimi, "Start Talking to Hezbollah," *New York Times*, August 18, 2006.

2. Lara Deeb, "Deconstructing a 'Hizbullah Stronghold,'" *MIT Electronic Journal of Middle East Studies* 6 (Summer 2006): 115.

3. There are eighteen religious sects in Lebanon.

4. Mai Ghoussoub, *Leaving Beirut: Women and the Wars Within* (London: Saqi, 1998), 21.

5. Interview, Dahieh, Beirut, July 25, 2007.

6. Alastair Crooke, *Resistance: The Essence of the Islamist Revolution* (London: Pluto, 2009), 191.

7. Interview with Na'im Kassim, deputy secretary-general of Hizbullah, Beirut, September 19, 2002.

8. The National Pact of 1943 "sought to define the balance between Christian and Muslim concerns. . . . It stipulated that Lebanon should remain independent and bound neither by its European nor its Arab ties, with Christian Lebanese respecting Lebanon's Arab character and refraining from any alliance or protection from a Western power, whilst Muslims in return would agree to accept Lebanese sovereignty and refrain from any attempt to integrate Lebanon into a wider Arab or Islamic state." See David McDowall, *Lebanon: A Conflict of Minorities* (London: Minority Rights Group, 1983, revised 1986), 11.

9. Michael C. Hudson, *Arab Politics: The Search for Legitimacy* (New Haven: Yale University Press, 1977), 286.

10. Ghassan Salame, "'Strong' and 'Weak' States: A Qualified Return to the *Muqaddimah*," in Giacomo Luciani, ed., *The Arab State* (London: Routledge, 1990), 47.

11. Ibid., 48.

12. Samir Khalaf, *Beirut Reclaimed: Reflections on Urban Design and the Restoration of Civility* (Beirut: Dar an-Nahar, 1993), 79.

13. Kamal Salibi, *A House of Many Mansions* (London: I. B. Tauris, 1988), 180.

14. Khalaf, *Beirut Reclaimed*, 87.

15. Miriam Cooke, *Women Write War: The Centring of the Beirut Decentrists*, Papers on Lebanon 6 (Oxford: Centre for Lebanese Studies, July 1987), 3.

16. Ghoussoub, *Leaving Beirut*, 19.

17. Cooke, *Women Write War*, 3.

18. Samir Khalaf, *Civil and Uncivil Violence in Lebanon: A History of the Internationalization of Communal Conflict* (New York: Columbia University Press, 2002), xi.

19. Ghoussoub, *Leaving Beirut*, 19.

20. Miriam Cooke, *War's Other Voices: Women Writers on the Lebanese Civil War* (Cambridge: Cambridge University Press, 1988), 123.

21. Interview, Nabatiyyeh, May 2, 2007.

22. Augustus Richard Norton, *Hezbollah: A Short History* (Princeton, NJ: Princeton University Press, 2007), 14.

23. Evelyne Accad, "Sexuality and Sexual Politics: Conflicts and Contradictions for Contemporary Women in the Middle East," in Chandra Talpade Mohanty, Ann Russo, and Lourdes Torres, eds., *Third World Women and the Politics of Feminism* (Bloomington: Indiana University Press, 1991), 245.

24. Interview with the director general, Ministry of Social Affairs, Beirut, February 20, 2003.

25. Interview with female academic, Beirut, May 31, 2003.

26. Interview, Beirut, April 16, 1994.

27. Interview, Beirut, August 1, 2007.

28. From the "File of Female Martyrs," prepared by Saqar Abu Fakh and Daud Faraj.

29. Interview, Sidon, April 17, 1994.

30. Interview, Baalbek, August 2, 2007.

31. Lara Deeb, *An Enchanted Modern: Gender and Public Piety in Shi'i Lebanon* (Princeton, NJ: Princeton University Press, 2006), 36.

32. Interview, Bint Jbeil, February 22, 2003.

33. Interview, Bint Jbeil, February 21, 2003.

34. Murtada Mutahhari, *The Rights of Women in Islam* (Tehran: World Organization for Islamic Services, 1981), 69.

35. Ibid., xxviii.

36. Interview with Hizbullah member, Beirut, January 26, 1993.

37. Meeting with Sayyid Hasan Nasrallah, secretary-general of Hizbullah, Beirut, June 9, 2003.

38. Interview, women's affairs office of Amal, Beirut, June 10, 2003.

39. Mutahhari, *The Rights of Women in Islam*, 65.

40. The philosophy of resistance of Hizbullah, quoted in Crooke, *Resistance*, 187.

41. Erika Friedl, "Ideal Womanhood in Postrevolutionary Iran," in Judy Brink and Joan Mencher, eds., *Mixed Blessings: Gender and Religious Fundamentalism Cross-Culturally* (New York: Routledge, 1997), 150.

42. Lara Deeb, "'Doing Good, Like Sayyida Zaynab': Lebanese Shi'i Women's Participation in the Public Sphere," in Armando Salvatore and Mark LeVine, eds., *Religion, Social Practice, and Contested Hegemonies: Reconstructing the Public Sphere in Muslim Majority Societies* (New York: Palgrave Macmillan, 2005), 94.

43. Meeting with Sayyid Hasan Nasrallah, secretary-general of Hizbullah, Beirut, June 9, 2003.

44. Miriam Cooke, "Arab Women, Arab Wars," in Fatma Muge Gocek and Shiva Balaghi, eds., *Reconstructing Gender in the Middle East: Tradition, Identity, and Power* (New York: Columbia University Press, 1994), 157.

45. James C. Scott, *Weapons of the Weak: Everyday Forms of Peasant Resistance* (New Haven, CT: Yale University Press, 1985).

46. Interview with female academic, Beirut, June 9, 2003.

47. Interview with female academic, Beirut, May 31, 2003.

48. Interview, Beirut, July 30, 2007.

49. Interview, Ayta Shaib, May 2, 2007.

50. Deeb, "'Doing Good, Like Sayyida Zaynab,'" 101.

51. Interview, al-Dahiya, July 25, 2007.

52. Julie Flint, "Crushed Hopes and Shattered Senses," *Guardian*, July 31, 1993.

53. Augustus Richard Norton, *Amal and the Shi'a: Struggle for the Soul of Lebanon* (Austin: University of Texas Press, 1987), 15.

54. Ibid., 16.

55. Ibid.

56. Majed Halawi, *A Lebanon Defied: Musa al-Sadr and the Shi'a Community* (Boulder, CO: Westview, 1992), 129.

57. Ibid., 135.

58. Norton, *Amal and the Shi'a*, 47.

59. Halawi, *A Lebanon Defined*, 138.

60. Ibid., 126.

61. Fouad Ajami, *The Vanished Imam: Musa al Sadr and the Shia of Lebanon* (London: I. B. Tauris, 1986), 27.

62. This "war" began in the mid- to late 1960s, after the creation of the Palestine Liberation Organization (PLO) to "liberate" Palestinian territory and permit the refugees to return.

63. Asad Abu Khalil, "Druze, Sunni, and Shiite Political Leadership in Present-Day Lebanon," *Arab Studies Quarterly* 7, no. 4 (1985): 47.

64. Interview, Beirut, June 2, 1993.

65. Halawi, *A Lebanon Defied*, 181.

66. Meeting with Randa Berri, Beirut, April 1994.

67. Interview, Nabatiyya, January 24, 1993.

68. Interview, Maarake, southern Lebanon, January 23, 1993.

69. Interview, southern Lebanon, January 23, 1993.

70. Interview, Tyre, January 23, 1993.

71. Interview, Nabatiyya, January 24, 1993.

72. Interview, Amal women's affairs office, Beirut, June 10, 2003.

73. Norton, *Amal and the Shi'a*, 207.

74. Interview with Zaynab Jaradi, Maarake, January 24, 1993.

75. Bouthaina Shaaban, *Both Right and Left Handed: Arab Women Talk About Their Lives* (London: Women's Press, 1988), 86.

76. Ibid.

77. Interview, Nabatiyya, January 24, 1993.

78. Shaaban, *Both Right and Left Handed*, 95.

79. Ibid., 86.

80. Ibid.

81. Ibid., 89.

82. Shimon Shapira, "The Imam Musa al-Sadr: Father of the Shiite Resurgence in Lebanon," *Jerusalem Quarterly*, no. 44 (Fall 1987): 128.

83. Amal Saad-Ghorayeb, *Hizbu'llah: Politics and Religion* (London: Pluto, 2002), 15.

84. A. Nizar Hamzeh, "Lebanon's Hizbullah: From Islamic Revolution to Parliamentary Accommodation," *Third World Quarterly* 14, no. 2 (1993): 323.

85. From an "Open Letter Addressed by Hizbullah to the Downtrodden of Lebanon and the World," February 16, 1985, 6.

86. Ibid., 9.

87. Ibid., 4.

88. Interview with Ibrahim al-Amin, al-Harakat al-Islamiyya fi Lubnan, Beirut, 1984.

89. *Al-Ahd*, Safar 10, 1406 (quoted in Saad-Ghorayeb, *Hizbu'llah*, 76).

90. Deeb, "Deconstructing a 'Hizbullah Stronghold,'" 117.

91. Khomeini's theory of *Wilayat al-Faqih* (the "guardianship of the jurisprudent") comes from his belief in the need to establish an Islamic republic.

92. Jeroen Gunning, "Hezbollah Reappraised: A Study into Hezbollah's Public and Hidden Transcripts in Post-Ta'if Lebanon," MSc thesis, School of Oriental and African Studies, University of London, September 1995.

93. Hamzeh, "Lebanon's Hizbullah," 321.

94. Deeb, "Deconstructing a 'Hizbullah Stronghold,'" 116.

95. International Crisis Group, "Lebanon: Hizbollah's Weapons Turn Inward," *Middle East Briefing* No. 23, May 15, 2008.

96. Senior Hizbullah leader, quoted in Crooke, *Resistance*, 177.

97. C33 TV Lebanon, May 1996 (quoted in Saad-Ghorayeb, *Hizbu'llah*, 82–83).

98. Norton, *Hezbollah*, 76.

99. Crooke, *Resistance*, 197.

100. Ibid., 177.

101. Hizbullah, "Open Letter."

102. Interview, female academic, Beirut, July 26, 2007.

103. Interview, Umm Ghassan, Beirut, January 26, 1993.

104. Hala Jaber, *Hezbollah: Born with a Vengeance* (New York: Columbia University Press, 1997), 90.

105. Meeting with Nasrallah, Beirut, June 9, 2003.

106. Interview, Nabatiyya, May 2, 2007.

107. Interview, Beirut, January 1993.

108. Julie Peteet, "Icons and Militants: Mothering in the Danger Zone," in Therese Sahiba, Carolyn Allen, and Judith A. Howard, eds., *Gender, Politics, and Islam* (Chicago: University of Chicago Press, 2002), 140.

109. Interview, Nabatiyya, April 28, 2007.

110. *Al-Hawadith*, March 19, 1999, quoted in Saad-Ghorayeb, *Hizbullah*, 128.

111. Shaaban, *Both Right and Left Handed*, 92.

112. Peteet, "Icons and Militants," 147.

113. Interview, Nabatiyya, May 2, 2007.

114. Interview, Beirut, September 19, 2002.

115. Interview, Beirut, September 19, 2002.

116. Interview, Beirut, September 19, 2002.

117. Meeting with Nasrallah, Beirut, June 9, 2003.

118. Interview, Bint Jbeil, February 22, 2003.

119. Norton, *Hezbollah*, 137–138.

120. Crooke, *Resistance*, 185.

121. Rashid Khalidi, "The Terrorism Trap," *New York Times*, July 22, 2006.

122. Norton, *Hezbollah*, 139.

123. Deeb, "Deconstructing a 'Hizbullah Stronghold,'" 121.

124. Interview, female academic, Beirut, July 26, 2007.

125. Interview, Beirut, July 25, 2007.

126. Interview, Ayta Shaib, May 2, 2007.

127. Interview, Bint Jbeil, July 26, 2007.

128. Interview, Bint Jbeil, July 27, 2007.

129. Interview, Bint Jbeil, July 27, 2007.

5

Islam and Resistance:
Iraqi Women

In this chapter, we present the experiences of Iraqi women living in exile in Jordan and Syria. These women were forced to leave their homes as a result of political and religious conditions prevailing during and after the 2003 US invasion of Iraq and the ethnic strife that followed. Given the situation that they confronted, most of the women were sympathetic toward, or part of, the resistance movement against the US occupation and subsequent governments, which were established on the basis of collaboration with the US authorities. Of course, much investigative work is needed on the internal dynamics of the complex political environment within Iraq, but there is also a need for focused evaluations of the refugee crisis generated by the conflict, and the plight of Iraqi women warrants study in its own right.

The study undertaken here is important because it is the first to profile the lives and experiences of refugee women caught in the Iraqi conflict zone.[1] These women recount their experiences and responses to conflict, for example, the way faith empowered them to combat the daily violence they encountered. We note that Iraqi women, as is to be expected, do not all share the same views of the occupation or the current government and that a large number of women are working inside Iraq in multiple ways to rebuild their lives, either because they have no choice or because they have made the conscious decision on principle to remain in their homes despite the enormous challenges facing them. However, the voices of women sympathizing with the resistance have been largely ignored or overlooked. In this book we highlight part of the Iraqi people's struggles for a more inclusive political stability.

This case study of Iraqi women in exile draws on sociohistorical data, including primary and secondary sources. Contacts established with representatives of two resistance movements (the Iraqi National Foundation Congress, or INFC, and the Association of Muslim Scholars, or AMS) in Syria and Jordan snowballed, allowing access to other opposition groups and enabling thirty-five volunteer women (twenty in Syria and fifteen in Jordan) to engage in qualitative conversational interviews with us as researchers.[2] The data were collected over two months (February and March 2011). A minimal, semi-structured framework was used that allowed a free-flowing conversation to occur on such themes as experiences encountered during and in the wake of the invasion, family and interpersonal relations, psychological and emotional coping strategies, modes of resistance, and the role of faith. Transcription, translation, and thematic analysis of the data followed, and patterns of consensus and contradiction were identified. All names have been changed to protect the interviewees.

We begin the chapter with a contextualizing overview of the sociopolitical situation in Iraq after 2003, the emergence of the resistance movement, and the role of women; then, we critique the research on this subject. In the second half of the chapter, we address the experiences of Iraqi women during and after the 2003 invasion, with a particular focus on the coping and empowerment strategies of resistance based on national and religious modes of identity.

Contextualizing the Situation in Iraq After 2003

In March 2003, the United States and Britain invaded Iraq. The destruction wrought by the war and subsequent occupation caused havoc, resulting in countless civilian deaths, the radical degradation of the nation's infrastructure, and the virtual meltdown of the country's socioeconomic structures. Iraqis now call the invasion "the second destruction," the first being the devastation of Iraq's Abbasid state and society by the Mongols in 1258. "This is not a liberation," said one of the interviewees, Umm Ahmed. "This is another form of the Mongol invasion."[3]

Emergence of the Resistance Movement and the Role of Women

According to the representative of the AMS in Amman, the kind of resistance that developed in response to the invasion was an instinctive form of resistance, and it has deepened continuously to the present time.[4] Despite the withdrawal of British and US forces from the major cities, most Iraqis believe that the US occupation is still very much being enforced and that the current government is a proxy of the United States, an occupational government designed to serve US rather than Iraqi national interests. In the words of the spokesperson for the National Front for Jihad and Liberation, "The Iraqi resistance does not believe that the Americans will withdraw through negotiations or by any political means. Therefore, the resistance will continue until the last American bases and last American soldiers are out of Iraq."[5] This view is echoed by the head of the Women's Will Association, Hana Ibrahim: "The political process in Iraq is an illegitimate process; it is a continuation of the occupational project; as long as there are American bases, the resistance will continue. The Iraqis have the right to choose all forms of resistance, including armed resistance."[6] Another voice, that of Suha, a twenty-four-year-old student at the University of Jordan, reflected the typical attitude of women toward the current government: "This is a sectarian government, and it is mainly serving the occupational project that aims at dividing Iraq into ethnic and sectarian provinces. Resisting this government is essential, for it is responsible for the prolonga tion of the American presence in Iraq up to the present time."[7]

Most of the women we interviewed in Jordan and Syria sympathize with and support the resistance. For them, fighting for the resistance was an eminently just cause: "The resistance did not go to America to fight them, the resistance was defending itself and the Iraqi people on Iraqi soil," said Umm Ali.[8] They spoke about the resistance with respect and admiration and were proud of its achievements: "The resistance is our pride and dignity," said Umm Zahra.[9]

Violent conflict is not something new for Iraqi women. Before the recent occupation, they were forced to confront the consequences of the brutal and debilitating Iraq-Iran War (1980–1988), followed by the Gulf War (1990–1991). Their engagement with the consequences of these conflicts was both instinctive—the defense of their homeland—and self conscious, with modes of activity that were clearly defined and intelligently articulated. The role of women during these conflicts was essential; it fell to them, in large part, to keep the wheels of society moving while so much of the nation's manpower was channeled to the war effort, bearing in mind the eight long years (1980–1988) when such a high proportion of Iraqi men were forced to go to the war front, and were either killed or wounded. Therefore, when Iraqi women hear about the assumption that women are excluded from society, they are affronted, and refute the misconception with vehemence. Their long-standing objective engagement with a socioeconomic fabric strained, if not torn apart, by violent conflict, together with their own personal narratives, their subjective expression of the premises of their activity, and the ways in which they have understood their activity, come together to belie the stereotype of the oppressed, excluded, and muted Muslim woman. These women would find not only inaccurate but also absurd the suggestion that they are the powerless victims of a patriarchal society.

Various forms of resistance throughout the country emerged in response to the occupation; they ranged from armed resistance to peaceful and communal acts of protest, and women were active participants in all aspects of the movement. Peaceful forms of opposition by organized political forces as well as spontaneous civil protest took place against the occupation and its policies. Resistance efforts in this context included peaceful demonstrations, passive noncooperation, and criticism and exposure of the occupation policies in fiction, painting, poetry, and the media, in general and on the Internet. Hana Ibrahim commented on the nature of the resistance:

> Iraqi resistance is unique in the sense that it started immediately after the invasion. This is something that has never happened before in other parts of the world. For most often, when an invasion takes place, some time is needed for the occupied nation to produce a resistance movement, the nation has to register the act, absorb it and then respond to it. In Iraq that did not happen; the resistance was instinctive and spontaneous, and it preceded the political ambience that supported it.[10]

The resistance movement cut across ethnic and religious divides. It included men and women from groups that constituted the social fabric of Iraqi society, which united the opposition forces.[11] The movement had broad grassroots support and increased in extent and intensity; some asserted that the movement "was born not only of ideological, religious, and patriotic convictions, but also as a response to the reality of the brutal actions of this occupation and its administration. It is a response to arbitrary break-ins, humiliating searches, arrests, detention, and torture."[12] It could be argued that the nature of the resistance was in general the result of a blend of nationalist and religious elements that reflected the social, ethnic, and religious composition of Iraq, but it was also fed by the specific values of Islam and how these values were seen to be relevant within the context of modern Iraqi politics. In the modern history of Iraq, Islam has typically been conceived in terms of personal choice rather than as a tool of governance. Therefore, within the context of the resistance, there was no sharp distinction between nationalism and religion: the operative "personal choice" was simply to end the occupation, and both patriotic sentiment and Islamic identity alike dictated this imperative. It is the consensus on this imperative that accounts for the fact that diverse social and political groups were able, in large part, to tolerate each other's differences and collaborate for the sake of the common goal: to end the occupation.

Although there were many opposition groups, two resistance movements were eventually "formalized" amid the mayhem that engulfed Iraq after the invasion: the Iraqi National Foundation Congress, and the Association of Muslim Scholars. Both were well known for their integrity, transparency, and clarity of aims and objectives, namely, to end the occupation and to eliminate all aspects of its legacy. Their leaders commanded respect among broad sections of the Iraqi people primarily because of their national loyalty and patriotic history. As stated earlier, access to other opposition groups and to participants for the study was obtained through these two associations.

The Iraqi National Foundation Congress

The INFC is an alliance consisting of more than twenty-two political parties and independent organizations, including women's organizations and civil society organizations, chief among which were the Society for Iraqi Jurists and the Association of University Lecturers, which had among their members female professionals. Among the prominent members of the INFC were Jawad al-Khalisi, a notable Shiite scholar and head of the Khalisi school, a seminary that was set up in 1911 by his grandfather, who led the Shiite resistance against the British occupation in the 1920s; Muthana Harith al-Dari, a member of a distinguished Sunni family historically opposed to foreign occupation; and Wamidh Nadhmi, former professor of political science at the University of Baghdad and long-standing Arab nationalist. The INFC was created in 2004 as an anti-occupation movement and included people who refused to take part in any political process that would legitimize the occupation and its government. They called for an immediate and unconditional withdrawal of the occupation forces; stressed the unity and integrity of the Iraqi territory and its people, irrespective of religious, denomination, and ethnic identity; and declared their right to resist by all means, including armed resistance. They believed that the occupation and its government were behind the disunity and destruction of the country, especially the ethnic and sectarian schisms, and called for the establishment of independent local and national committees to observe and study the cause of sectarian crimes and deal with them in a constructive way.[13] The head of the Women's Will Association, whose organization was part of this group, explained why the INFC believed that both the occupation and its government were behind the sectarian and ethnic conflicts that tore the country apart:

> We were accepting of each other. We—Muslims, Christians, Sunnis and Shi-
> ites, Arabs and Kurds, and all other ethnic groups—lived together peacefully.
> The occupation and its government wanted to divide Iraq on an ethnic and
> sectarian basis, they wanted to politicize both the Shi'a community and the
> ethnic Kurds, but they did not succeed, for historically Iraq, unlike Lebanon,
> never entertained the idea of sectarian and ethnic division. We as women are
> against such a policy.[14]

This sentiment was supported by a number of our interviewees. The following statement by Umm Muthana may be taken as typical: "We are one
social fabric; it is the occupation government that is encouraging sectarianism and ethnic division, and I am against this policy."[15]

The reality of the occupation and its government on the ground did not
allow the INFC to work freely in society. Various forms of punishment
were inflicted on those who were involved in the anti-occupation movement; under such circumstances members of this movement were forced to
go into exile, go underground, or assume low-profile roles.[16]

The Association of Muslim Scholars

The AMS emerged as an Islamic resistance movement opposed to the
invasion. It was originally founded on April 14, 2003, five days after the
invasion, by a group of thirteen religious scholars, but later expanded to
include intellectuals, politicians, doctors, engineers, lawyers, and university professionals. Its current secretary-general is Harith al-Dari (not to be
confused with Muthana Harith al-Dari, founding member of the INFC,
mentioned above), a respected religious scholar, whose grandfather
fought the British occupation of Iraq in the early part of the twentieth
century.[17] His charisma and tenacity in the face of many threats and much
pressure earned him great respect and trust,[18] which positively affected
the AMS's reputation.[19] The AMS has branches in most Iraqi cities, and
offices abroad in countries such as Jordan, Syria, Egypt, Turkey, and
Yemen that are staffed by dedicated persons.[20] Inside Iraq, it runs social,
educational, medical, and charity programs dedicated to helping Iraqis in
need of shelter, food, clothing, schooling, and medical care.[21] Its offices
abroad work to mobilize Arab, Muslim, and world opinion against the
current government and also to attend to those Iraqi exiles who need
financial and medical help.[22] Apart from a human rights section that doc-
uments human rights abuses inside Iraq, the AMS also has an effective
education and media section, geared primarily toward resisting the occupational government. It has a satellite TV channel, al-Rafdan,[23] based in
Cairo, which broadcasts political, religious, and educational programs,
live interviews, and documentaries on life inside Iraq.[24] The AMS pub-

lishes a website and a newspaper titled *Al-Bas'ir*,[25] as well as research projects, monographs, short articles, and press releases that focus on the current situation in Iraq and issues related to the broader Arab and Muslim world. One of the publications worth mentioning is "Statements of the Association," which regularly highlights the events, especially breaches of human rights, that have taken place in Iraq since 2003 and explains the AMS view on how to restore stability and unity in Iraq in a way that will accommodate all its ethnic, religious, and political groups.[26] The AMS also cooperates with human rights groups to bring attention to the multiple crises affecting the country.[27]

Although members of the AMS are predominantly from a Sunni background (including members of Arab, Kurd, and Turkmen origins), its policies and strategies cut across religious, sectarian, ethnic, and political boundaries. Also, the internal system of the association is open to everyone irrespective of any political, religious, or ethnic loyalties. The AMS works actively with other opposition forces, including the INFC, and prominent individuals such as the Shiite scholar al-Khalisi, and Ayatollah Ahmed al-Hasani al Baghdadi,[28] who opposed the occupation and criticized Ayatollah Ali al-Sistani for his support of the current political process; al-Baghdadi is also an ardent opponent of Iran's role in Iraq.[29] The AMS has good relations with secular nationalist forces and other non-Muslim groups such as Christians, Sabians, and Mandaeans, who agree with AMS principles on the issue of the illegality of the regime.[30] The AMS rejects ethnic and sectarian division and asserts the historical coexistence and respect between the various groups of the society; it also prohibits any attacks on Iraqis, whatever their religious, sectarian, or ethnic backgrounds, and seeks to cooperate with religious leaders and politicians to contain attempts that could lead to civil unrest. In addition, it condemns terrorism and makes a clear distinction between legitimate resistance and indiscriminate attacks that terrorize innocent people.[31]

The AMS refused to be part of or acknowledge the political process.[32] It called for the immediate and unconditional withdrawal of all foreign troops, opposed federalism and upheld the unity and sovereignty of the country, and emphasized the right to resist the occupation by all means, including armed resistance. On the basis of this political and moral support, thirteen armed resistance groups met in 2009 to form a united front and went on to appoint Harith al-Dari as their representative on the international scene.[33] Because of the association's public support for the armed resistance, many of its members were threatened, forcing some, including the secretary-general, Harith al-Dari, to leave Iraq and live in exile.[34] But this situation has not had any impact on the role of the AMS, including women's activities inside or outside Iraq.

Problematization of This Research Project

Despite the importance of the subject, there are very few studies on the situation of women in Iraq.[35] Research on women within the context of Islamist politics and national resistance is even more rare, whether in English or Arabic, which makes the present book all the more important. When we asked ourselves why there is such neglect of this subject, we thought of many factors that might explain the absence of interest in the subject, the most important being the policy adopted by the Bush administration vis-à-vis the resistance. From the beginning the US government denied the existence of any indigenous opposition to the occupation and insisted that the majority of Iraqis were overjoyed to be liberated from the dictatorship of Saddam.[36] US officials declared that the reports mentioning resistance were referring to weak and sporadic actions from loyalists of the old regime.[37] As such, they were deemed not to represent a substantial and coordinated resistance movement. The United States continued to stress that if there was a problem, it pertained to "isolated and uncoordinated remnants coupled with small numbers of terrorists moving into the country from elsewhere in the Arab world. In no way were these representative of the mood of Iraqis as a whole."[38] Paul Bremer, the head of the Coalition Provisional Authority in Iraq, concurred with the administration, stating that these activities were led by "those few remaining individuals who have refused to fit into the new Iraq [and] are becoming more desperate."[39] These assumptions were to prove inaccurate: a full-scale national and Islamic resistance movement evolved that was to severely stretch US-led forces, and it consisted of ordinary Iraqi people comprising various components of Iraqi society.[40] This point is important, given the fact that both the United States and the Coalition Provisional Authority tended to give the impression that the resistance was composed of only radical foreign fighters and members of the Sunni minority in the areas of the Sunni triangle or the "death Triangle,"[41] primarily because they "fared better than did other groups under the Hussein regime" and their opposition was ascribed to "the eclipse of their relatively privileged status"; it was this, US officials argued, that "propelled disproportionate numbers into opposition."[42] In doing so, they gave the impression that the opposition was confined to a relatively small geographical area with vested personal interests.

However, the spread of the opposition movement to other major cities, such as Mosul, Kirkuk, Baghdad, Basra, Amara, Diwaniya, and Najaf, clearly contradicted the official US assertion that the resistance was centered in and around the Sunni triangle.[43] For the United States to admit that there was real internal resistance would have meant discrediting one of the main pillars used by the coalition forces to justify the invasion, namely, the liberation of the Iraqi people; it would be even worse for them to admit that significant numbers of Iraqi women supported the resistance.[44] To take one instance, just one year after the invasion, even those female exiles who received funding from the United States and the UK to return home and establish organizations promoting women's rights made dismal reports of the situation of Iraqi women in the postinvasion era.[45] In this context, it is important to consider how US slogans regarding liberation, the promotion of democracy, human rights, and women's freedom (key issues for the invasion) have been viewed by some analysts, especially in the Muslim world, as not having been as vigorously pursued as the policies for economic control and regeneration. The disingenuous pursuit of such aims served to reinforce the theory of the clash of civilizations between the West and the rest of the world, especially the Muslim world. As Nadje Sadig al-Ali and Nicola Christine Pratt argue, "These notions construct an 'us versus them' mentality that underpins and helps to perpetuate the War on Terror [because] within the discourse of US officials, as well as other Western politicians, democracy, human rights, and women's rights distinguish the United States and its Western allies from the 'rest.' They are used as markers of 'civilization' as well as reasons for 'civilizing' others."[46]

Under the tight security that characterized the Coalition Provisional Authority, it would be virtually impossible for the representatives of the resistance to identify themselves or release information on the resistance to any researcher interested in working on the subject. In response to the view that there was no resistance, Aisha Ahmed, a social and political activist, stated in 2011, "The resistance is alive, but it is deliberately besieged. Why do they want to convince us that Iraqis do not deserve to resist? Our country was occupied and it is logical that we should resist. Also, our religion and heritage encourage us to resist—why, then, do they want to deny us the right to resist?"[47]

The US government focused on the elements of foreign Islamic radicalism within the context of the resistance to avoid drawing attention to the shortcomings of any espoused aims to democratize the politically oppressive forces within Iraqi society. In keeping with their image of avowed aims being thwarted, US officials would often point to radical Islamists who entered Iraq and joined members of the old regime to destroy the "democratic process brought about by America." Undeniably, the fact that borders were unguarded immediately after the invasion allowed some radical Islamists to enter the country easily, chief among whom were elements of the terrorist group al-Qaeda, but it is questionable whether their number was as significant as that projected by the Bush administration.[48] According to some, the administration seized upon this issue and exaggerated the number of foreign fighters in order to advance its policy of prosecuting the war on terror in Iraq.[49] Security analyst Paul Rogers stated that the number of foreign fighters was very often inflated by the US government in order to give the impression that there was no real indigenous opposition to the occupation, thus deflecting attention from the internal resistance and linking Iraq to the wider global policy of the war on terror.

> Although the presence of foreign Islamic paramilitary forces in Iraq was not substantial during the first year of the war, there was a marked tendency in Washington to over-emphasise their presence, even to the extent of saying that Iraq now represented the core geographical region for the conduct of the war on terror. In the words of George W. Bush, the aim was to "bring 'em on," in the sense that they would congregate in Iraq and there be eliminated. A central part of the war on terror would therefore be fought 6,000 miles from the USA.[50]

Iraqi women intellectuals understood the discrepancies between the avowed aims of the Bush administration and the reality of their lives under occupation. As el-Ali and Pratt amply explained, Iraqi women were among the most literate in Arab society from the 1950s onward and were valued as a necessary component of the workforce, which had been much depleted because of the wars waged by Saddam Hussein and his Baathist regime. Although they suffered as a whole due to the oppressive policies and practices of his regime, they were not hapless victims of male oppression. When they were asked about the connection between the resistance and terrorism, the women we interviewed did not accept the implied equation: Randa Ahmed, a doctor living in Syria, explains,

> When they speak of the resistance they say these are terrorists, or Baathists or loyal Saddamists, but this is not true. We know the reason why they say so; they want to justify the invasion, especially for those who came with them. America and its allies say that they brought freedom to the Iraqis; we tell them you brought destruction and you are invaders and we are proud resisters.[51]

By linking the resistance with foreign terrorism, the United States, one could argue, discredited the resistance as a legitimate movement worthy of academic investigation; it also prevented any attempt by any credible researcher to have access to fair and balanced information on the movement. What lent this policy credibility was the special situation of the resistance movement inside Iraq. In the chaos and lawlessness that followed the invasion, criminal gangs, some radical foreign fighters, and different militia groups belonging to competing religious and political parties brought havoc to the country. They indiscriminately targeted civilians throughout the country, making it difficult to tell who was a terrorist, an insurgent, or a resistance fighter. This certainly tainted the image of the resistance, not only inside Iraq but also regionally[52] and internationally, and discouraged interested researchers from contemplating any attempt to work on or with the resistance under such circumstances: "In Iraq the word 'resistance' is forbidden," reported Amal Hassan, a refugee in Syria and mother of two children. "If a person is suspected of being a member of the resistance, or even supporting the resistance, the person will be killed or arrested and charged with terrorism under section 4 (*Irhab,* on terrorism) of the law."[53]

The criminalization of resistance activities meant that there was no clearly defined and stable base of resistance inside the country where interested researchers could fairly easily meet with representatives of the movement: "We are not like Hizbullah in Lebanon or Hamas in Gaza. Talking about the resistance entails charges of terrorism and subsequent capital punishment," said Umm Iman, a political activist living in Syria.[54]

Moreover, the resistance has its own problems: it consists of many disparate groups that are united only against the current government. Some of them may have joined an umbrella organization, especially those who have accepted the secretary-general of the Association of Muslim Scholars as their "mediator" or the "spokesperson" on their behalf, but certainly they do not form a cohesive united front with a clear and defined political program.[55] This, according to Muhammad Bashar Al-Fadhi, the spokesperson for the Association of Muslim Scholars, "may have had a negative effect on the overall situation of the resistance, but by the same token," he added, "it has helped the resistance not to be identified as one single group which could be easily targeted."[56] Given this situation, organizations such as the AMS and INFC are particularly important in gaining access to opposition groups for the purpose of conducting research.

Beyond Iraq's borders, there is no real support for the resistance: "There is no single country in the world that has seriously supported the Iraqi resistance. We rely solely on ourselves and we will achieve our goals by liberating our country from the current government," said the spokesperson of the National Front for Jihad and Liberation.[57] In Syria and Jordan, "We are not allowed to play an effective political role," the media representative of the Association of Muslim Scholars in Damascus told us.[58] Saudi Arabia cannot afford to upset its special relationship with the United States, and Iran has vested interests in not entertaining the resistance primarily because the Tehran government supports the current Iraqi political process that is dominated by groups nurtured in Iran. We have offered multiple reasons that the research and literature associated with women and the national resistance in Iraq are so limited. The significance of the present study lies in its ability to provide a forum in which women's voices about resistance to the current regime in Iraq can be heard. The rest of this chapter, therefore, is devoted to giving expression to those voices as they describe their personal experiences and their coping strategies.

We seek to expose the extent of the violence witnessed or experienced by many Iraqi women on a daily basis throughout the many conflicts and intend to cast light on the impact of this violence on the lives of women and their families. The women also air their views of the resistance movement and reveal the manner in which they felt empowered by the ambience of the resistance. Throughout the following section, the voices of the women interviewed take precedence.

Experiences of Iraqi Women During and After the 2003 Invasion

The interviews regarding women's experiences during and after the invasion reveal how both women and their families have been traumatized. These painful experiences touched every aspect of their lives and played an important role in their views and reactions to the resistance. They are highlighted below thematically.

Resigned but with a Defiant Mood to Resist

The view that all Iraqi people would not resist and instead would welcome the coalition forces as liberators proved to be incorrect.[59] Haifa Zangana claims that even before the invasion, there were already defiant elements among Iraqis: "Baghdad isn't Saddam's property, it is ours and we shouldn't leave it."[60] She adds that some of those who were abroad, especially in neighboring countries, decided to risk their lives and return home, and when they were asked for the reason, they answered, "to defend Iraq" or "to be with my family."[61] When women were asked to recall their mood just a few days before the invasion and describe their situation and what they did in the face of imminent attack, the majority of the responses revealed worries, hopes, but also defiance. Umm Hamza, who lived in Baghdad at the time and now lives as a refugee in Syria, said,

> I was worried about what would happen if America attacked, worried about my family, my relatives, my friends and my country. I hoped and prayed many times that Bush would change his mind. We could not afford to have another war. We were already tired of years of wars and crippling sanctions. I tried to be optimistic and advocated a policy of peace among the people, but was also determined that, if they attacked, we would resist.[62]

And Umm Shatha stated,

Just before the attack, we (as an educated women's group) met and advocated a policy against the war. We organized demonstrations in collaboration with women peace advocates from around the world, and we carried paintings saying that women are creative and women create lives and because of that we are against the war. We made it clear that the policy of war is a policy of death and destruction. But by the same token we, as Iraqi women, prepared ourselves to resist if they would attack.[63]

Evaluation of the Invasion

With the start of military operations, the optimistic mood that coalition forces would march through the country easily soon changed when signs of tough resistance, especially in the south of the country, including in the cities of Umm Qasr and Nasiriya, took the coalition forces by surprise. This level of opposition, according to Toby Dodge, "reflected a factor that continues to dominate Iraq: nationalism."[64] It sprang from their sense of responsibility for defending their lands but also from their awareness that US forces came to take over Iraqi oil and other natural resources rather than liberate them. Many of the women interviewed believed the Americans had entered Iraq because of its oil wealth. Umm Sondos had this to say: "America came in because of our oil and other natural resources; they did not come because they wanted to liberate us."[65] And Umm Aisha agreed: "Iraq is rich in oil and gas, and America wanted to benefit from this wealth."[66]

According to AMS spokesperson al-Fadhi, the resistance started immediately in the aftermath of the fall of Baghdad; initially, it was a peaceful resistance with demonstrations first in Baghdad, especially in the Adthmiyyah neighborhood on April 18, 2003.[67] That was followed by another peaceful demonstration, this time in the city of Fallujah, 35 miles west of Baghdad. On April 30, 2003, US troops fired into a crowd, killing sixteen people and thus paving the way for real confrontation.[68] Some had argued that at first, many Iraqis "had hoped for a measure of truth in the claims made by the United States to justify the invasion, and for a measure of intelligence from the occupiers. Had there been such, the resistance would have followed a different profile and trajectory."[69] But that was not to be the case.

The incident in Fallujah, together with a series of polices deliberately adopted by the occupying forces, left no room for peaceful opposition and ultimately cleared the way for an overall resistance movement that in due course became strong and engulfed the rest of the country. First, the decision by Paul Bremer, head of the Coalition Provisional Authority, to abolish the army, the police, and security personnel on the assumption that they belonged to the old regime had the result of depriving more than 300,000–400,000 people of jobs, salaries, and pensions. It was argued that many of

those affected by the decision became disenchanted and eventually susceptible to the views of the resistance movement.[70] This was followed by
another controversial decision, the disbanding of the Baath Party—known
as the de-Baathification Decree, which continues to propel the resistance.
The decree stated that all people who held jobs

> in the top three layers of management in every national government ministry,
> affiliated corporations and other government institutions (e.g., universities and
> hospitals) shall be interviewed for possible affiliation with the Ba'ath party.
> . . . Any such persons determined to be full members . . . shall be removed
> from their employment. This includes those holding the more junior ranks of
> . . . [member] and [active member], as well as those determined to be senior
> party members.[71]

The decree had major ramifications. The majority of party members,
especially those at the lower levels, had joined the party because it
improved their employability (that applied across religious, ethnic, and sectarian divides). It is estimated that 500,000 to 1 million qualified people,
including teachers, doctors, lawyers, and professionals, found themselves
overnight without jobs and without any future security as a result of the
decision. Not only was a substantial section of the professional classes
deprived of a livelihood—people who were innocent and had no blood on
their hands—but also the country itself was deprived of the expertise and
services of those professionals, which were desperately needed for the postinvasion reconstruction process. Worse, the commission responsible for the
implementation of the decision was supervised by Ahmed Chalabi, who
took advantage of the situation to achieve his political ambitions to punish
and purge his personal enemies, in the process spreading fear and engaging
in witch hunts among certain groups.[72] Hence, large numbers of ordinary
middle-class professionals were forced to become refugees as a result of
this policy, people who could otherwise have remained and contributed to
the reconstruction of the country if the occupation had been less totalitarian
in its rejection of everyone connected to the Baath Party. It would appear
that the United States did not understand the adage "Two wrongs do not
make a right." Certainly, the Baathists were wrong to tyrannize the popu-
lace of Iraq and force everyone to join the party if they wanted to advance
in their careers, but the US policy was a kind of mirror image of this
tyranny: rejecting everyone in the party instead of focusing on the leaders,
those really responsible for forcing the Iraqi people into a straitjacket called
the Baath Party. It would have been so much more farsighted if the United
States had exercised tolerance toward the ordinary card-carrying Baathists,
who were acting under orders, not giving them, who probably hated the
Baathist regime as much as anyone else, and who may well have welcomed

US troops as liberators if the Americans had allowed them to contribute to the new Iraq. The United States might then have been seen as not only having liberated ordinary, non-Baathist Iraqis from Saddam's tyranny but also having liberated the majority of the members of the Baath Party from their Baathist overlords. But as we show later in the chapter, US policies alienated even the non-Baathist professionals, not just out of nationalist and Islamist sentiment but because of the specific, heavy-handed, if not brutal way in which the United States stamped its authority on the Iraqi people.

Lamenting the implications of these two decisions, former senior adviser to the US Department of State David Phillips stated, "The Bush administration had committed one of the greatest errors in the history of US warfare: It unnecessarily increased the ranks of its enemies . . . who would re-emerge to lead the insurgency against U.S. troops. Mistakes disbanding the armed forces and concerning de-Baathification would have lasting and far-reaching ramifications."[73] One of the worst impacts of the decision was the legitimization of the killing of Baathists, through de-Baathification or *ijtethath*, which means "uprooting," "weeding out," or "killing" in Arabic. Hence killing Baathists has become legitimate in Iraq; many, including women, have been targeted by government militias under this pretext.

The Impact of US Policy on Families

Many of the women interviewed had their lives changed by these decisions. Umm Asrar described her experience: "We could not understand why they relieved him suddenly of his job," she said about her husband, who was a police officer. "Overnight we found ourselves with no source of income, and with four kids it was a great shock for us. At the age of thirty-four it was very difficult for him to retire, so we sold our flat and came here to Syria. We opened this small grocery store to earn a living, but it is hardly generating enough money to allow us to live with dignity."[74]

Umm Ma'dah, whose husband was working in the security service, echoed the same puzzlement and feeling of despair: "We were worried about what would happen. My husband was expecting the worst and that was what happened. He was not only released from his job but was also hunted for his life, and we did not know why. We were lucky that we managed to escape to Syria and now our lives are at least safe, but our living conditions are very difficult when you live as a refugee."[75]

Umm Waheed, sixty-five years old, whose husband worked as an engineer for the ministry of the military industry, described her experience as hell:

We had no idea what to do. He [her husband] lost his job, and his life was on the line. We left everything behind: our home, our car, our family, and our homeland. We went to Jordan and asked for refugee status but were denied, and then we had to go to Syria, where we managed to get refugee status. My husband did not do anything wrong, he did not harm anyone, and we are at a loss as to why we were treated that way. We were looking forward to a good retirement, but now we live in despair.[76]

Islam as a Source of Spiritual Sustenance and Psychological Empowerment

The Muslim world in general and the Middle East in particular are places where modes of life generally continue to be dominated by religion. Islam is still dynamic and can play an important role in allowing people to cope with difficulties. Most Muslims believe that religion is supposed to provide a sense of constant assurance that everything that happens is by the will of God; therefore, people find solace in the traditional quranic virtue of *readh*, which refers to tranquil acceptance of the will of God, whether bad or good. In this context, when the women were asked what sustained them in the face of their difficulties, all of them said it was religion that kept them going; they felt that they were empowered by their faith: "It is my faith in Allah that has kept me out of insanity," said San'a, a university lecturer now living in Jordan who lost her job in Iraq because she was a member of the Baath Party. She continued, "Islam gives you serenity and tranquility and empowers you to face severe difficulties. I should be working at home and benefiting my country at a time when it needs me badly, but I am unable to do so."[77] The same sentiment was echoed by Umm Abbas: "Without my faith in Allah I would not have [survived] the unspeakable difficulties I have endured."[78]

Cultural Misunderstanding

Most of the women interviewed mentioned their distress at the lack of cultural sensitivity on the part of the US authorities,[79] especially the way women were treated, and at the lack of manners common among US soldiers when dealing with ordinary Iraqi people: "The Americans do not like us, and they do not respect us," said Huda Ahmed, a secondary school student in Amman. "Very often they used abusive language such as 'Fuck you,' 'Fuck Iraqis,' and 'Fuck Iraq.'"[80]

"When they burst into our house," Umm Salaam said, "they terrorized everyone, including children. They went into the bedroom and threw away everything they laid their hands on—our clothes, our pictures, and all other private and intimate things." She added, "It was a shocking experience that I will never forget."[81]

Umm Hisahm recalls her ordeal when soldiers raided their house:

> One night the American soldiers suddenly raided our house, and they started immediately beating my husband in front of me and the children. I begged them to leave him alone, but they did not listen. The children were crying, seeing their father being beaten by the soldiers. It was an awful sight; as you know, in our culture the father is a respected figure and is the head of the family, and to see him being humiliated in this way in front of his wife and children was very difficult to bear. When they did not stop beating him, I suddenly dropped unconscious on the floor and since then I have contracted epilepsy.[82]

Detention, Torture, and Rape

The most traumatic issue for the women we interviewed was the abuse that took place at Abu Ghraib prison. Soon after the invasion, US forces reopened the prison, the symbol of oppression and death under the previous regime.[83] The building was redesigned and used as the main detention center in Baghdad for people suspected of being involved in the armed resistance or for top Baathist officials. By late 2003, about 8,000 detainees, including women and children, had been imprisoned there. According to the International Committee of the Red Cross, most of them were innocent.[84] Once again, the prison became the symbol of torture and death, described as

> a place where, in some cases, torture resulted in death. Where photographs and videos, kept as memorabilia, show breaking chemical lights and pouring the phosphoric liquid on detainees; pouring cold water on naked detainees; beating detainees with a broom handle and a chair; threatening male detainees with rape; allowing a military police guard to stitch the wound of a detainee who was injured after being slammed against the wall in his cell; sodomizing a detainee with a chemical light and perhaps a broom stick; and using military working dogs to frighten and intimidate detainees with threats of attack, and in one instance actually allowing a dog to bite a detainee.[85]

The women we interviewed also spoke of torture resulting in death, whether in Abu Ghraib or elsewhere in Iraq. The following comes from Umm Bakr, a mother of three daughters and two sons:

> My twenty-year-old eldest son was a member of the resistance. When they captured him, they put him in Abu Ghraib prison. For six months he was heavily tortured in an attempt to force him to give information about the resistance, but he refused. When they realized that they could not extract any information

from him, they decided to kill him. . . . Fearing for the life of my now only
son and the life of my three daughters, we decided to flee to Amman. My only
conciliation for his loss is that he died as a martyr.[86]

Similarly, Umm Zeyad, who originally comes from Basra and now
lives in Syria, recounted, "My brother was detained and tortured. When he
was released, he decided to take them to court. To silence him, they killed
his father."[87] And Umm Atyiah revealed that she "spoke against the government. The second day, they detained my cousin as a way to silence us.
It is very frightening, but we have to resist. Fear is a natural thing. I fear
for my children and for my husband, for if they will take him I will be
finished."[88]

The release of the disturbing photos showing US soldiers violating
human rights and the Geneva Conventions by torturing and humiliating
Iraqi prisoners sent shock waves throughout the world. In Iraq, where the
pictures were widely circulated, most people believe that the prominent
US officials and commanders who were behind these acts have not been
brought to justice. As a result, "few Iraqis [are] now willing to trust American claims of protecting human rights or supporting the development of
democratic institutions."[89] Umm Abeer's reaction is more typical: "When I
saw the pictures, I could not believe that the American soldiers could do
something like this. They say that they trained their soldiers to respect others and be mindful and aware of human rights, but it seems that they did
not learn anything."[90] Umm Lumah, a refugee living in Syria, asked, "Is
this the freedom and democracy they brought to us? I no longer trust
them."[91] Patrick Hagopian explains that the sexualized, humiliating positions assumed by prisoners in the photos could not have been dreamed up
by naive guards; rather, they were orchestrated by pro-war neocons who,
just before the war, had circulated the idea of exploiting Arab men's vulnerability to sexual indignity as a means of terrorizing the Iraqi people and
subjugating them. The idea was borrowed from Raphael Patai, who wrote
a book entitled *The Arab Mind* in which he alleged that the veiling of
women and the rules of segregation that govern the relationships between
men and women have made sex a prime mental issue in the Arab world.
This book "became the bible of the neo-cons on Arab behaviour."[92] Those
who devised this strategy, Hagopian says, aimed to inflict the maximum
humiliation on Muslims and Arabs, who, according to Patai, "were self-
conscious about their sexuality and proud of their masculine dignity. Thus,
photography was not just the means by which the torture was recorded; it
was an instrument of torture in itself. The interrogators hoped that fear of
exposure before their family and friends would turn the prisoners into pli-
ant informers."[93]

Women's detention, torture, and rape were especially painful issues for Iraqis and remain one of the most intense and painful points of discussion among the interviewees. Because of the concept of honor, women who are assaulted are disposed to keep silent and not seek help publicly. Abdulhamid Al-ani, the AMS representative in Damascus offered this explanation:

> The weakest point in man's ability to withstand any pressure is the attack on his women's honor. When the Americans wanted to find the whereabouts of the men; they took their wives, sisters, mothers, or daughters. This is because women in our culture are regarded as the symbol of family honor, if they lose their honor through rape; the entire family loses its respect and reputation. Therefore, most Iraqi women who were detained, tortured, and raped did not come out and speak about it publicly. There are a few exceptions, for example the case of Abeer and Nadia. The former was burned by those who committed the act, while the latter went into hiding for fear of being killed by her family. Here in Iraq, it is not like the situation in the West where women can go public to defend themselves against those who rape them.[94]

Hence, when some Iraqi women were detained, tortured, and raped, the shock was deepened by the contrast between such atrocities and the US claims to be giving Iraqis freedom. According to Hana Ibrahim, head of the Women's Will Association,

> They told us that they came to offer us freedom. We tell them that freedom is not a ready-made thing to be offered. Freedom is something that can be created, made and gained from within. We did not ask them for freedom. We are responsible for our freedom. Tanks do not bring freedom and bullets do not bring freedom. The occupation did not bring freedom. It brought torture and rape for many Iraqi women.[95]

When the US handed over Abu Ghraib prison on August 15, 2006, to the occupation government, the situation in the prison deteriorated further, forcing the UN to report just over a month after the handover, that

> Detainees' bodies showed signs of beating using electrical cables, wounds in different parts of their bodies, including in the head and genitals, broken bones of legs and hands, electric and cigarette burns . . . bodies found at the Medico-Legal Institute often bear signs of severe torture including acid-induced injuries and burns caused by chemical substances, missing skin, broken bones (back, hands, and legs), missing eyes, missing teeth and wounds by power drills or nails.[96]

Umm Saad described her ordeal: "My eighteen-year-old son did not do anything. After school, he used to help his ailing father in the grocery we owned. He did publicly criticize the current government. One late night the security forces raided our house and took him. After two months of anxious waiting we finally received his dead body from the hospital near us. His body showed clear marks of violent abuse."[97]

Hagopian stresses that abuse and torture were widespread, not only in US detention centers in Iraq but also in other US-controlled facilities around the world, and these behaviors were consciously tolerated by both political and military leaders: "It appears . . . that abuse permeated US detention facilities in a number of countries, facilitated by the permissive approach to the treatment of prisoners advocated by the nation's political and military leaders."[98] Even worse, he goes on, these forms of abuse take place "in some jurisdictions in the United States [where] there is now a prison culture that tolerates violence and it's been there a long time."[99]

One of the reasons that US forces escaped criminal prosecution is their immunity under both Iraqi and international law.[100] This issue is very important since those who committed crimes against innocent people were not brought to justice. In this context, Umm Iman, a teacher living in Amman, recalled what happened to a teenage boy she saw in 2005:

> One day I was driving in the west of Baghdad and suddenly we were told that we had to give way to American tanks. While we were waiting for the tanks moving ahead, I saw an American soldier point his gun into a car next to me; in that car there was a mother and her seventeen-year-old son. Suddenly that soldier shot the boy in the head, killing him immediately, leaving his mother holding him in disbelief. I watched the tanks moving on as if nothing happened. I will never forget this incident, and wonder who would find justice for this boy.[101]

Sectarian Strife

The exacerbation of social unrest brought about by government strategies also led to an increase in sectarian violence throughout the country. The invasion heralded the disruption of the social fabric of Iraqi society, a disruption brought about by a politically manufactured divide between the various groups in Iraqi society. Historically, this divide was constructively handled by Iraqis themselves in a way that ensured harmonious coexistence and even positive integration such that the phenomenon of intermarriage between Kurds and Arabs and Shia and Sunnis was markedly on the rise. It is estimated that before the invasion, intermarriage involving members of the major ethnic groups and Islamic sects had reached 25 percent of the total population.[102] After the occupation, so-called dormant sectarian divisions were encouraged because of the way in which the new government was formed, and this ultimately led to the destruction of indigenous modes of coping with ethnic and cultural differences among the Iraqi people. The inability of the occupying forces to control violence stemming from, among other factors, the government's divisive policies resulted in widespread killings, abductions, and forced displacements, as a result of which every social, ethnic, and religious group in the overall social fabric of the Iraqi society was severely traumatized.

"During the 'civil strife,' I lost my nephews and nieces, my cousins, and my brothers-in-law. Namely, most of my extended family," said Umm Montaha from Basra (now living in Syria). She continues, "In our area we used to live in harmony as one family. But suddenly everyone changed, neighbors no longer trusted each other, and finally we were forced to leave. It is not easy to be forced to leave your house, your extended family, and your homeland."[103] Umm Muhammad added, "My husband and I grew up in [Shaljyah] west of Baghdad and were living happily with the neighbors, but things changed and we no longer felt that we were living in a safe place. One night a militia gang raided our house and told my husband to leave the area or he would lose his life. That night we had to leave. We were lucky that they did not kill him."[104]

Following the invasion, state institutions were looted by organized gangs, and the occupying forces seemed incapable of protecting them. This, in addition to the disbanding of the army, police, and security forces, led to a total collapse of state institutions and key civil society structures, forcing people to seek protection within their communities. Self-reliance within community groups had worked well during the years sanctions had been imposed (1991–2003) because the state still provided some kind of over-arching structure, despite its policy of violently suppressing any activity deemed to be subversive. However, these groups had limited resources and were only successful within the framework of existing state institutions such as the police force. After the emergence of organized gangs and the ensuing corruption, those communities were left alone to fend for themselves in the face of attacks and evictions carried out by gang militias and death squads under the pretext of sectarianism.[105] They were also left on their own to overcome the desire for revenge that came after they witnessed atrocities committed against their own fellow citizens. Many communities can withstand a great deal because their neighborhoods are tightly knit, but they need professional and civil society structures to endure the kind of onslaughts that occurred after the invasion. According to Zangana, "the people who could set up and manage such structures have been systemati-cally evicted or physically eliminated since the occupation, and communi-ties have been forced to fall back on deeper but weaker resources."[106]

In the absence of an effective state structure and in order to sustain a sense of community, some mosques took the initiative and started providing some basic services, such as food, classes for school, and clinics for medication. But even these initiatives were very often blocked or dismantled when US troops and Iraqi soldiers would raid mosques on the charge that they harbored "insurgents." In certain cases, imams were executed or detained, and ordinary people were killed.[107] In this context, let the following account suffice: "On Tuesday, troops from the Iraqi army, supported by US helicopters, raided a mosque in the heart of old Baghdad. The well-respected muezzin Abu Saif and other civilians were executed in public. Local people were outraged and attacked the troops. At the end of the day, thirty-four people had been killed, including a number of women and children. As usual, the summary execution and the massacre that followed were blamed on 'insurgents.'"[108]

Forced Displacements

Forced displacements, whether inside or outside Iraq, and their impact on women and children were among the most common themes discussed by the women we interviewed: "All women are affected by forced displacement. When I came here to Syria, I was in shock. For a year I felt that I was dislocated. I could not compose myself; I suffered from depression and isolation," said Umm Omar, a schoolteacher living in Syria.[109]

Umm Leila told a similar story, emphasizing its effect on her children:

> I was very worried about the impact of moving to another place on my children; my son and daughter were thirteen and fourteen years old, respectively, when we were forced to leave. The displacement meant that there was no stable home for them and no stable schedule for school. I was worried about their reactions and education. It was not easy to suddenly move. We had to prepare them. The move affected them psychologically: for a while they felt sad and depressed and could not understand why they had to move.[110]

Collective Punishments

The response of the US government and its military commanders to the activities of the resistance had severe ramifications for ordinary people. In every case, the responses were characterized by heavy retribution, including collective punishments that often led to the death of innocent people. Take, for example, the case of the city of Fallujah, which led the initial armed resistance. After more than two months of aerial bombardment in the fall of 2004, US forces staged a second attack on the city. British forces supported the attack with hundreds of troops moved from the south to form part of a "ring of steel" around it. Under air cover and supported by artillery, US troops entered the city to clean up the area from "the insurgents." The assault on the city caused widespread destruction: hundreds of civilians were killed, and thousands of its residents became refugees. On November 7, 2005, Italian correspondent Sigfrido Ranucci released news that the United States had used white phosphorus weapons in dealing with the resistance. The authenticity of the report was based on an interview with a former US soldier who took part in the assault and admitted that he "heard the order to pay attention because they were going to use white phosphorus on Fallujah. In military jargon," the soldier goes on, "it's known as Willy Pete. . . . Phosphorus burns bodies, in fact it melts the flesh all the way down to the bone. . . . I saw the burned bodies of women and children. Phosphorus explodes and forms a cloud. Anyone within a radius of 150 meters is done for."[111] One of our interviewees, Umm Saja, reported,

> For weeks and weeks Fallujah was bombarded and besieged from everywhere; for days and days women, children and elderly people were trapped in their homes. There was no way to get out of their houses to get essential needs, and when women tried to open outside doors to check on their children or attend to their needs, the Marines pointed guns to their heads and killed them. Seventy-two women were killed by shots in the forehead by marines in Fallujah for no reason except that they opened their home doors to look for the children. The effect of those scenes during which I saw human beings struggling to save their lives has changed me forever. I no longer feel like an ordinary woman with rosy dreams. I saw the truth that shook me to the core.[112]

* * *

The sections above reveal multiple forms of violence experienced by women during the war and civil conflicts that engulfed Iraq. Their stories testify to the vehemence of the occupation and the civil strife and their impact on the livelihood of both women and their families. The violence of the war in Iraq far exceeded that described in western media. Various forms of violence were witnessed firsthand by the relatively silent women of Iraq, now exiled from their country. These insights are painful but powerful in enhancing our understanding of the lasting legacy of displacement and broken families that is the reality for many Iraqi people. Women's testimonies of violence also reveal to us why the majority of those we interviewed support the resistance both in word and deed and why they felt strongly about the need for the success of the resistance.

The following section focuses on the women's testimonies of agency, revealing differences in the ways they coped with their situations and looking at the role of Islam in their actions.

Coping Strategies:
Resistance, Islam, and Empowerment

In this chapter, we foreground the voices of Iraqi women, exiled after the US invasion, with the purpose of increasing our understanding of how people survive in a serious conflict. In war men are normally profiled more than women, and coverage of Iraq has reflected this. But the women were the mothers, wives, daughters, and sisters who lived the terrors of the invasion and aftermath and who needed to find ways through their disrupted lives. In this section, we highlight the ways in which survival was achieved and the role of faith in general and Islam in particular in their success and empowerment. It is worth mentioning briefly that a small number of Iraqi women supported the occupation and the establishment of its government. Those women openly decried any form of resistance, which they equated with terrorism: "The ongoing attacks against coalition soldiers remind us that the war to free Iraq is not over. Ba'athists and other anti-democratic forces in the region want to maintain Iraq in a state of chaos. They hope their attacks will pressure us to retreat. We must not allow that to happen: If our enemies succeed in Iraq, it will be a victory for tyrants and terrorists worldwide."[113] They also advance the view that Iraqi women needed to be liberated.

Most of the women interviewed disagreed with them and regarded these women as "collaborators" promoting US interests rather than the interests of the Iraqi people, especially those of women.[114] As Hana Ibrahim said, "We never accepted the view of those new liberal women who justified the invasion; we told them that the liberation of women was organically linked to the liberation of their country. Women's issues could not be separated from the resistance against the occupation."[115] The women we interviewed were critical of them and argued that those women had failed to understand the feelings of ordinary Iraqi women[116] or to show real concern about their needs and priorities before or after the occupation: "Those women had never understood the situation of Iraqi women because they did not live inside the country. They lived abroad and knew of our situation only through the media; they did not share our suffering," said Umm Asmahan, a mother of one daughter.[117]

They also opposed the rhetoric used by the collaborators that Iraqi women were passive and needed help, referring to it as a shallow understanding of the history of the Iraqi women's movement and stressing that Iraqi women were historically active in public life and could be found in schools, the media, politics, and so on.[118] They insisted that before the invasion, there was space available for women's advancement in society, that there was significant mobility for women and great opportunities for them to take part in building their country. Even if the political environment was brutal and oppressive, there was nonetheless a socioeconomic ambience in which women were empowered in practically all significant dimensions of society.[119] Iraqi women's achievements were described by the UNICEF report in 1993 as one of the best in the Arab world at the time.[120] Clearly, the women interviewed reacted strongly against the women who supported the invasion and did not regard them as a genuine voice serving women's rights: "These women do not represent us. They represent their own political parties, they use us to advance the agenda of their parties, and there is [a] great difference between those who represent women's rights and defend them as such and those who use women's issues to propagate party politics," said Umm May, a schoolteacher living in Amman.[121]

As we stated earlier, the majority of women we interviewed rejected the invasion and opted for resistance, either direct or indirect or both. For ordinary Iraqi women, life during the occupation and civil strife involved different forms of struggle: surviving their daily lives, meeting their basic needs (food, water, gas, electricity, and medicine), keeping their families together, and coping with the status quo were all forms of resistance to the mayhem of political and social instabilities. Hence, the concept of resistance among Iraqi women acquired a broader meaning than is usual and blended with spiritual elements. Two of the women we interviewed explained how their faith sustained them. Umm Anas described the difficulty of caring for a special needs child:

> Our daily life was like living in hell: every day we planned how we would cope with our daily needs, how we could get the food, the gas and the medicine we needed. My son was disabled, and he needed special medicine. His father used to run around to the chemists to make sure that we had enough for him; sometimes we were lucky, but most of the times we were not lucky, and my boy had to suffer. Another issue was the lack of electricity, and with a boy with special needs that was a real struggle. In summer, especially, when it was hot, I used to put him in a bucket of water all day; otherwise he would not stop crying. It was our faith in Allah that kept us going.[122]

Umm Anfal was widowed after the occupation: "I lost my husband, and with three kids I had to start working. Every day I went to work, I would kiss and hug the kids for fear of not seeing them again. By the time I was home and they were back from school, I used to thank God for our safety."[123]

Most women, especially those who lived in the capital, spoke of the worries they and their families endured when they had to go to work, not knowing whether they would be safe till the end of the day or not, and how they called to Allah for protection. One said her main worry was whether she would face car explosions or indiscriminate shootings; another described how her father used to wait for her in the main street and prayed to God for her safety.

In response to these daily struggles, the women developed strategies to resist the occupation; there were many strands of resistance. Although traditionally men carried the weapons, women did take part in the actual struggle, according to Hana Ibrahim:

> We as a nation were prepared to resist. Our Islamic beliefs and upbringing encouraged us to fight the occupation, and from the beginning we said that if they entered our country, we would fight them. For example, just before the invasion, we [the Women's Will Association] produced a special edition of our magazine *Gender,* and we put on the main page a picture of a woman holding a gun, and it says that resistance is the answer to the occupation.[124]

Iraqi women took part in the armed resistance, but the extent of their involvement has not been fully documented.[125] Many women spoke of using weapons; one fought alongside her son; another defended herself for fourteen days when her town came under attack. Despite examples of direct involvement in the war, the majority of women interviewed said that women's role was to support the men who do the fighting. They stressed that women should not fight, that their role was to help the fighters, but if there were not enough men, then women could fight. "In our culture men are responsible for keeping us safe, and although Islam allows women to take part in the battles, it is the men who should carry the weapons and fight," said Umm Amal.[126]

Women's support roles involved protecting the fighters, helping with carrying or hiding weapons, detonating explosives, taking or passing messages, helping fighters mentally and psychologically, supporting them financially (through selling their jewelry or farm products), and keeping life as normal as possible for the families in the absence of men. Women also encouraged their sons to fight, and when they died, they accepted the event with satisfaction on the basis that they were martyrs.[127] On the latter role, Umm Aisha said, "Those women deserve respect and veneration. They felt that their religious and national duty called on them to encourage their sons to fight for they sensed that there was a bigger issue that demanded their sacrifices—that was to liberate their homeland. This is a fresh way of thinking and a new understanding of the concept of Jihad."[128]

The supportive roles of women extended beyond conflict zones to help those ordinary people who were caught in between factions and became victims of violent conflict. For example, women protested the dismissal of their relatives from jobs, asked for the release of detainees from prisons, demanded information on their missing loved ones, organized social gatherings to help families with basic needs (food, clothes, and even generators to supply electricity), trained other women (especially widows) in skills that might generate some income, ran training sessions on first aid to help clinics with their daily needs of supplying and collecting blood and other essential medical requirements, offered advice on social issues such as divorce and domestic violence (which had become epidemic as a result of mounting poverty, forced displacement, and lack of general security), and offered classes for children who were unable to reach schools. The women also identified and reached out to those families who had lost their loved ones and were left with no regular financial support.[129] They stressed that there were hundreds of those collective efforts throughout the country and their benefits cut across religious, ethnic, and sectarian boundaries.[130] "As a group of women, we used to identify the families in the areas that suffered most and provide them with material help. We used to visit those who lost their loved ones and shared their bereavements. Moreover, we helped those children who could not attend school by opening classes and teaching them," said Umm Montaha.[131]

Apart from social survival strategies, women also spread information about the situation for women in Iraq. Hana Ibrahim explained,

> In the face of constant harassment and loss of liberty we politicized and activated our issue as women and stressed that our liberation was linked directly with the liberation of our country. We as women were not isolated from what was taking place in our country. So we decided to issue a newspaper that highlighted to the public all forms of suffering facing women under occupation. It was not an easy task. We did not have financial help to keep it going, so we did all the work in our homes, from writing to design to final production. To get the proceeds needed, we used to sell the paper to our friends, but also we distributed it at the checkpoints; it was a very risky job. Imagine you produce an anti-occupation newspaper while you were under the occupation.[132]

Cultural resistance offered another outlet for contesting the more subtle forms of hegemony of the occupation. Many Iraqi women artists, poets, musicians, documentary filmmakers, singers, and actors affirmed and reinvented their collective memory, history, and cultural identity: "The occupation wanted to change our thinking and our way of life. We decided to fight back and make people aware of this cultural hegemony so that they would oppose such hegemony. We held poetry workshops to create poetry of resistance," said Umm Yasmeen.[133] Young women, especially, played an important role by highlighting their sufferings under occupation on blogs and elsewhere on the Internet.[134] "I used to mobilize the nation and highlight our suffering to the world through the Internet," said Umm Ali.[135] Some Iraqi women, especially those with talents and professional skills, practiced passive resistance, refusing to get involved in any initiatives led by the occupation. "I am a qualified civil engineer. I used to work in Mahmudiyah, south of Baghdad, as a designer for a government company. I designed many bridges and repaired some of those damaged during the Gulf War. After the invasion, I decided to give up the job and not cooperate," said Umm Raghad.[136]

Underpinning the strong support for all forms of resistance, including armed resistance, at least among the women interviewed in Syria and Jordan, were many factors. Most important was their sense of religious duty: they felt that their country had been illegally occupied and therefore they had the right to defend themselves and their faith: "Islam instructs us as Muslims to fight back if we are attacked, and if we are killed while we are defending our country, we will be rewarded in the hereafter," said Umm Nurayn.[137] There was also a deep sense of humiliation caused by the invasion, which manifested itself in various ways, such as the portrayals of Iraqi women as passive, oppressed, and in need of liberation. "We were liberated before they came," said Umm Suha. "We had one of the best education systems in the region, and it was free for everyone. Women worked everywhere in hospitals, universities, schools, companies, farms, everywhere."[138]

It is essential to recall here the way Iraqi women were treated under the occupation. They were regularly abused directly and indirectly; they were often arrested and detained, and while in prison, they were beaten and tortured.[139] In Abu Ghraib alone, women were systematically abused, raped, and "photographed naked . . . [and] forced at gunpoint to bare their breasts," including "an Iraqi woman in her 70s [who] had been harnessed and ridden like a donkey."[140] Some women were put in solitary confinement for twenty-three hours a day with no forms of relief or entertainment. Those who became pregnant were released and then disappeared because they had either been killed (having lost their honor) or committed suicide.[141] Those arrested were either relatives of Baathists or ordinary women; the latter were often used as bargaining chips to force male relatives to inform on rebels or give themselves up. In addition, women were kidnapped, raped, and killed by militias, including government militias, and these crimes were never investigated by the government.[142] Around 600 women were assassinated, including 350 female doctors who worked in the medical and humanitarian sectors.[143] Women were also killed randomly during house raids or at checkpoints.[144] Trafficking of Iraqi women for the sex trade in the surrounding countries and beyond became a major issue, and with the violence and kidnapping that accompanied such activities, it was estimated that between 2003 and 2010 about 4,000 Iraqi women disappeared, one-fifth of them under the age of eighteen.[145]

Displacement, especially outside the country, traumatized Iraqi women; for them, home was no longer safe because occupation forces were pursuing them; hence they supported the resistance to regain their lost spaces. This testimony by Umm Ali recounts a typical life-changing crisis when an interviewee was forced to flee her country:

> We were with the children visiting our in-laws in the north of Baghdad. We left home at 10 PM, and we were there by 11 PM; by 12 PM we received an urgent call from our next-door neighbor informing us that the American and Iraqi armies had raided our house looking for my husband and destroying anything they could lay their hands on. We had to flee that night to Amman. We still do not know why they were after my husband, but we lost everything, the house, my jewelry, and the wheelchair of my disabled boy. We have to support the resistance because they are protecting our home land, our nation, and our dignity.[146]

The by-products of the occupation directly affected women's personal situations. This was highlighted by the UN envoy to Iraq in January 2011, who warned that one in five women in Iraq ages fifteen to forty-five was subjected to violence from their male relatives, and a staggering 50 percent of marriages were ending in divorce, a phenomenon never heard of in Iraq before the invasion. More than 70 percent of Iraqi women and girls opted out of going to school and college for fear for their lives; over 2 million widows were left alone to fend for themselves,[147] and the pre-invasion family law that offered women some measure of equality and freedom was undermined by the emergence of an authoritarian conservative culture that glaringly subordinates women to male authority.[148] These were some of the factors that compelled women to have recourse to violence and support violent conflict.

Despite their suffering, most women interviewed were resolute about supporting the resistance: "I am proud of the resistance. It forced the occupation forces to withdraw from our country; the resistance stopped the American plan to control Iraq and the rest of the neighboring Arab countries; the resistance proved that Islam is still alive; it restored to Islam its youth; and it demonstrated that Islam and Muslims are able to defend themselves," said Umm Mahmood.[149]

What was the impact of war, resistance, and Islam on women? The majority of women interviewed said that it was positive; despite what they had endured, they came out stronger and more assertive. They stressed that Islam and the resistance have empowered them, partly because they have overcome their ordeals and survived. Also, they now occupy a public space and are able to challenge and question certain attitudes and policies. However, one has to see if these kinds of political and public empowerment will positively affect women's broader conditions, especially those connected with economic, social, and cultural policies and the power structure at both state and societal levels. Judging by recent developments in the "Arab spring" countries, there will not be great improvement. Power is not a zero-sum game. One can gain in one domain and lose in others. In reality, Iraqi women's rights have suffered a setback because of the ways in which the fractured state under US control has responded to social unrest and the ongoing instability in the country.

Conclusion

There is no doubt that the occupation led to the emergence of an Islamist and nationalist resistance, and significant numbers of Iraqi women have supported and were involved in the resistance. Despite the attempt to ignore and eliminate the resistance, the women we interviewed manifested a remarkable resourcefulness and various strategies of resistance, although all had experienced a life crisis in which fleeing their homeland was the only way to survive. All were positive about the resistance movement: "The resistance is alive and will continue to resist until the last American base is closed, and will not accept any other forms of occupation, whether Iranian or otherwise, after the Americans have completed their final withdrawal," said Abdul Nasser al-Janabi, the speaker of the National Front for Jihad and Liberation.[150] The women interviewed said that resisters were demonized as terrorists in order to deny any indigenous resistance and any right to resist. Many Iraqi women suffered all kinds of abuse: arrest, torture, rape, intimidation, collective punishments, destructions of their towns and cities, random killings, and displacements. As a way of overcoming these difficulties, they said that they trusted in God and continued in good faith for the benefit of their homeland: "Women's resistance has added a new understanding to the concept of Jihad in Islamic thought," said Umm Salwa.[151] For the women interviewed, the resistance continues despite the official withdrawal of the occupation forces; the legacies of the invasion persist, and its government is still active and operative. Their hopes for swift change are rising, and their efforts are gaining further momentum with the current strides toward democracy and self-determination that have been taken in the Arab spring. In this chapter, we have raised the profile of women's engagement in that struggle by highlighting the voices of Iraqi women who have articulated their own direct and indirect roles in responding to, coping with, and inwardly overcoming the oppressive hegemony produced by the occupation of their country. We have helped to refute the assertion, or blind assumption, that Arab women are passive, helpless victims in need of liberation by force, showing it to be either a mode of wishful thinking or a self-justifying fallacy.

Notes

1. Nadje Sadig al-Ali has done some work in this context. See al-Ali and Nicola Christine Pratt, *What Kind of Liberation? Women and the Occupation of Iraq* (Berkeley: University of California Press, 2009).

2. There are many opposition movements representing various groups, but we chose these two for practical and legal reasons.

3. Interview, Damascus, Syria, February 5, 2011.

4. Interview, Amman, Jordan, March 3, 2011.

5. Interview, Damascus, February 6, 2011.

6. Interview, Damascus, February 8, 2011.

7. Interview, Amman, March 8, 2011.

8. Interview, Damascus, February 10, 2011.

9. Interview, Damascus, February 10, 2011.

10. Interview, Damascus, February 14, 2011.

11. See Association of Muslim Scholars (AMS), Education and Media Section, "An Open Message to the Fighters in Iraq," 2007, 16–18.

12. Haifa Zangana, *City of Widows: An Iraqi Woman's Account of War and Resistance* (New York: Seven Stories Press, 2007), 20.

13. Ibid., 129–131.

14. Interview, Damascus, February 14, 2011.

15. Interview, Damascus, February 15, 2011.

16. Zangana, *City of Widows*, 131.

17. Born in 1941 in the town of Abu Ghraib to a distinguished religious family, Harith al-Dari was initially given a religious education by private tutors. Afterward, he went to school first in Fallujah, and then in Baghdad to further his religious education. Upon finishing his primary education, he went to Al-Azhar University, where he earned a BA, an MA, and a PhD. He taught in various universities and religious institutions, in Iraq, Jordan, and the United Arab Emirates. He published and lectured widely. In 2003, he was elected as secretary-general of the newly formed AMS. Email communication with the representative of the AMS in Damascus, Syria, August 28, 2011; more information on al-Dari can be found also on the AMS website, www.iraq.amsi.org.

18. See, for example, some of his high-profile roles and meetings in Association of Muslim Scholars, Education and Media Section, "Activities of the Association of Muslim Scholars in Iraq," 2010, 329–349.

19. See, in this context, the comments written by a group of Arab intellectuals, researchers, and well-known journalists in AMS, Education and Media Section, "Writings on the Association," 2007, 5–58.

20. In 2007, the AMS was forced to close its main branch in Umm al-Qura in Baghdad. The AMS also was and continues to be prevented from opening branches in Najaf, Karbala, Sulymaniah, and Erbil. Interview with AMS representative in Damascus, February 8, 2011.

21. See, for example, AMS, "Activities of the Association," 15–23, 353–356.

22. Interview with the representative of AMS in Damascus, February 16, 2011.

23. The AMS used to have a radio station called Umm al-Qura in Baghdad, that focused on the association's political, social, and educational role, but was forced to close it down. The building was taken over by the government. Interview with the representative of the AMS in Damascus, February 16, 2011.

24. Email communication with the representative of the AMS in Damascus, Syria, September 4, 2011.

25. For a brief summary of the history, aims, and objectives of the newspaper, see Harith al-Mofraji, "Al-Bas'ir: Story and History," AMS, Education and Media Section, 2010.

26. All AMS statements can be found on its webpage, www.iraq.amsi.org.

27. See AMS, "Activities of the Association," 248–316.

28. Al-Baghdadi is one of the eminent grand ayatollahs within the context of the Shiite establishment in Iraq; he has followers both inside and outside Iraq. He has published more than thirty books. His overt criticism of the occupation, its government, and Iran's role in Iraq put his life in danger and forced him to live in exile in Syria. Interview, Damascus, February 20, 2011.

29. Interview, Damascus, February 20, 2011.

30. The Sabians and Mandaeans are followers of John the Baptist, or the Prophet Yahya in Islam.

31. See, for example, some of the AMS statements in this context: 16, 17, 18, 21, 22, 23, 28, 32, 35, 36, 50, 75, 76, 77, and 78 from 2004; 84, 106, 107, 128, 134, 156, 157, 158, 161, 174, 175, 183, 197 from 2005; and 204, 205, 211, 244, 249, 251 from 2006.

32. In contrast to other Islamic groups, such as the Islamist Party, which accepted the political process. See the AMS statement in this context, number 169, 2005.

33. Interview, Amman, March 8, 2011.

34. See AMS statements 9, 11, 22, 24, 27, 38, 39, 40, 44, 47, 49, 51, 55, 56, 60, 61, 62, 53, 66, 69, 70, 71, 72, 79, and 82 from 2004; 87, 89, 92, 99, 102, 103, 104, 114, 122, 124, 129, 130, 152, 162, 168, 185, 186, and 198 from 2005; and 206, 234, 242, 247, 252, 261, 264, and 267 from 2006.

35. There are a handful of studies in this context. See al-Ali and Pratt, *What Kind of Liberation?*

36. There were clear indications from the early days of the occupation that Iraqis (with the exception of people in the Kurdish north) showed no sign of rejoicing: "There was not a widespread welcoming of liberation [during] the early weeks of the war. . . . What was surprising, and indeed discouraging to coalition forces, was the lack of welcome [even] in those substantial parts of central Iraq and almost the whole of the south-east of the country that were populated primarily by Shia communities." See Paul Rogers, *Iraq and the War on Terror* (London: I. B. Tauris, 2006), 12.

37. The view advocated by the administration, that the initial stage of the resistance was led by Baathists loyal to Saddam, was accepted without challenge even by intellectuals and academics. See, for example, V. Spike Peterson, who says, "while resistance was initially concentrated in groups supportive of Saddam Hussein and/or the Ba'ath party, resentment of the invasion quickly drew various other groups into attacks on US and coalition forces." Peterson, "Gendering Informal Economies in Iraq," in Nadje Sadig al-Ali and Nicola Christine Pratt, eds., *Women and War in the Middle East: Transnational Perspectives* (London: Zed, 2009), 47.

38. See Paul Rogers, *A War Too Far: Iraq, Iran, and the American Century* (London: Pluto, 2006), 60.

39. Ibid., 69.

40. See Haifa Zangana, "The Iraqi Resistance Only Exists to End the Occupation," *Guardian* online, April 12, 2007.

41. Zangana claims that the term was used to uphold the atrocities of the occupation, especially the killing of civilians because "in the Sunni Triangle, it is not easy to determine who is a combatant and who is not. And this sometimes results in unintended consequences that the military says it can't avoid. Civilians sometimes get caught in the crossfire. They get shot, or worse, they get killed." See Haifa Zangana, "There Is More Than One Triangle of Resistance," *Guardian* online, September 14, 2006.

42. See Carl Conetta, *Vicious Circle: The Dynamics of Occupation and Resistance in Iraq* (Cambridge, MA: Project on Defense Alternatives, Commonwealth Institute, 2005), 22.

43. For more, see Zangana, "There Is More Than One Triangle of Resistance." Paul Rogers also said that "it is clear that the insurgency is deeply embedded in much of the country and is certainly not limited to the so-called 'Sunni triangle' north of Baghdad." Rogers, *Iraq and the War on Terror*, 88.

44. Just before the war, and to lend the invasion some form of legitimacy, George Bush announced, "The Iraqi people gotta know, see, that they will be liberated." Similarly, Tony Blair agreed with him and declared, "To Iraqis we say we'll liberate them." Quotes are taken from Zangana, "The Message Coming from Our Families in Baghdad," *Guardian* online, April 3, 2003.

45. See, for example, the article by Hozan Mahmoud, the UK representative of the Organisation of Women's Freedom in Iraq, "An Empty Sort of Freedom," *Guardian*, March 8, 2004.

46. See al-Ali and Pratt, *What Kind of Liberation?* 5–6.

47. Personal interview, Damascus, February 20, 2011.

48. It is relevant in this context to recall that one of the pretexts used by the Bush administration to invade Iraq was the stress on the link between al-Qaeda and Saddam's regime, despite the fact that "there appears to be little evidence that Al-Qaida had links with the Iraqi regime; on the contrary, its ideology was violently opposed to secular Ba'athism, so that the movement and the regime were enemies rather than conspirators." See Patrick Thornberry, "It Seemed the Best Thing to Be Up and Go," in Alex Danchev and John Macmillan, eds., *The Iraq War and Democratic Politics* (London: Routledge, 2005), 122.

49. According to al-Ali and Pratt, the invasion of Iraq (and beforehand Afghanistan) formed part and parcel of the US empire-building strategy that aimed at the following: controlling other courtiers and their resources through military interventions; reshaping and repositioning power relations within and between the United States, its allies, and its adversaries to ensure US preponderance; and confirming US supremacy through economic power, moral and cultural authority, and military might. See al-Ali and Pratt, *What Kind of Liberation?* 5.

50. Paul Rogers, *Iraq and the War on Terror*, 20.

51. Interview, Damascus, February 21, 2011.

52. One could refer to the case of Zarqawi (who, as a member of the terrorist group al-Qaeda, gained a foothold in Iraq after the US invasion of the country in 2003) and his role in alienating public opinion in Jordan after the suicide bombing at a wedding party in Amman that killed a considerable number of innocent people.

53. Interview, Damascus, February 17, 2011.

54. Interview, Damascus, February, 17, 2011.

55. The AMS was concerned enough about this in 2007 to issue a message to the resistance, advising the movement to attend to this important issue. Interview with the representative of the AMS, Amman, March 21, 2011.

56. Interview with the representative of the AMS, Muhammad al-Faydhi, Amman, March 14, 2011.

57. Interview, Damascus, February 22, 2011.

58. Interview, Damascus, February 23, 2011.

59. This impression was nurtured and passed on to the Americans by Saddam's opponents, some of whom had developed a close relationship with the US government and were, until the invasion, supported and funded by the US government. Chief among them was Ahmed Chalabi, who was sentenced in absentia by a Jordanian court to twenty-two years in prison in 1992. The story goes back to 1977 when Chalabi moved to Jordan after he finished his study in the United States. With the agreement of the Jordanian authorities he set up Petra Bank, which he headed. In 1989, news spread of his misconduct, upon which he fled with his wife and children to live in London. The Jordanian court found him guilty of thirty-one charges, "including embezzlement, theft, forgery, currency speculation, making false statements, making bad loans to himself, to his friends, and to his family's financial enterprises in Lebanon and Switzerland." Jane Mayer, "Ahmed Chalabi, the Manipulator," *New Yorker,* May 29, 2004, www.archive.truthout.org/article /ahmed-chalabi-the-man, accessed May 19, 2013. During the preparation stage for the US invasion, his Iraqi National Congress (INC) "became a one-stop shop for information on Iraq." His role in convincing the Bush administration to venture into Iraq is described by former senior adviser to the US State Department David Phillips: "Smart U.S. officials allowed Chalabi to spin them because they badly wanted to believe what he said. Suspending their disbelief, some envisioned Chalabi as a Mesopotamian Spartacus mobilizing vast legions to take over and reshape Iraq. Chalabi systematically provided the rationale for going to war and promised that coalition forces would be greeted as liberators." See David Phillips, *Losing Iraq: Inside the Postwar Reconstruction Fiasco* (New York: Basic Books, 2005), 68.

We have to stress the exceptional case of the Kurdish part of Iraq, however, which continues to regard the US-led invasion as a liberation. This is no doubt in large part due to the violently oppressive measures taken by Saddam Hussein to suppress the Kurds from the 1970s onward.

60. See Zangana, "The Message Coming from Our Families in Baghdad."

61. Ibid.

62. Interview, Damascus, February 28, 2011.

63. Interview, Damascus, February 28, 2011.

64. See Toby Dodge, "War and Resistance in Iraq: From Regime Change to Collapsed State," in Rick Fawn and Raymond A. Hinnebusch, eds., *The Iraq War: Causes and Consequences* (Boulder, CO: Lynne Rienner, 2006), 214.

65. Interview, Amman, March 20, 2011.

66. Interview, Amman, March 20, 2011.

67. Interview, Amman, March 15, 2011.

68. See AMS, "An Open Message to the Fighters in Iraq," 6.

69. Zangana, *City of Widows*, 127.

70. Some US officials expressed concern about the wisdom of the decision (the British also were not happy but did not do anything to stop it), stressing, "There are a number of [officers] who are very good, courageous, and determined people, which, if given the chance, would be part of the solution in Iraq. These are proud

officers with enormous energy and capability. If we harness their capability, it'd be a good thing." See Phillips, *Losing Iraq*, 152.

71. Cited from Abdullah Thabit, *Dictatorship, Imperialism, and Chaos: Iraq Since 1989* (London: Zed, 2006), 98.

72. Ibid.

73. See Phillips, *Losing Iraq*, 153.

74. Interview, Damascus, February 24, 2011.

75. Interview, Damascus, February 24, 2011.

76. Interview, Damascus, February 26, 2011.

77. Interview, Amman, March 3, 2011.

78. Interview, Amman, March 3, 2011.

79. In this context, we can also refer to the attempt to replace the old flag with a new one that excludes the phrase "God Is Great," or the decision by the members of the Coalition Provisional Authority, who were appointed by Paul Bremer, to consider the date of the formation of that council (April 9, 2003), which coincides with the date of the fall of Baghdad, as a national day for Iraq. For the former, see Conetta, *Vicious Circle*, 4; for the latter, see AMS "An Open Message to the Fighters in Iraq," 27.

80. Interview, Amman, March 17, 2011.

81. Interview, Amman, March 17, 2011.

82. Interview, Amman, March 17, 2011.

83. The prison was empty because the previous regime had ordered the release of all prisoners just before the invasion.

84. See Haifa Zangana, "Foreword: Abu Ghraib: Prison as a Collective Memory," in Louise Purbrick, Jim Aulich, and Graham Dawson, eds., *Contested Spaces: Sites, Representations, and Histories* (Hampshire: Palgrave Macmillan, 2007), xiii.

85. The quote is from Zangana, "Foreword," xiv.

86. Interview, Amman, March 19, 2011.

87. Interview, Damascus, February 22, 2011.

88. Interview, Damascus, February 22, 2011.

89. See Thabit, *Dictatorship, Imperialism, and Chaos*, 100.

90. Interview, Amman, March 19, 2011.

91. Interview, Damascus, February 22, 2011.

92. Patrick Hagopian, "The Abu Ghraib Photographs and the State of America: Defining Images," in Louise Purbrick, Jim Aulich, and Graham Dawson, eds., *Contested Spaces: Sites, Representations, and Histories* (Hampshire: Palgrave Macmillan, 2007), 22.

93. Ibid.

94. Interview, Damascus, February 28, 2011.

95. Interview, Damascus, February 27, 2011.

96. Zangana, "Foreword," xiv. This description reminds me of the brother-in-law of a friend, who was kidnapped, tortured, and killed; when they picked him up at the hospital morgue, his face was mutilated beyond recognition.

97. Interview, Amman, March 25, 2011.

98. Hagopian, "The Abu Ghraib Photographs," 28.

99. Ibid., 29.

100. This explains the reality of the occupation. They knew that they would not be accountable before Iraqi or international law.

101. Interview, Amman, March 25, 2011.

102. See Muhammad Bashar al-Fadhi, *The Illusion: The Outcome of the Political Process Under the American Occupation of Iraq* (Amman: Dar al-Jeel al-Arabi, 2007), 111.

103. Interview, Syria, February 7, 2011.

104. Interview, Amman, March 30, 2011.

105. It is important, in this context, to stress that despite attempts by politicians, parties, and their warring militias to force civil war on the country, ordinary Iraqi people, together with the resistance forces, succeeded in averting a full-scale civil war, as happened in Lebanon in the 1970s.

106. Zangana, *City of Widows*, 18.

107. See, for example, the statement by the Association of Muslim Scholars on January 2, 2004, in which it stated that US troops had raided a mosque south of Baghdad (Umm al-Tubool), arrested the imam and members of the committee of the mosque, desecrated the place, scattered copies of the Quran on the floor, and thrown away the turbans of the imam and the members of the committee. In that same week, US troops arrested another three imams in the capital. All of these imams who were arrested, the statement adds, had no connection with the resistance, and some of them are known to advocate peaceful resistance. See *Statements of the Association of Muslim Scholars*, compiled by Muhammad Bashar al-Fadhi, Part 1 (Amman: Dar al-Jeel al-Arabi, 2008), 56. AMS statements can be found at www.iraq-amsi.org.

108. See Zangana, "The Iraqi Resistance Only Exists to End the Occupation."

109. Interview, Damascus, February 28, 2011.

110. Interview, Damascus, February 28, 2011.

111. See Zangana, *City of Widows*, 95.

112. Interview, Amman, March 12, 2011.

113. See Haifa Zangana, "Colonial Feminists from Washington to Baghdad: Women for a Free Iraq: A Case Study," in Jacqueline S. Ismeal and William W. Haddad, eds., *Barriers to Reconciliation: Case Studies on Iraq and the Palestine-Israel Conflict* (Lanham, MD: University Press of America, 2006), 73.

114. Most of these women lobbied very hard for the invasion of Iraq.

115. Interview, Damascus, February 13, 2011.

116. One of the representatives of this group went to President Bush to thank him for his efforts and leadership that led to the "liberation" of her own people. See Zangana, *Colonial Feminists from Washington to Baghdad,* 63–84.

117. Interview, Amman, March 13, 2011.

118. For more detailed information on this subject, see Zangana, *City of Widows*, 28–78.

119. We know that the situation deteriorated in the few years just before the invasion as a result of the comprehensive sanctions imposed on Iraq, which affected the health, education, and well-being of women and children. It also led to the emergence of social conservatism that restricted the personal rights women had previously worked to gain.

120. See the report cited in Haifa Zangana, "The Three Cyclops of Empire-Building: Targeting the Fabric of Iraqi Society," in Amy Bartholomew, ed., *Empire's Law: The American Imperial Project and the "War to Remake the World"* (London: Pluto, 2006), 253.

121. Interview, Amman, March 10, 2011.

122. Interview, Amman, March 10, 2011.

123. Interview, Amman, March 10, 2011.

124. Interview, Damascus, February 29, 2011.

125. This was confirmed by AMS spokesperson Muhammad al-Fadhi in an interview in Amman on March 29, 2011.

126. Interview, Amman, March 29, 2011.

127. Email communication with the office of the AMS, Damascus, April 18, 2011.

128. Interview, Damascus, February 11, 2011.

129. See, for example, the initiatives of the women's section of the AMS in "Activities of the AMS," 323–325.

130. See, for example, Women's Will Association and the Women's Dawn Committee. Although they differ in character and style, since the former is more intellectual and cultural and the latter is more social and educational, both are homegrown and geared toward peaceful activism. Also, the Women's Will Association is an independent group, whereas the Women's Dawn Committee works within the AMS, but again, both work for the preservation of the national unity of Iraq and its people. For more, see Zangana, *City of Widows*, 133–138.

131. Interview, Damascus, February 14, 2011.

132. Interview, Damascus, February 16, 2011.

133. Interview, Damascus, February 26, 2011.

134. See the famous stories of life under the occupation by a young Iraqi woman who called herself "Riverbend," in "Baghdad Burning," http://river bendblog.blogspot.com.

135. Interview, Damascus, February 25, 2011.

136. Interview, Amman, March 19, 2011.

137. Interview, Damascus, February 25, 2011.

138. Interview, Damascus, February 25, 2011.

139. For some accounts of Iraqi women's experiences in prison, see AMS, "Statements of the Association," nos. 740 (December 5, 2010), 741 (December 9, 2010), 746 (January 8, 2011), and 755 (February 7, 2011). Some women, especially those detained in government-run prisons, spent around four years without anyone attempting to investigate the reasons for their detentions. See rare footage inside an Iraqi women's prison, Sebastian Walker, October 7, 2007, www.youtube.com/watch ?v=E08uwRZL&rw&feature=relmfu, accessed on September 9, 2011.

140. Luke Harding, "The Other Prisoners," *Guardian*, May 19, 2004.

141. Ibid.

142. For more information, see Peter Beaumont, "Hidden Victims of a Brutal Conflict: Iraq's Women," *Observer* online, October 8, 2006; and Ruth Rosen, "The Hidden War on Women in Iraq," ZNET online, July 13, 2006.

143. On the assassination of Iraqi professionals of both sexes, see Hussein al-Rashed and Saif al-Inbouri, "The Iraqi Scientific Competencies That Were Assassinated After the American Occupation of Iraq," Working Paper, Al-Umma Centre for Studies and Development, 2010, 8–42.

144. See AMS, *Human Rights Annual Report, 2010–2011*, October 20, 2011.

145. See Iman Abou Atta, "The Occupation Goes On," Labour briefing online, accessed April 23, 2011.

146. Interview, Amman, March 25, 2011.

147. See AMS, *Human Rights Annual Report*. See also Ikram Centre for Human Rights, "Iraq After Seven Years of Occupation: Facts and Figures," 2010; contact Ikram at ikram2006@yahoo.com.

148. The interpretation and application of the law have been largely left to the mullahs, especially in the rural areas, where one sees the emergence of underage marriages, temporary marriages (though practiced only among Shiites; historically,

Iraqi Shiites never practiced this form of marriage), strict sex segregation, and strict dress codes. These days in most Iraqi cities, especially in the south where the mullahs dominate the scene, one sees slogans posted on the streets stating the following: "We warn [women] against uncovering, and if they do not comply we will punish them. And God witnesses that we have informed you [the women]." Interview, Amman, March 23, 2011.

149. Interview, Amman, March 23, 2011.
150. Interview, Damascus, February 29, 2011.
151. Interview, Damascus, February 29, 2011.

6

The Violence of Occupation: Palestinian Women in the West Bank and Gaza Strip

In December 2008, in response, it was claimed, to the firing of rockets across the border into southern Israel, the Israeli army invaded the nominally "independent" Gaza Strip, killing a disproportionate number of civilians, causing mass destruction of homes and infrastructure, and provoking a humanitarian crisis.[1] The stated aim was to put an end to the resistance—or, as the Israelis saw it, the "terrorist" activities of the Palestinian Islamist party Hamas. This raises the question of what "resistance" means in the context of military occupation and colonization and how it has affected notions of national identity, especially for women. For Palestinians, resistance "represents a refusal to 'normalize' injustice"[2]; Palestinian men and women have been resisting first the British occupation and then the Zionist colonial project since the early twentieth century. It is regarded as an obligation for everyone and a foundation of their existence as a national entity. But since the late 1990s, some have argued that Hamas in Gaza has distorted the notion of "national identity." How accurate is this claim? Could it be that, far from damaging feelings of identification with the nation, Hamas has reinvigorated national resistance? The violence of the Israeli onslaught in 2008–2009 increased support for Hamas, but at the same time, the lack of a political process and the absence of security for ordinary Palestinian families has generated intense soul-searching about the degradation of identity and the failure of religious parties to conduct a "moral struggle."

Recent developments suggest that the Palestinian nation is in crisis and that the 2008–2009 war between Israel and Hamas in the Gaza Strip, far from asserting Hamas's strength, merely confirms the hopelessness of the current situation. This prompts us to ask how Palestinians' sense of self has changed as a result of Islamist involvement in the conflict. What effect did the 2008–2009 Gaza war have on how Palestinians perceive themselves as a nation and, especially, on the practice of resistance? How has the Israeli-Palestinian conflict, described as "a transformative political event in the Middle East,"[3] contributed to the Palestinian "story of unfulfilled desires"?[4] We will try to answer these questions with reference to Amartya Sen's argument that "many of the conflicts and barbarities in the world are sustained through *the illusion of a unique and choiceless identity*."[5] For Palestinians, their "choiceless identity" may be not so much an "illusion" as foisted upon them by the imperatives of the struggle and the actions of those who oppose them. As in the July–August 2006 war between Israel and Hizbullah in Lebanon, the phenomenon of Islamic resistance in the Palestinian territories has been represented as fanatical, violent, and, above all, male. There are reasons that this image has taken hold of the popular imagination, but as we argue in this chapter, it fails to do justice to the Islamic resistance movement in Palestine. In reality, this movement reflects the diversity and complexity of Palestinian society, including—importantly—the voices and activities of women.

The significantly increased use of violence by the Israeli state and army since the start of the second Palestinian intifada (uprising) in late September 2000 and then, in January 2006, the resounding victory of Hamas in the Palestinian parliamentary elections, which caused a withdrawal of international support and aid, has had a profound effect on notions of national identity. As the current stalemate leads to ever-deteriorating living conditions for the civilian population, there is a growing feeling that "the national dream has ended."[6] In the battle of rhetoric and competing claims, by linking the Palestinian liberation struggle with Islamist terrorism, Israel has succeeded in denying to Palestinians their legitimate right of resistance. Palestinian identity, unlike that of Lebanese Shiites, is contested and their right to exist is constantly threatened.

In a departure from the framing of liberation as a primarily secular endeavor, the Palestinian struggle is now articulated more explicitly in terms of Islamic resistance. In this chapter, we examine the experiences of Palestinian women from the perspective of a conflict between victimization and agency, and we ask what effect the Islamization of their society is having on women's ability to resist and survive the long-running Israeli occupation. First, what has been the impact of Islamic resistance on women's ability to cope with the effects of violent conflict on themselves and their children? Second, what changes have occurred in women's behavior and responses since the start of the second intifada, and how are they affecting gender dynamics? Third, has women's activism improved their rights within the family and in the public sphere? In other words, how have women resisted "different forms of power," and how have they sought to protect the nation?[7] We argue that patriarchal nationalism is being challenged and reinscribed by women's strategizing and determination, and yet, since the Palestinian revolution has shown few tangible results, especially in the area of women's rights, the resistance project cannot be judged wholeheartedly successful.

Women and the Nation

For Palestinians, nationalism developed not only because they have a strong attachment to their territory and because they share "religion, language and customs and other nationalistic symbols, but because their history of expulsion, of dispossession and, more recently, the Israeli Occupation have sharpened and heightened their nationalistic feelings."[8] How can these "nationalistic feelings" best be characterized? One would imagine that they are the preserve of all Palestinians. Yet Joseph Massad describes Palestinian nationalism as a "masculine-based nationalism"; by examining its evolution, he seeks to show "the process through which masculinity itself is lived within the modality of nationalism—indeed, how masculinity is *nationalized*."[9] He is intimating, in effect, that nationalism has been constructed to exclude half the population. As Frances Hasso argues, "men often construct nationalist narratives on the basis of gender differences, with national agency and citizenship assumed to be masculine prerogatives defined in contrast to femininity."[10] Writing in 1986, the late Edward Said also noted "the crucial absence of women" in the Palestinian national narrative. With few exceptions, he remarked, women seem "to have played little more than the role of hyphen, connective, transition, mere incident."[11] The Palestinian national narrative is the story of a nation thwarted and threatened with obliteration, which has sought to practice various forms of resistance or accommodation, but they have been too little or inappropriate or ignored.

What exactly is meant by "identity," in the context of violence, dispossession, and struggle? Said argues that the "construction of identity . . . involves the construction of opposites and 'others' whose actuality is always subject to the continuous interpretation and reinterpretation of their differences from 'us.'"[12] It is important to distinguish here between a shared or collective identity and the "inescapably plural identities" of individuals.[13] By considering the differences between national identification and what Stuart Hall calls the "stable core of the self," we seek to understand how Palestinian women in the West Bank and Gaza Strip enact notions of identity construction and preservation.[14] Identity, as Julie Peteet suggests, is dynamic, "a process of becoming rather than simply being."[15] Hall agrees that "instead of thinking of identity as an already accomplished fact," we should think of it, instead, as "a 'production' which is never complete, always in process."[16] Michel Foucault, too, has argued against a "timeless identity," suggesting instead that identities are plural and partial.[17] However, these "competing interests and identities create conflicts."[18] Identity processes become "coercive. We are labelled, named, known by identities that confine us, regulate us and reduce our complexity."[19]

This coercion is especially pronounced for women, who are often compelled to occupy symbolic and even inflexible roles. By labeling women as persistent victims or preservers of tradition, we are in danger of limiting their capacity for active involvement. It should be recalled "that the high level of political (as well as social) activity performed by women in early Islam could not have been achieved without . . . the recognition of the political ability or competence of women. . . . Women were regarded as fully-fledged citizens capable of participating in all political activities (including . . . taking part in Jihad)."[20] According to a tradition attributed to the Prophet's wife, A'isha, "although jihad for women may be 'without fighting,' it remains jihad."[21] Palestinian women could fairly be described as following in this well-established female tradition. At the same time, as "women fight colonial occupation, they become conscious of their own oppression within a patriarchal culture."[22] With "the birth of a national consciousness . . . women's roles begin to change; as they participate in the struggle, [they] break down traditional barriers."[23]

Michael Broning argues that a "key concept" for Palestinian notions of resistance is *sumud*, "which can be translated as perseverance or steadfastness."[24] Palestinians demonstrate *sumud* in their daily lives "as they perform what would amount to normal everyday tasks in other places."[25] This echoes James Scott's argument about "everyday acts of resistance." It was reiterated over and again in interviews as women spoke about "getting on with life," looking after their homes, and taking their children to school; each "confronts the violence of occupation constructively, thereby rendering the acts of daily life into a form of resistance."[26] Since 2000, *sumud* has been conceived "in a more proactive fashion, as a rejection of immobility and a refusal to let the army's roadblocks disrupt life."[27]

A History of Struggle

At the start of the twentieth century, Palestine was part of the Ottoman Empire, ruled from Istanbul. The majority of the population were peasant farmers (*fellahin*), residing in hundreds of villages and hamlets. Their relatively tranquil existence began to be disrupted by the arrival in their country of politically motivated Jewish immigrants. In response to anti-Semitism in Europe in the late nineteenth century, a group of Jewish intellectuals led by Theodor Herzl proposed the creation of a Jewish national state. Early Jewish nationalism, or Zionism, quickly focused on Palestine, the ancient biblical homeland of the Jewish people, as an appropriate site to develop the new state. Zionist ambitions were supported by the Balfour Declaration of 1917, in which the British government promised its "best endeavours" to facilitate the establishment of "a national home for the Jewish people" in Palestine. Jewish "pioneers" began to enter the country in ever-increasing numbers. Before the Zionist immigration drive, Jews made up approximately 4 percent of the total population; by the end of World War I, the number had risen to 11 percent.

In the wake of the war and subsequent collapse of the Ottoman Empire in the early 1920s, Britain was assigned control over Palestine through a "mandate" system. The period of British rule, which essentially favored the "civilized" Zionist incomers over the "primitive" indigenous inhabitants, proved disastrous for the Palestinians. It witnessed both the rise of Palestinian nationalism, as an "embattled" nationalism, and the birth of the resistance movement. Liah Greenfield argues that "national identity" derives from membership in a "people" rather than residence in a particular state.[28] The emergence of a distinct Palestinian identity coincided with Zionist claims to the land. There was a close linkage, therefore, between feelings of national belonging and the increasingly urgent imperative to resist the colonization of their land.

As Nels Johnson suggests, the "presence of Zionist settlement and the supportive Mandate policies set the primary socio-economic context" for the first serious Palestinian rebellion (1936–1939).[29] This revolt, which was inspired by the teachings of Shaikh Izz al-Din al-Qassam, demonstrated the close link between religion and national struggle for Palestinians. In his dying moments, Qassam declared that "this is a *jihad* for God and the homeland" and urged his followers to "die as martyrs."[30] Although this link was not always explicit, it started to be articulated more insistently as an authentic identity in the late 1980s.

At the end of World War II and in the aftermath of the Holocaust in Europe, the British acknowledged that they were no longer able to control the situation of escalating violence in Palestine; they handed the problem over to the newly created United Nations. By this time, although numerically still superior, the Palestinians lacked an army, effective weaponry, and organized leadership. The UN partition plan of 1947 awarded 57 percent of Palestine to the proposed Jewish state, even though Jews represented only 33 percent of the population and owned a mere 7 percent of the land. For

Palestinians, the partition plan "was an illegal and illegitimate attempt to divide" the country.[31] They believed "it was unfair that the Jewish immigrants, most of whom had been in Palestine less than 30 years, and who owned less than 10 percent of the land, should be given more than half of Palestine including the best arable land," and therefore rejected the proposal.[32]

The all-out war that followed resulted in the creation of the state of Israel in May 1948 and the uprooting of the majority of Palestinians from their land. While Jews refer to this event as their "war of independence," for Palestinians it is regarded as *al-nakbah* (the catastrophe), during which approximately 780,000 of them were transformed into stateless refugees. Their resistance had proved ineffective against a considerably superior and well-armed enemy. For the next twenty years, Palestinians "were in a state of shock and despair," their nationalism "for the most part muted."[33] In the meantime, the new Israeli state thrived and, as Zalman Amit and Daphna Levit argue, refused all opportunities for peace.[34]

In June 1967, perceiving a threat from neighboring Arab states, Israel staged a preemptive strike, in the process seizing control of the remaining remnants of mandate Palestine still in Arab hands: the West Bank, Gaza Strip, and East Jerusalem. By this time, Palestinians in exile had started to organize themselves politically and militarily; the Palestine Liberation Organization (PLO) was founded in 1964, and Palestinian guerrillas staged cross-border raids into Israel. Nonetheless, the occupation of 1967 was a terrible blow to national aspirations, and from that time Palestinians have existed under a harsh regime. There have been a number of attempts to negotiate a just and peaceful end to the conflict but, as Amit and Levit suggest, there is no peace between Israelis and Palestinians after sixty-two years "because Israel never wanted to achieve peace with its Palestinian neighbours."[35]

After twenty years of Israeli occupation, Palestinians in the West Bank and Gaza Strip staged another revolt. The first intifada (1987–1993) was essentially nonviolent. It "focused on acts of civil disobedience through strikes, mass demonstrations, funeral marches, tax boycotts . . . [and] symbolic acts."[36] These "acts of resistance," as Broning notes, "were complemented by efforts to create an independent and self-reliant Palestinian polity."[37] The intifada led to the first serious attempt to reach a comprehensive peace deal; the 1993 Oslo Accords between the PLO and the government of Israel, whereby Palestinians were granted a degree of autonomy in the West Bank and Gaza Strip and permitted to create a self-governing Palestinian Authority (PA), were greeted with cautious optimism by observers around the world. The first Palestinian elections were held in early 1996, bringing the secular Fatah party of PLO leader Yasir Arafat to power; Arafat himself was elected president. More difficult issues, such as borders, water resources, the status of Jerusalem, and the question of Palestinian refugees, were postponed until a later date. Although many Palestinians initially welcomed the agreement, believing that it would eventually lead to an independent state, their hopes were soon dashed and what Amit and Levit call "Israeli rejectionism" eventually prevailed. Israel dragged its feet, failing to implement the step-by-step approach agreed to at Oslo; for their part, Palestinians became increasingly exasperated and, in September 2000, to no one's surprise, a second intifada began in the West Bank and Gaza Strip. There have been no significant negotiations since that time between the two sides, although many abortive ones.

Throughout the Palestinian national struggle, women have played an active role, and it is possible to trace a trajectory of growing activism and assertion among women. To begin with, during the British colonial period, women of the largely elite classes tended to focus on social welfare projects, although the stirrings of political awareness were evident as early as the 1920s, when women joined in mass demonstrations against British control and the threat of mounting Jewish immigration. The first Arab Women's Congress was organized in 1929 to protest the unjust practices of the colonial regime. Strum argues the "Palestinian women's movement has always been inextricably intertwined with the Palestinian liberation movement."[38] In her view, women's groups "from the late 1920s through 1947 concentrated on playing a backup role for male revolutionaries."[39] However, this disregards the role of agency, both in terms of women's attitudes toward the perceived invasion of their country and the measures they took to resist it. Although Palestinian nationalism was essentially patriarchal, it incorporated and "reinscribed new meanings to women's domesticity," thereby providing "an impetus for women to defy social and cultural norms and become involved in realms of activity from which they had previously been excluded."[40] There is some evidence, as Ellen Fleischmann argues, that women "created their own indigenous feminisms."[41]

After the forced dispossession of the Palestinians by the new state of Israel in 1948, women adopted unfamiliar roles in exile. Gradually, the dispersed community began to organize itself. The spread of female education and opportunities for employment outside the home, coupled with the determination of women to play a part in the national struggle, has meant that many women have been able to engage in an increasingly wide range of activities, from humanitarian projects to political involvement and, in some instances, armed struggle. In the 1980s, four women's committees were formed, each attached to one of the main Palestinian political parties (Fatah, the Palestinian Front for the Liberation of Palestine, the Democratic Front for the Liberation of Palestine, and the Communist Party). In addition, "a variety of women's NGOs . . . emerged in the 1990s [to work] specifically on women's issues."[42] During the first intifada, many women came out of their homes to engage in nonviolent resistance, which included street demonstrations and confrontations with the Israeli army, the provision of alternative schooling and import-substitution projects; initially, at least, the intifada "restored a positive self-image, high self-esteem, and national pride."[43] Some "believed that victory in the political sphere had the potential to be aligned with corresponding changes in society."[44] However, a woman interviewed by Cheryl Rubenberg in the West Bank had a different perspective: "I became very active in politics . . . before the *intifada*. When it began, I participated in demonstrations, strikes, committees, and confrontations. But then the elite women came from the city and began to tell us how to organize . . . and I felt very humiliated."[45] Her words illustrate the conflict between the grassroots response of many women in Palestinian society and the deliberate campaigns of organized political groups, which has tended to alienate some women at the popular level.

"Everyday Forms of Resistance"

After the Palestinian Authority was set up in 1994, secular women's groups began to organize in terms of female participation in the anticipated independent Palestinian state. But, in what has been described as a "profound political crisis of Palestinian nationalism," women's activism started to decline; as in other newly emerging states, politics has tended to be appropriated by men.[46] Nonetheless, women fought hard to have their concerns incorporated into the constitution and legal framework of the state. In the first parliamentary elections in 1996, which were boycotted by the Islamist parties, five women were elected to the Palestinian Legislative Council (PLC). However, following the eruption of violence at the end of September 2000, women's organizing was replaced by the basic requirements of survival in the face of mounting repression and crisis. Women focused on "more mundane everyday practices [that] can also be viewed as acts of resistance."[47]

Religion also became more prominent. As Umm Adel in Ramallah recalled, "During the first intifada, men and women were alike, fighting together, working, teaching; they were neighbors together. But now, with Hamas, we start to see the separation of men and women; this is their ideology, but it was not like this in Prophet Muhammad's time."[48] Dalal, a political activist in Ramallah, agrees that "Islamic groups are now joining the political struggle." She added, if we look at what is happening in Gaza, it is a struggle for power. People were feeling despair over the peace process and corruption and so religious groups took advantage of this. But now there is no law at all. These groups gave very little to women; their vision is not about women's rights; they help with money and food and help them to find jobs if they are widows; and they instruct them to be with God, to cover their heads.[49]

But Souad, a journalist in her thirties, articulates a different perspective on the involvement of Islamic parties. "Islam teaches women to be patient, she said, "they are sure that God will help and this satisfies them. Islamic groups are not a threat to the state. If one studies Islam correctly, it gives women more than secularism; more rights are given to women by Islam, and more freedom."[50] One can hear in their words the debate about the role of Islam in society and whether it is a help or a hindrance to women's rights. What happens when religious groups try to involve themselves in politics?

The second intifada witnessed dramatically increased levels of violence and the entry of women into more controversial forms of protest, including suicide bombing. In the face of severe Israeli repression during the first intifada, Palestinians showed "impressive restraint,"[51] but many have concluded that, if "Israel makes no significant compromise, the Palestinians have no option but violence to end decades of occupation."[52] Umm Walid in Hebron, whose son had been killed by the Israelis, insisted that

> a woman is entitled to become a shahida [female martyr]. It is not violence against Israel. One cannot call it violence. If a woman kills herself, it is because she had a bad experience with Israel. There is no conflict between religious and secular groups; when Israel attacks, everyone—whatever their ideology—unites to defend the community.[53]

Souad in Ramallah agreed that the role of women changed in the second intifada. Women now carry out military operations: "they help the fighters when the Israelis enter the city. As the mother of a martyr or the wife of a prisoner, women also help in practical ways."[54] Similarly Nur, a twenty-one-year-old student at Birzeit University, concurred that "women in Palestine assume all roles: they are fighters, they sacrifice themselves for their children, their husbands, their land, their religion—they can be anything."[55] The defiance of these women's words, in common with many of our interviewees, indicates both a refusal to accept the designation of "victim" and also the breadth of women's scope of action. The first intifada, however, was notable for the breadth and intensity of women's participation. A marked difference was observed in the second, as women became largely absent from the front line. Penny Johnson and Eileen Kuttab argue that there is a strong link between the marginalization of women from the public and political spheres.[56] According to Umm Nader in Ramallah, "In the old days everyone took part because the Israelis were at our doorsteps. Women confronted them face-to-face and we didn't need to leave our neighborhoods. Now they're only at the entrances of the cities. So we have to travel to confront them, and very few women will do that."[57] The pressures resulting from the violence "have taken their toll on the family unit . . . particularly in terms of its authority structure and ability to provide order, discipline, security, and—perhaps most importantly—protection."[58] Umm Nabil, who is forty-two years old and lives in the Balata refugee camp in Nablus, remarked that the 1987 intifada was better because they were fighting only the Israeli army; since the 2007 "civil war" between Fatah and Hamas, Palestinian groups have been fighting each other. "Now one can easily see a gunman," she said, "now everyone carries a gun and they are using them against each other." Before, she added, she felt safe and felt her children were safe, but now she cannot let them go into the street.[59]

However, despite their nonparticipation at flashpoints, women have not been able to avoid the violence. Even the home is no longer a place of security: there have been instances since 2001 in which women have been killed in their own homes, often as accidental victims caught in the crossfire. The overall effect, it has been suggested, has been negative for women in terms of their progress on rights and entitlement; it also tended to separate their areas of activity from those of men. At the same time, it provoked expressions of solidarity. In response to an Israeli assault on Gaza in 2006, for example, unarmed women came out into the streets to defend their families. According to Hamas member of parliament Jameela al-Shanti in Beit Hanoun,

> Yesterday at dawn, the Israeli air force bombed and destroyed my home. I was the target, but instead the attack killed my sister-in-law, Nahla, a widow with eight children in her care. In the same raid, Israel's artillery shelled a residential district in the town . . . leaving 19 dead and 40 injured, many killed in their beds. One family, the Athamnas, lost 16 members in the massacre: the oldest who died, Fatima, was 70; the youngest, Dima, was one; seven were children. . . . It is not easy as a mother, sister, or wife to watch those you love disappear before your eyes. Perhaps that was what helped me, and 1,500 other women, to overcome our fear and defy the Israeli curfew last Friday—and set about freeing some of our young men who were besieged in a mosque while defending us and our city against the Israeli military machine.[60]

The Israeli army responded by opening fire on the women, killing two and wounding more than ten, and then "denigrated their action into 'an action supporting Palestinian Terror.'"[61] This is a familiar pattern, whereby Palestinian resistance is portrayed as "terrorism" and then demonized or ignored hy Israel and the west. But women are taking a stand, like the women in Gaza, against the chaos that is engulfing their society. In the words of Naila Ayesh, director of the Women's Affairs Centre in Gaza, "I think the Palestinian women feel, now, more seriously and worry about what's going on in our society. . . . These women now go out of their homes asking to be part of stopping this violence inside our society."[62] The widespread violence and constant fear experienced by Palestinian women provides some explanation as to why they seek empowerment through Islamic forms of resistance.

Women and Violence in the West Bank and Gaza Strip

The imbalance of power between Palestinians and Israelis has meant that conventional warfare is out of the question, and therefore Palestinians have been forced to seek alternative methods to wage their anticolonial struggle. They have tried nonviolent protest (the first intifada was largely nonviolent) and diplomatic negotiation (as exemplified by the Oslo peace process), but these tactics have failed to end the occupation or to halt the creeping colonization of their land. Since the 1960s, Palestinians have also adopted various forms of militant action. The PLO used armed struggle as a key element of its strategy. Many Palestinians, including women, have reached the conclusion that violence is now the best option they have to end the occupation; yet it too has yielded little success, other than to brand the Palestinians as irrational terrorists rather than "partners for peace."Although PLO resistance was located largely in secular nationalist discourse, increasingly since 2000, Palestinians' "recourse to violence finds justification in the militant Islamist ideology and its concept of *jihad*," and, we argue, this has served as both a comfort and a source of protection.[63] Yet, even though Palestinian violence may be an unsurprising response to the aggressive policies of the Israeli occupation, it has contributed to an image of Islam, at least in western eyes, that appears barbaric and intolerant. However, "to stigmatize Islam and Muslims as the equivalent of modern-day 'barbarians' to the exclusion of the role of Western powers, serves only to 'mythologize' Euro-American democracies as forces of peace and good in the global arena."[64] As a result of their decision to link their struggle to the language and symbols of Islam, groups such as Hamas have been equated with the extremism of al-Qaeda. The Palestinian terrorist serves a useful rhetorical purpose, to confirm a lack of civilization and Israel's claim of the absence of "a partner for peace." When the terrorist is a woman, her act tends to reinforce still more the image of an irrational and inhumane people.

Women's efforts to involve themselves in the national struggle have been hampered by the violence of everyday life. In the absence of protection mechanisms, women have seen many of their rights eroded. Violence against Palestinian women occurs on several levels, but most of the women interviewed agreed that the worst forms of violence are those inflicted by the Israeli occupation. First, they say, Israel stole their land, and then it tried to delegitimize their national identity and extinguish all hopes for self-determination. Since the beginning of the occupation in 1967, Israeli policies in the West Bank and Gaza Strip have been harsh and punitive, including house demolitions, expulsions, arbitrary arrest, and collective punishment. Women suffered as the occupation invaded the private sphere, and as "women returned to the fold of the patriarchal and extended family structure, their progress was halted and the economic survival of the family took precedence."[65] At the same time, in many cases, as their husbands were killed or imprisoned, many women have been forced to become the heads of their households and sole protectors of their children; this has given them another sort of power.

Israeli violence against population centers since the start of the second intifada has created fear and despair among Palestinians. In the words of a woman in the West Bank town of Beit Sahour whose home was shelled for five straight days at the beginning of October 2000,

> The tension has taken over my life—I no longer have the patience or stamina to help my children with their homework, and I am overly sensitive about the most trivial things. . . . What happened has taken a piece of my heart and has severely altered my state of mind. . . . The cruelty of the shelling, and the terrible fear for our lives have robbed me of my ability to be happy.[66]

Amina, a young married woman in Gaza City, expressed similar feelings of helplessness in the face of Israeli aggression; she said she sat and watched the television for hours, crying and ignoring her children. People feel desperate, she explained, even if they have jobs and food.[67] Palestinian women and girls have been killed and injured while attempting to go about their daily business or even inside their own homes. Women have died or been forced to give birth at Israeli military checkpoints because they have been denied access to ambulances.[68]

But women also suffer as a result of discriminatory practices and traditions. A report by the United Nations Economic and Social Council, released in December 2011, revealed that "high levels of poverty, unemployment and related frustration have contributed to an increase in tension, and ultimately violence, within families" in the West Bank and Gaza Strip. The situation is particularly serious in Gaza: "Gaza is under a closure. The economic situation is very bad. There is a high percentage of poverty and unemployment. There is frequent violence from Israeli attacks. All of these circumstances affect the level of violence against women."[69] A 2009 report published by the Gaza-based Palestinian Women's Information and Media Centre discovered that 77 percent of Palestinian women reported being subjected to verbal violence on a regular basis, 71 percent reported psychological violence, 52.4 percent had experienced physical violence, and 14.5 percent reported sexual violence.[70] In other words, as one commentator remarked, women are the victims of double discrimination—"at the hands of male society and by Israel"[71]—and therefore violence "becomes a means not only to defend against a military or security threat, but more profoundly, against any action that is or may be interpreted as an act of opposition. Violence is [therefore] a tool to preserve the status quo in terms of power, values and priorities."[72]

Palestinian society is a patriarchal and conservative one, which means that the "burden of living under military occupation is compounded by the additional responsibilities imposed on them by their own society."[73] Although patriarchy, "representing a gender and age hierarchy based on the household as a productive unit, has in recent decades been challenged by social transformations sweeping the regions in which it prevails," gender issues have generally been subordinated to the national struggle.[74] According to a woman in Gaza, since the nationalist discourse is the predominant one, no woman can speak out about the violence she faces.[75] Therefore, women are caught in a contradiction between wishing to play a full part in the struggle and having to follow the lead of men, both in public and private matters. In cases of marital breakdown, for example, it is considered inadvisable for a woman to seek a divorce because she may lose her children, her home, and even the respect of the community. According to Shadia Sarraj of the Women's Empowerment Project in Gaza, there is no acknowledgment of the honor or dignity of women.[76] Since Palestinians lack a functioning legal system, some men have taken advantage of the situation in order to pursue their own agendas. Men feel frustrated and powerless and may, in some instances, take it out on their wives. The man sees himself as the supporter of his family, and when he is unable to fulfill his responsibilities, his pride is injured. But this discrimination needs to be deconstructed and understood in the context of human rights abuses and the inability of the Palestinian population to protect itself. It is true that the helplessness of men has led to increased levels of violence against women, but it has also given women access to new areas of activity. It is undeniable that patriarchal structures have been reinforced, but women's scope for resisting these structures has also increased.

This raises the question of whether women's activism and survival strategies represent a form of feminism. By distinguishing between feminist attitudes and feminist behaviors, Randa Nasser, Fidaa Barghouti, and Janan Mousa argue that "women are not consistently feminist in all domains"; they "may be more likely to achieve access to rights and opportunities than

they are to gain control over their bodies and destinies or to change traditional female roles. This likelihood need not be strictly due to a society's
'backward patriarchal' cultural values or to women's involvement in
national liberation movements . . . it may be due, rather, to a specific sociohistorical context related to the legacy of colonial rule and its present hegemony."[77] Most of the women we interviewed in the Palestinian territories
did not articulate their concerns in terms of feminism, yet their actions
often appeared to be informed by feminist praxis.

Islam and Islamism in the Palestinian Territories

Islam has always occupied a central position in Palestinian politics. But it
is "one of the many elements of Palestinian identity," or "Palestinian-ness,"
and one that has been used in a variety of ways since the early twentieth
century.[78] Until the late 1920s, it was "an expression of the dominant class
interests and outlook."[79] Between 1929 and 1939, as we have argued,
"Islam as a populist idiom" appeared in response to the combination of
"despair, political frustration and growing awareness of both national identity and class tensions."[80] After the *nakbah* of 1948, the immediacy of Islam
as a tool of popular resistance faded; instead, it became a link with the
familiar and helped to define identity. Gradually, the secular nationalist ideology of the PLO replaced Islamic political activism. However, at the grassroots level, Islam remained an important source of comfort and protection
and also an indicator of the community's morality.

   The origins of Islamist movements in the Palestinian territories can be
traced back to the Muslim Brotherhood, which was founded by Hasan al-
Banna in Egypt in 1928. At their convention in Haifa in late 1947, the
Palestinian Muslim Brotherhood declared that it would "bear its full share
of the cost of resistance."[81] Following the establishment of the state of
Israel the following year, the Muslim Brotherhood movements in the West
Bank and Gaza Strip began to develop in significantly different ways.
While "the Palestinian Brethren in the West Bank did not constitute an
effective political force," the "Gazan Brothers stood at the forefront of military and political engagement."[82] After the formation of the nationalist
Fatah movement (led by Yasir Arafat), it became Fatah, rather than the
brotherhood, that "clearly embodied the aspirations of the Palestinian people for liberation."[83] For its part, the Muslim Brotherhood focused on educational, social welfare, and faith-based activities. According to Khaled
Hroub, the period from the start of the Israeli occupation in 1967 until 1975
represented "the phase of mosque building," and the period from 1975
through the late 1980s constituted "the phase of social institution build-

ing."[84] These endeavors succeeded in mobilizing young people and students and laying the foundations for popular action. In the early 1980s, Islamic Jihad, which "constituted a marriage between Islam and the gun," emerged with its commitment to armed resistance.[85]

Since the mid-1980s, as secular politics have failed to end the occupation, there has been a renewed interest in Islamic activism. Since the outbreak of the first intifada, and even more since the second, Palestinian resistance has been increasingly influenced by the language and symbols of revivalist Islam. Hamas (Harakat al-muqawwama al-Islamiyya, or the "Islamic resistance movement") was officially established in August 1988 when the Muslim Brotherhood decided to turn to violent resistance. Its "covenant [*mithaq*] is a remarkable document in that it contains many of the ideological ambiguities and contradictions which have plagued the Islamist movement in Palestine, including the proper response to Palestinian nationalism and nationalist organizations, the question of political activism versus social transformation, and the role women should play in the struggle."[86]

The move "from prioritizing Islamic revival to privileging armed struggle" was made in response to the growing hardships of life on the ground in Gaza and the start of the first intifada in 1987.[87] As a result of "the socioeconomic and political transformations produced by the Israeli Occupation," Hamas "shifted from an exclusionary religious movement into a powerful rival and alternative to the secular Palestinian national movement."[88] Jeroen Gunning argues that, as Hamas "became more adept at carrying out resistance activities during the first Intifada, its political influence increased."[89] The group strongly opposed the Oslo peace process and, as a result of its rejectionist stance, attracted more support and started to defeat Fatah in elections for chambers of commerce and student unions.

To understand how women are situated within the framework of resistance, we need to appreciate the various meanings of "resistance," or jihad, in the Palestinian context. The Arabic word jihad "literally means 'striving' [and provides] a motivation to fight for justice and against abuse of power."[90] It has also been "a potent system for popular mobilization" and is not solely linked to violence.[91] Palestinians resist the occupation, as we have argued, in a diversity of ways, most of which are nonviolent. Inevitably, the more spectacular forms of resistance, in which violence is a factor, tend to dominate the headlines in the west. As a result, some observers argue that Islamist notions of resistance have been unbalanced, especially by the emergence of the Palestinian female suicide bomber, perceived as either a new and effective form of resistance or a deviation from social values. There are, however, historical precedents for the involvement of women in resistance. During the lifetime of the Prophet Muhammad, several women are recorded as having taken part in battles: Nusayba, the daughter of Ka'b, fought with Muhammad in the Battle of Uhud (625 CE); and Safiya, the Prophet's aunt, took up a sword during the Battle of the Khandaq (627 CE). David Cook argues that women "were aware of the high spiritual merit accorded to the [male] *jihad* fighter, and wanted to participate in the fighting."[92] This is in line with notions of communal solidarity, repeated many times in our interviews with West Bank women.

In Article 12 of its 1988 covenant, Hamas stated that "resisting and quelling the enemy has become the individual duty of every Muslim, male or female. A woman can go out and fight the enemy without her husband's permission."[93] But there are conflicting views on whether it is acceptable for women to enter the battlefield. The late Lebanese scholar Sayyid Muhammad Hussein Fadlallah, for example, argued that Islam does not require women to participate formally in war. Fighting is not imposed on women; instead, Islam tells women to accompany the soldiers but to stay in the background.[94] From this we can infer that, although it is preferable for women to "stay in the background," performing activities in support of male fighters, the situation in the West Bank and Gaza Strip has deteriorated to such an extent that it demands a determined response from all Palestinians.

A resistance struggle based on religion brings both problems and benefits. In Islam, there are clearly established rules for the engagement and conduct of war and no legal precedent for attacking civilians.[95] In other words, "the religion of Islam does not provide any basis for suicide bombing."[96] Therefore, anyone seeking to ground violent action in religion faces a dilemma. Religion is also a popular tool of legitimation, however, and has therefore been able to mobilize large numbers of Palestinians who may feel alienated by politics, including women who responded enthusiastically to Hamas's grassroots activities. Many women reported that they found the inclusive approach of Hamas a refreshing change from the more elite and corrupt practices of Fatah; they also welcomed the methods used by Hamas, such as meetings organized in women's homes.

Although it has become commonplace, in Israel and the west, to describe Palestinian resistance as "terrorism," we need to ask what effect both the culture of destructive violence, especially in the period following the start of the second intifada, and also the denigration of their liberation struggle, are having on Palestinian society and its "collective national reality"?[97] In order to explore this question fully, it is necessary to appreciate the role of morality. An important indicator of identity for Palestinians is religion, specifically Islam. Before the outbreak of the first intifada and the emergence of Hamas, the Muslim Brotherhood in the West Bank and Gaza worked to create "the preconditions for an Islamic moral order."[98] A broad cross-section of Palestinians, across age, class, gender, and geographic divides, supported and participated in the first intifada and felt it to be a moral struggle, but their support for the second intifada was more ambivalent. Many Palestinians were uncomfortable with the rising levels of violence and particularly the way in which Islam was used to justify the morally dubious "sacrifice" of the suicide bomber.

Some observers have remarked on feelings of moral decay that are beginning to afflict the community. Dalia, an activist in Ramallah, explained that "political parties who cover themselves with Islam spoil religion. People will lose confidence. The people who work in politics in Palestine have a lot of work to do to give people confidence back in the national struggle. They need to renew their vision. Popular resistance should be peaceful, not a few people fighting."[99] It is here that the Islamist movement has come to play an increasingly significant role. According to Islah Jad, a professor at Birzeit University, the Islamist parties have never used bribes; instead, they relied on motivation and internal conviction. In the 2006 elections, people reported that members of Hamas were not corrupt; they were seen as moral and as trying to build a model human being, which attracted many Palestinian voters.[100] In the opinion of Maha, a student at the university, people voted for Hamas "because they need to see changes in all aspects of life."[101] However, although their instincts may have been moral, the environment in which they have been forced to operate since their election victory in 2006 has had a corrosive effect on their ability to practice good governance. Thus, their efforts, rather than promoting a more moral society, have seemed coercive, and some have even accused them of slipping into the corrupt habits of the former Fatah administration.

Nonetheless, even though some women have expressed dismay at the creeping Islamization of their society and fear that they may be in danger of losing some of their hard-won rights, others—such as Maha and some of her university friends—have felt empowered by the Islamic model. Jad argues that Hamas's gender ideology has been forced to adapt; thus, the rigid division of labor "confining women to the domestic sphere as the reproducers of a 'moral' nation," has been relaxed, "enabling women to occupy a wider space in the public arena."[102] In the January 2006 election, out of the seventy-four seats won by Hamas, six were won by women. According to one of the elected women, "We are going to show the people of the world that the practice of Islam in regards to women is not well known."[103] Her assertion, we argue, lies at the heart of understanding why many Palestinians have turned to a specifically "Islamic" form of resistance and why many women feel both comfortable with and empowered by this form of activism.

However, the extreme violence of the second intifada also provoked a hitherto unfamiliar response from women in the shape of the female suicide bomber, which some have interpreted as a troubling development. According to Mervat, a doctor in Ramallah,

> During the intifada, the Islamic movement started to use political issues and this is why they became popular. The method they use is to brainwash people so they will blow themselves up; the leadership of Hamas has used these young people in a cynical way, and this has had the worst impact on the Palestinian image in the world. . . . A poor woman, single parent, whose son blew himself up, she cried and asked what she had done wrong. The use of motherhood as a political cause is inhuman.[104]

The issue of motherhood raises awkward questions about the moral community. Although women as mothers "are a collective moral representation of a community testifying to the abusive nature of occupation," they are also confronted with seemingly impossible dilemmas.[105] The trauma of losing a son does not only come from the loss of this child but "also from the political and social repression they experience."[106] As Nadera Shalhoub-Kevorkian observes, losing "a child to a just political cause does not obviate the maternal feelings of these mothers towards their children."[107] Umm Walid in Hebron, whose son was killed by the Israelis in the early days of the second intifada, naturally mourns her son—her home is full of photographs of him in the heroic pose of a Hamas fighter—but she also sees his sacrifice, and her own, as part of a larger tradition of *sumud*.

Terrorism or Resistance?

Caught between the competing narratives of Jewish entitlement and Arab self-determination, Palestinian national identity has developed characteristics of struggle, resistance, and defeat. In response to dislocation, Palestinians began to construct a narrative of heroism that, as Laleh Khalili remarks, "was the valorization and militarization of masculinity."[108] At the same time, Hamas's "path to resistance" was "located in the feelings and emotions of the people."[109] Many of the women interviewed in the West Bank expressed a sense of belonging and inclusion. Umm Mustafa, for example, who voted for Hamas in 2006, asserted that "the role of women in Hamas is very wide. They are regarded as strong and important."[110] Sherifa agreed that "much of the power of Hamas came from the efforts of women. They helped them to be elected. Islam is a very important component of their culture and heritage; women are more in favor of Islam sometimes than men. They feel they belong."[111] This fits with both the notion of a more inclusive environment in which the mobilization of women took place and also with

Sadiki's argument of a "global solidarity bound by faith and faith-derived value of resistance."[112] In this analysis, the "resisters are not only trustees of occupied lands, but also, and above all else, trustees of an ideal 'city of God' which they are commended to build by 'enjoining the good' and 'resisting evil.'"[113] Women are accommodated in this "community of resistance" both ideologically and in practice. Through their unwavering involvement in the national struggle, in traditional and more innovative ways, and their insistence on the right to resist, women have rejected a purely maternal role; they have become "fully operational people," people, in Cynthia Cockburn's words, "who may have 'bloodstained hands.'"[114]

Partly as a result of women's "bloodstained hands," there is no denying that Palestinian national identity has been shattered and demoralized. Far from being "a primary form of belonging," it is now associated with shame, victimization, and failure. The international community, in the view of many women interviewed in the West Bank, "is not interested at all; they have an image of the Palestinian as a 'terrorist' who fires missiles into people's homes."[115] The "shameful" aspect of identity has increased as a result of Palestinian "Islamist terrorism," as this term has been defined by Israel and the United States and, although most Palestinians categorically reject the automatic and dismissive linkage between Islam and terrorism, they recognize an underlying narrative of loss of dignity. That is why some Palestinians applauded the attacks of September 11, 2001; although they were appalled at the loss of life, these acts provoked "a hidden sense of pride and empowerment."[116] But Islamism is also associated with resistance, which, as Haidar Eid observes, "is not only the ability to fight back against a militarily more powerful enemy, but also an ability to creatively resist the occupation of one's land."[117] Thus, Hamas "sees resistance as the means to generate the feelings that go into building community cohesion and self-respect."[118] In this respect, as many of our interviewees' narratives reveal, Hamas has been successful.

The period since September 2000, and the "final nail in the coffin" of the Oslo "peace process," has witnessed an increase in militant activities by Islamist groups such as Hamas and Islamic Jihad. It is interesting to note that the politics of Islamism is viewed by many Palestinians as a source of hope, as authentic resistance as opposed to the sellout tactics of the PLO, because Islamism "is not a monolithic phenomenon but is very much context-specific."[119] In the context of the Palestinian struggle against Israeli occupation, Hamas, as a "culturally authentic" resistance movement, has become a barometer of political discontent.[120] Its practice of jihad has been fiercely debated. Nilufer Gole argues that the "call for jihad entails both meaning of making an effort on the path of God, ranging from a warrior military sense to a more moral version, encompassing individual interiorized effort and community improvement. Martyrdom is associated with the warrior interpretation of jihad and the devotion to the community's defences."[121]

According to Mariam Saleh, a member of Hamas elected to the Palestinian Legislative Council, although resistance is usually associated with military force, it can also mean other sorts of support activities such as giving money or teaching others about jihad, or steadfastness (*sumud*) in the face of suffering.[122] For Islamists such as Hamas, jihad, in the sense of "any effort on the path of Islam," is considered to be one of the basic values of an Islamic order.[123] These understandings are in line with "everyday forms of resistance" and the notion of "just getting on with life," much repeated by the subjects of our research.

Since their national rights have been systematically repressed by the Israeli occupation and the apparent disinterest of the international community, some Palestinians have adopted desperate measures. The practice of Islamic resistance as an anticolonial struggle takes the form of armed attacks, suicide bombings, and kidnappings to combat Israel as an invader and occupier. But it has a broader context in line with a "devotion to the community's defences." Hamas and Islamic Jihad, like Hizbullah in Lebanon and Islamist groups elsewhere in the Arab world, are far more than armed militias. They are also political parties and social welfare networks. They respond to a longing by the Palestinian national collectivity for justice and dignity, and although some of their responses have been counterproductive, they regard the right to resist, as enshrined in international law, as an entirely legitimate one. Their response has been severely tested by the controversial use of women as "human bombs."

Writing the "History of Their Liberation with Their Blood"

> *We do not have a choice between purity and violence but between different kinds of violence.*[124]

In contrast to the optimistic energy of the first intifada, when women were fully engaged in multifaceted resistance and had some expectation of a better future, the situation in the West Bank and Gaza Strip has been steadily deteriorating since 2000 and has caused large numbers of Palestinians to lose hope. As a result, we suggest, some women have been attracted by Islamic activism as a model of modernity or, as it is sometimes described, the "Islamization of modernity": Rubenberg argues that the "emergence of the Muslim Sisters in the West Bank reflects an attempt by observant women to demonstrate their capacity for agency through the development of Islamic solutions to women's social problems."[125] Roy, too, confirms that the "Islamic movement is creating a discourse of empowerment," which has certainly extended to women.[126] This was not always the case. In its early days, Hamas adopted a more coercive approach, including a campaign during the first intifada to impose Islamic dress on women, thus throwing into question "the fundamental linkage between gender liberation and the possibility of a progressive and democratic future."[127] Hamas's behavior—and this impression can be gleaned from its founding covenant—resulted from impatience, the need to "purify" society without paying any heed to individual concerns. Since then, it has undergone a transformation and, accepting the need to be pragmatic, has adopted a more gradualist approach to the Islamization of society. Women's responses, too, have changed.

Palestinian women are involved in resistance operations on several levels, all of which need to be carefully considered in order to understand why a woman living under Israeli occupation or control, despite the restrictions of a traditional society, may choose or be persuaded into an act of violent self-sacrifice. First, women's daily lives in the West Bank and Gaza Strip are conducted in an environment of relentless and frequently indiscriminate violence and increasing hopelessness. Women and their children are victims of profound insecurity and helplessness. The "permanent war" being waged by Israel has led to what Martin Shaw calls the "brutalization of state and society."[128] Under such circumstances, some argue, the emergence of the suicide bomber can be seen as an unsurprising response to oppression. This raises the question of the impact on this deeply conservative society of what has been described as a "culture of death."[129]

Second, many women in the West Bank and Gaza Strip have lost family members or seen their homes destroyed as a result of violent hostilities between Palestinians and Israelis. For example, Souad, the Ramallah journalist, saw her home demolished in 2005 after her husband was arrested. The Israelis came to her house at 3 AM, she said; it was unexpected; they called everyone out of the house and told her to enter with them, to show them the house, a "human shield." In the ensuing destruction, she lost everything: all her memories, all her things were gone, and she became "a person without history."[130] Souad's experiences are an example of victimhood, the inability to defend oneself, and although they did not cause her to turn to violence, they reinforced her conviction that only groups such as Hamas and Islamic Jihad have the moral courage to confront Israel and end Palestinian humiliation. In general, women like Souad are regarded as innocent victims, forced to watch helplessly as their lives and families are shattered; others have become the mothers or widows of martyrs, a status that is celebrated in Palestinian society and conforms to traditional understandings of "a woman's place." The "maternalist position" equates women with motherhood and peace.[131] It raises the question of religion as a tool of motivation or mobilization, or a signifier of honor.

Third, some women have started to adopt patterns of behavior that appear unsettling to Palestinian society's sense of propriety. A small minority have *chosen* to engage in militant anti-occupation activities (defined by Israel and its supporters, including the United States and the European Union, as terrorism), and we would like to consider why women have chosen to carry out martyrdom operations and why their decisions, on the one hand, may seem to challenge the fundamental values of society but, on the other, seem to support the development of Sadiki's "community of resistance" in the face of overwhelming odds. Since the reemergence of conflict in 2000, as fear and hopelessness have become increasingly significant factors, women's space for maneuver began to diminish. The response of the majority of women was to focus on their familiar roles of support and caring. In the words of a health professional, "We have taken on the traditional role of doing relief work and handing out food and clothing to families of martyrs." However, she added that "we are also using these activities to speak to mothers and wives about bettering their education . . . and becoming more independent."[132] Another response has been passivity and withdrawal; many women report feeling "helpless" or "unable to cope," as Amina in Gaza City testified. A final choice available to women is to sacrifice their own lives to fight the occupation; we should add that this "choice" has been made by a very small number of women. For example, in November 2006, Fatma al-Najar, a woman in her seventies, blew herself up in the Jabaliya refugee camp in the northern Gaza Strip, slightly injuring three Israeli soldiers. According to her daughter, "she was a religious woman. She did this to fight the Israelis and get them out of our land."[133]

While the international community appears to have little interest in the resolution of the Palestinian-Israeli conflict and continues to defer to "negotiations between the two parties involved," the vexed question of Palestinian suicide bombing has attracted considerably more attention. Those who commit these acts are regarded by some as terrorists or evil and by others as heroes and martyrs, although even some of those who condemn such violence concede that Palestinians have few other options at their disposal against the powerful Israeli army of occupation. Most of the suicide bombers since the mid-1990s have been young men, but since 2002, a small number of women have embarked on suicide-martyrdom missions.

An adherence to Islam and religious justifications for acts of violence have been cited by women martyrs by way of explanation. However, the question of whether suicide bombings are valid in the case of occupied Muslim lands, such as Palestine, has generated a number of contradictory interpretations, which suggests "that the desire to support female suicide bombing stems more from strategic and tactical arguments than any theological premise."[134] Many observers condemn these acts as terrorist and unacceptable, both in terms of humane practices and also of Islamic teachings. "Terrorism" has been defined as "the intentional use of political violence against civilians and civilian sites."[135] But the definition "is marred by acrimonious debates," and "it is important to underline that terrorism is a *means* or method used to achieve political objectives and does not refer to the objectives themselves."[136] In early Islam, jurists "developed a sophisticated discourse on the proper limits of the conduct of warfare, political violence and terrorism. . . . The Qur'anic prescriptions simply call upon Muslims to fight in the way of God, establish justice and refrain from exceeding the limits of justice in fighting their enemies."[137] Commentators refer to this discourse to argue that the "proper limits" have been exceeded by suicide attacks on civilians. However, Palestinians respond that they are obliged to undertake jihad to correct an unjust situation. Azam Tamimi argues that despite "its sanctity in Islam, life can be sacrificed for the sake of ending oppression. Both the Qur'an and the *hadith* . . . exhort Muslims to resist oppression and struggle against it."[138] But it remains a contentious area, especially for women. Kholoud al-Masry, the deputy mayor of Nablus, observed that the two reasons why Palestinian women are becoming stronger are, first, a belief in the Islamic resistance; and, second, the imperative they feel to end the occupation and reclaim Palestinian land.[139]

According to the Covenant of Hamas, "There is no greater patriotism than a situation in which the enemy takes over Muslim land. Then the *jihad* turns into a religious obligation for every Muslim man or woman. The woman goes out to battle without her husband's permission and the slave without his master's permission."[140] The question of using Islam as a justification for violence has been explored by various "experts" seeking to discover "why certain women turn to martyrdom."[141] There is a widespread belief that women, much more than men, "tend to choose self-sacrifice as an exit from personal despair" or because they have broken social taboos.[142] Rather than agents, they are identified predominantly as victims. However, we intend to challenge the dominant "understandings" of why women might choose to act in this way by presenting the life stories of women in the West Bank. In terms of resistance, Palestine is often regarded as an exceptional case in which resistance is felt to be an obligation for everyone. However, for women, it is inevitably more complex. The link between women and peace, or nonviolence, and women's maternal role has meant that the violent woman is seen as in some way deviant or unconventional.

Osama Hamdan, who represents Hamas in Lebanon, espouses this view. In an interview in 2007, he said that Palestinian women living under occupation support militant activities, although they do not usually carry them out. Instead, he explained, women must take responsibility for their families when the men are killed or imprisoned, and these roles are of equal, if not greater importance.[143] In 2008, the BBC's Middle East correspondent interviewed an eighteen-year-old woman in Gaza who had volunteered to undertake a suicide mission. She described the opportunity as "a gift from God." As the correspondent observes, the "use of Palestinian women as suicide bombers was once thought of as immodest—and therefore un-Islamic—but that changed, the militant groups say, because of shortage of male candidates and because women were better able to get close to their targets"; in addition, female bombers "have much greater propaganda impact."[144]

In a somewhat sensationalized account, journalist Barbara Victor argues that Palestinian women suicide bombers are "an example of the exploitation of women taken to a cynical and lethal extreme."[145] This argument is not uncommon. There is a widespread belief that women, much more than men, "tend to choose self-sacrifice as an exit from personal despair" or because they have broken social taboos.[146] Reacting to the constraints of their society, women are said to "have channelled their frustration . . . into criminal behaviour" or have taken the opportunity "to affirm themselves as human beings after having failed or been denied the ability to affirm themselves as women."[147] Rather than agents, they are identified predominantly as victims. Our analysis is intended to highlight the dominant narrative of Israel and the west. For example, in response to protests by women in the Gaza town of Beit Hanoun in November 2006 and their attempt to protect a group of resistance fighters trapped inside a mosque, an Israeli government spokesman announced, "The militants used women as human shields. This is a clear example of the use of an innocent population for terror."[148] This language has become so commonplace that it is rarely questioned by western media sources.

It is important to reiterate that, out of the many suicide attacks against Israeli military and civilian targets carried out by Palestinians since 2001, very few have involved women and even fewer have been orchestrated by Islamist groups; nonetheless, these acts have been subjected to intense scrutiny. The tiny minority of Palestinian women have been perceived by some as having destabilized the notion of "appropriate roles" in this conservative society. The violent *man* is expected, but the violent *woman* is more likely to be regarded as transgressing against the norms and values of society. Palestinians argue, however, that they are not engaging in unprovoked violence but, rather, practicing their legitimate right of resistance and self-defense. As a "community of resisters," their perspective on the situation, as one of the unjust victimization of a disempowered people, gives some women the confidence to embark upon extreme action. It is necessary to understand how such narratives are constructed and justified. By referring to theories of Islamic militancy and also by exploring women's experiences of violent conflict, we argue that resistance is a necessary method of survival in a situation in which human security is severely compromised and the powerlessness of women and men constantly reiterated. It is a complex and sensitive area, and our objective here is to "deconstruct the insidious and pervasive effects and mechanisms of violence and terror, underscoring how it operates on the level of lived experience."[149] In other words, we propose to challenge "gendered assumptions" and to destabilize "the construct of men as defenders of community and women as the protected."[150] For the purposes of this chapter, we are seeking to understand these women's actions from the perspective of liberation and agency.

Anat Berko and Edna Erez argue that some women combatants act "out of religious conviction" or feel the need to avenge the death of a family member,[151] whereas others see it as a way "to rebel against a strict patriarchal regime" or as "an opportunity to resolve a personal or familial problem."[152] Other scholars have described the self-inflicted violence of these women "as vengeance driven by maternal disappointments and humiliation."[153] Like Victor, Clara Beyler asserts that female suicide bombers "appear to be one of the most extreme forms of exploitation of women, who become objectified, even if they think that their choice is subjective . . . they become weapons in the hands of the men of the terrorist organizations."[154] When reporting the *shuhida*, the media tend to emphasize "the emotional over the ideological."[155] But there are other, more thoughtful ways of assessing this phenomenon that eschew the frameworks of both patriarchy and victimization as a means of understanding women's behavior.

At the same time, some critics have argued that the violence involved in Islamic resistance and the process of Islamization has hampered women's ability to participate in the national struggle. In communities that place an emphasis on appropriate gender roles, the emergence of the female suicide bomber in the Occupied Territories in 2004, and more recently in Iraq, must be regarded as a deviation from the fixed and long-standing conventions of Arab societies in general and Palestinian and Iraqi societies in particular. The idea that increasing numbers of Palestinian women are now prepared to die violently for the cause indicates either that the desperation of their nation's plight has unbalanced normal gender hierarchies or that the position of women in Palestinian society is undergoing radical change. It raises the question of what role Islam is playing in encouraging these young women to take such a drastic and "unnatural" step.

However, it is our contention that, by dismissing these women as "exploited" or the "tools of men," this type of analysis fails to take seriously either women's own agency or the pressures of the conflict. In reality, the situation is more nuanced. Its complexity can be gleaned from statements by the women martyrs themselves, which indicate political awareness and a clear understanding of their situation. For example, twenty-nine-year-old lawyer Hanadi Jaradat killed herself in a restaurant in Haifa in October 2003 "in revenge for the killing of her brother and her fiancé by the Israeli security forces," but also "in revenge for all the crimes Israel had perpetrated in the West Bank."[156] This indicates another motive for female self-sacrifice, the embodying of national pride and honor; it supports the claim that Palestinian women are writing "the history of their liberation with their blood."[157] Another young West Bank woman, who "martyred" herself in 2002, was shown on Arabic satellite television reading from a prepared statement in which she asserted, "I've chosen to say with my body what Arab leaders have failed to say."[158] In her martyrdom video, the second Palestinian *shahida*, Dareen Abu Aysheh, stated that the Palestinian woman's role "will not only be confined to weeping over a son, brother or husband; instead she will become a martyr herself."[159] Clearly, these women—far from being coerced by bullying men or a punitive society—are driven by a commitment to the liberation of their nation and the overriding demand of communal solidarity.[160]

Conclusion

As they continue to exist under a harsh occupation regime, in which their elected representatives have been prevented by sieges and sanctions from exercising their legislative powers, women have enjoyed few formal improvements in their daily lives; their activism has not had obvious concrete outcomes. The Hamas government has signaled an awareness of the need to address women's concerns, however. In addition, many women have felt themselves empowered by the grassroots activities of Islamist groups to play more meaningful and "appropriate" roles in the struggle, and, on occasion, roles that are less "appropriate." Although one cannot equate these activities with feminism, they exhibit evidence of increasing female agency.

In this chapter, we have considered the threatened nature of Palestinian national identity and also the ways in which resistance to Israeli occupation has become more violent. The violence is striking, on the one hand, because it is closely linked to Islamic symbols and moral codes and, on the other, because it has drawn in a number of women. This raises the question of what options are available to women for dealing with the crisis in their society. It is not sufficient to describe Palestinian society as "patriarchal" or "aberrant." We have argued that Palestinian women have not emerged from their homes in order to sacrifice their bodies for male vanity or through despair; they have done so through a commitment to communal protection in the face of overwhelming odds. Palestinians observed the response of the international community in 2008–2009 to the Israeli assault on Gaza and Israeli claims of "self-defense," and they concluded, as in the case of the 1982 massacres in Sabra and Shatila in Lebanon and the 2005 attack against the Jenin refugee camp in the West Bank, that the world has turned its back. Their only hope is in solidarity, the construction of a "community of resisters," and that, inevitably, includes women as much as men.

Notes

1. According to the Palestinian Centre for Human Rights, the fighting killed more than 1,419 Palestinians; of these fatalities, 252 were combatants, 40 percent were said to be children (412) and women (110). More than 5,000 were reported wounded, a large number of them civilians.

2. Alastair Crooke, *Resistance: The Essence of the Islamist Revolution* (London: Pluto, 2009), 225.

3. Hussein Ibish, "'Martyrs vs. Traitors' Myth Gains Currency in Gaza War's Wake," *Chicago Tribune*, January 25, 2009.

4. "The story of the Palestinian people since their *nakba* is a story of unfulfilled desires: the desire for normal life, for justice, for national independence and freedom." Mourid Barghouti, "He Is the Son of All of You," *Guardian*, August 16, 2008.

5. Amartya Sen, *Identity and Violence: The Illusion of Destiny* (London: Penguin, 2006), xv.

6. Sara Roy, *Failing Peace: Gaza and the Palestinian-Israeli Conflict* (London: Pluto, 2007), 173.

7. By "different forms of power," we mean the power exerted over Palestinian women by their position in the gender hierarchy, their roles in the family, and the ongoing violence of the Israeli occupation.

8. Tamar Mayer, ed., *Women and the Israeli Occupation: The Politics of Change* (London: Routledge, 1994), 64.

9. Joseph Massad, "Conceiving the Masculine: Gender and Palestinian Nationalism," *Middle East Journal* 49, no. 3 (Summer 1995): 469.

10. Frances S. Hasso, "The 'Women's Front': Nationalism, Feminism, and Modernity in Palestine," *Gender and Society* 12, no. 4 (August 1998): 442.

11. Edward W. Said, *After the Last Sky* (London: Faber and Faber, 1986), 77.

12. Edward Said, *Orientalism*, 2nd ed. (New York: Vintage, 1994), 331–332.

13. Sen, *Identity and Violence*, xiii.

14. Stuart Hall, "Who Needs 'Identity'?" in Stuart Hall and Paul du Gay, eds., *Questions of Cultural Identity* (Thousand Oaks, CA: Sage, 1996), 3 (emphasis added).

15. Julie Peteet, *Landscape of Hope and Despair: Palestinian Refugee Camps* (Philadelphia: University of Pennsylvania Press, 2005), 99.

16. Stuart Hall, "Cultural Identity and Diaspora," in Patrick Williams and Laura Chrisman, eds., *Colonial Discourse and Post-Colonial Theory: A Reader* (New York: Harvester Wheatsheaf, 1993), 392.

17. Michel Foucault, *Power/Knowledge: Selected Interviews and Other Writings, 1972–1977*, edited by Colin Gordon (London: Harvester, 1980).

18. M. E. Bailey, "Foucauldian Feminism: Contesting Bodies, Sexuality and Identity," in Caroline Ramazanoglu, ed., *Up Against Foucault: Explorations of Some Tensions Between Foucault and Feminism* (London: Routledge, 1993), 115.

19. Cynthia Cockburn, *The Space Between Us: Negotiating Gender and National Identities in Conflict* (London: Zed, 1998), 216.

20. Haifaa A. Jawad, *The Rights of Women in Islam: An Authentic Approach* (Basingstoke: Macmillan Press, 1998), 87.

21. Miriam Cooke, *Women Claim Islam: Creating Islamic Feminism Through Literature* (London: Routledge, 2001), 55.

22. Suha Sabbagh, "Introduction," in Suha Sabbagh, ed., *Palestinian Women of Gaza and the West Bank* (Bloomington: Indiana University Press, 1998), 18.

23. Ibid., 19.

24. Michael Broning, *The Politics of Change in Palestine: State-Building and Non-Violent Resistance* (London: Pluto, 2011), 135.

25. Samah Sabawai, "Truth, Non-Violence, and the Palestinian Hills," Australians for Palestine, australiansforpalestine.com/22195, 2010.

26. Nadia Yaqub, "Dismantling the Discourses of War: Palestinian Women Filmmakers Address Violence," in Moha Ennaji and Fatima Sadiqi, eds., *Gender and Violence in the Middle East* (London: Routledge, 2011), 233. For more about "everyday acts of resistance," see James C. Scott, *Weapons of the Weak: Everyday Forms of Peasant Resistance* (New Haven, CT: Yale University Press, 1985).

27. Lisa Taraki, "Introduction," in Lisa Taraki, ed., *Living Palestine: Family Survival, Resistance, and Mobility Under Occupation* (Syracuse: Syracuse University Press, 2006), xx.

28. Liah Greenfield, *Nationalism: Five Roads to Modernity* (Cambridge, MA: Harvard University Press, 1992), 7.

29. Nels Johnson, *Islam and the Politics of Meaning in Palestinian Nationalism* (London: KPI, 1982), 35.

30. Ibid., 44.

31. Simona Sharoni and Mohammed Abu-Nimer, "The Israeli-Palestinian Conflict," in Jillian Schwedler and Deborah J. Gerner, eds., *Understanding the Contemporary Middle East*, 3rd ed. (Boulder: Lynne Rienner, 2008), 187.

32. Greg Philo and Mike Berry, *More Bad News from Israel* (London: Pluto, 2011), 31.

33. Sharoni and Abu-Nimer, "The Israeli-Palestinian Conflict," 189.

34. Zalman Amit and Daphna Levit, *Israeli Rejectionism: A Hidden Agenda in the Middle East Peace Process* (London: Pluto, 2011).

35. Ibid., 11.

36. Broning, *The Politics of Change in Palestine*, 136.

37. Ibid., 136.

38. Philippa Strum, *The Women Are Marching: The Second Sex and the Palestinian Revolution* (New York: Lawrence Hill, 1992), 29.

39. Ibid.

40. Ellen L. Fleischmann, *The Nation and Its "New" Women: The Palestinian Women's Movement, 1920–1948* (Berkeley: University of California Press, 2003), 10.

41. Ibid., 11.

42. Cheryl A. Rubenberg, *Palestinian Women: Patriarchy and Resistance in the West Bank* (Boulder, CO: Lynne Rienner, 2001), 209.

43. Shadla el-Sarraj, "Screaming in Silence," in Marguerite R. Waller and Jennifer Rycenga, eds., *Frontline Feminisms: Women, War, and Resistance* (New York: Routledge, 2001), 19.

44. Nadera Shalhoub-Kevorkian, *Militarization and Violence Against Women in Conflict Zones in the Middle East: A Palestinian Case Study* (Cambridge: Cambridge University Press, 2009), 67.

45. Janeen, quoted in Rubenberg, *Palestinian Women*, 57.

46. Penny Johnson and Eileen Kuttab, "Where Have All the Women (and Men) Gone? Reflections on Gender and the Second Palestinian Intifada," *Feminist Review*, no. 69 (Winter 2001): 25.

47. Taraki, "Introduction," xx.

48. Interview, Ramallah, West Bank, June 13, 2007.

49. Interview, Ramallah, June 14, 2007.

50. Interview, Ramallah, October 31, 2007.

51. G. Sharp, "The Intifadah and Nonviolent Struggle," *Journal of Palestine Studies* 19, no. 1 (1989): 7.

52. Amit and Levit, *Israeli Rejectionism*, 163.

53. Interview, Hebron, West Bank, November 4, 2007.

54. Interview, Ramallah, October 31, 2007.

55. Interview, Birzeit University, Ramallah, November 3, 2007.

56. Johnson and Kuttab, "Where Have All the Women (and Men) Gone?" 24.

57. Umm Nader, Ramallah, quoted in "Palestinian Women Help Behind the Lines," Dainik Bhaskar Group (India's largest newspaper group), November 13, 2000, indiainfo.com.

58. Roy, *Failing Peace*, 49.

59. Interview, Balata camp, Nablus, West Bank, June 16, 2007.

60. Jameela al-Shanti, "We Overcame Our Fear," *Guardian*, November 9, 2006.

61. Eliza Ernshire, "Who Was Perpetrating the Terror? The Women of Beit Hanoun," *Counterpunch*, November 7, 2006, http://www.counterpunch.org/ernshire.11072006.html, accessed February 9, 2010.

62. Women Living Under Muslim Laws, "Palestine: Female Activists a Force in Male-Dominated Gaza," February 12, 2007, http://www.wluml.org/english/news fulltxt.shtml?cmd%5B157%5D=x-157-550222, accessed March 26, 2009.

63. Salwa Ismail, *Rethinking Islamist Politics: Culture, the State, and Islamism* (London: I. B. Tauris, 2006), 136.

64. Larbi Sadiki, "Reframing Resistance and Democracy: Narratives from Hamas and Hizbullah," *Democratization* 17, no. 2 (April 2010): 355.

65. Sabbagh, "Introduction," 17.

66. Maha Abu Dayyeh Shamas, "The Second Palestinian Intifada: Social and Psychological Implications of the Israeli Escalation of Violence," Women's Centre for Legal Aid and Counselling (WCLAC), Jerusalem, August 2001.

67. Interview, Gaza City, May 2001.

68. For further information about human rights abuses in the Palestinian territories, see Palestinian Centre for Human Rights (www.pchrgaza.org), Al-Haq (www.alhaq.org), Palestinian Human Rights Monitoring Group (www.phrmg.org), and Miftah (www.miftah.org).

69. Mona Shawa, head of the women's unit at the Palestinian Centre for Human Rights in Gaza City, quoted in Jillian Kestler-D'Amours, "Harsh Economic

and Social Conditions Contribute to Violence Against Palestinian Women," *Electronic Intifada*, August 20, 2012.

70. Kestler-D'Amours, "Harsh Economic and Social Conditions." She is referring to "77% of Gaza Women Face Violence," a report produced by the Palestinian Women's Information and Media Centre, Gaza, December 2009.

71. Malek Shubair, assistant public relations coordinator, Gaza Community Mental Health Project, quoted in "Palestinian Women Use Intifada to Better Their Lot," November 11, 2000.

72. Abu-Dayyeh Shamas, "The Second Palestinian Intifada."

73. A report on the situation of women's human rights during the second intifada, presented by the Women's Centre for Legal Aid and Counselling (WCLAC) and the Women's Studies Center (WSC) to the UN Human Rights Commission Fact-Finding Mission, February 16, 2001, 2.

74. Lisa Taraki, "Palestinian Society: Contemporary Reality and Trends," In *Palestinian Women: A Status Report* (Birzeit: Women's Studies Program, Birzeit University, 1997), 18.

75. Nahda Sh'hada, "Women in Gaza," *Zmag*, www.zmag.org, November 27, 2000.

76. Interview, Shadia Sarraj, Women's Empowerment Project, Gaza City, May 2001.

77. Randa Nasser, Fidaa Barghouti, and Janan Mousa, "Feminist Attitudes and Praxis Among Palestinian Women Activists," *Feminist Formations* 22, no. 3 (Fall 2010): 152.

78. Johnson, *Islam and the Politics of Meaning in Palestinian Nationalism*, 94.

79. Ibid., 98.

80. Ibid., 99.

81. Khaled Hroub, *Hamas: Political Thought and Practice* (Washington, DC: Institute for Palestine Studies, 2000), 17.

82. Ibid., 23.

83. Ibid., 28.

84. Ibid., 31.

85. Ibid., 32.

86. Glenn E. Robinson, *Building a Palestinian State: The Incomplete Revolution* (Bloomington: Indiana University Press, 1997), 151.

87. Jeroen Gunning, *Hamas in Politics: Democracy, Religion, Violence* (London: Hurst, 2009), 38.

88. Islah Jad, "Between Religion and Secularism: Islamist Women of Hamas," in Fereshteh Nouralie-Simone, ed., *On Shifting Ground: Muslim Women in the Global Era* (New York: Feminist Press at the City University of New York, 2005), 173.

89. Gunning, *Hamas in Politics*, 41.

90. Crooke, *Resistance*, 69.

91. Ibid.

92. David Cook, "Women Fighting in *Jihad?*"in Cindy D. Ness, ed., *Female Terrorism and Militancy: Agency, Utility, and Organization* (London: Routlege, 2008), 39.

93. Quoted in Robinson, *Building a Palestinian State*, 155.

94. Meeting with Sayyid Muhammad Hussein Fadlallah, Beirut, May 2, 1994.

95. M. A. al-Akiti, *Defending the Transgressed by Censuring the Reckless Against the Killing of Civilians* (Leicester: Aqsa Press, 2005), 34.

96. Margaret Gonzalez-Perez, "The False Islamization of Female Suicide Bombers," *Gender Issues* 28 (2011): 51.

97. Haidar Eid, "Gaza 2009: Culture of Resistance vs. Defeat," *Electronic Intifada*, February 11, 2009.

98. Lisa Taraki, "Mass Organizations in the West Bank," *Readings in Contemporary Palestinian Society*, vol. 2 (Birzeit: Birzeit University Press, 1989), 172.

99. Interview, Ramallah, June 14, 2007.

100. Personal interview with Islah Jad, Birzeit University, Ramallah, October 31, 2007.

101. Interview, Birzeit University, Ramallah, November 3, 2007.

102. Jad, "Between Religion and Secularism," 174.

103. Jamila al-Shanty, a professor at the Islamic University in Gaza, quoted in Ian Fisher, "Women, Secret Hamas Strength, Win Votes at Polls and New Role," *New York Times*, February 3, 2006.

104. Interview, Ramallah, November 3, 2007.

105. Julie Peteet, "Male Gender and Rituals of Resistance in the Palestinian Intifada: A Cultural Politics of Violence," in Mai Ghoussoub and Emma Sinclair-Webb, eds., *Imagined Masculinities: Male Identity and Culture in the Modern Middle East* (London: Saqi, 2000), 119.

106. Nadera Shalhoub-Kevorkian, "Liberating Voices: The Political Implications of Palestinian Mothers Narrating their Loss," *Women's Studies International Forum* 26, no. 5 (2003): 406.

107. Ibid.

108. Laleh Khalili, *Heroes and Martyrs of Palestine: The Politics of National Commemoration* (Cambridge: Cambridge University Press, 2007), 152.

109. Crooke, *Resistance*, 197.

110. Interview, Balata refugee camp, Nablus, June 16, 2007.

111. Interview, Nablus, June 16, 2007.

112. Sadiki, "Reframing Resistance and Democracy," 365.

113. Ibid.

114. Cynthia Cockburn, "The Gendered Dynamics of Armed Conflict and Political Violence," in Caroline O. N. Moser and Fiona C. Clark, eds., *Victims, Perpetrators, or Actors? Gender, Armed Conflict, and Political Violence* (London: Zed, 2001), 21.

115. Interview, Ramallah, October 31, 2007.

116. Nilufer Gole, "Close Encounters: Islam, Modernity, and Violence," July 3, 2006, http://mbarchives.blogspot.co.uk/2006/07/close-encounters-islam-modernity-and.html#!/2006/07/close-encounters-islam-modernity-and.html.

117. Eid, "Gaza 2009."

118. Crooke, *Resistance*, 197.

119. Roy, *Failing Peace*, 162–163.

120. Ibid., 168.

121. Gole, "Close Encounters," 5.

122. Interview, Mariam Saleh, Ramallah, November 1, 2007.

123. Gudrun Kramer, "Visions of an Islamic Republic: Good Governance According to the Islamists," in Frederic Volpi, ed., *Political Islam: A Critical Reader* (London: Routledge, 2011), 89.

124. Maurice Merleau-Ponty, *Humanism and Terror* (Boston: Beacon Press, 1969 [1947]), 107.

125. Rubenberg, *Palestinian Women*, 232.

126. Sara Roy, "The Transformation of Islamic NGOs in Palestine," *Middle East Report* 30, no. 1 (Spring 2000): 25.

127. Rema Hammami, "Women, the Hijab, and the Intifada," *Middle East Report*, May–August 1990, 24.

128. Martin Shaw, *The New Western Way of War* (Cambridge: Polity, 2005), 140.

129. Judith Miller, "The Bomb Under the Abaya," *Policy Review* (June–July 2007).

130. Interview, Ramallah, October 31, 2007.

131. Caron E. Gentry, "Twisted Maternalism," *International Feminist Journal of Politics* 11, no. 2 (2009): 235.

132. Aitemad Muhanna, a psychologist with the Women's Empowerment Project, Gaza Strip, quoted in "Palestinian Women Use Intifada to Better Their Lot," November 11, 2000.

133. Rory McCarthy, "Sisters, Mothers, Martyrs," *Guardian*, December 5, 2006.

134. Gonzalez-Perez, "The False Islamization of Female Suicide Bombers," 58.

135. Augustus Richard Norton, *Hezbollah: A Short History* (Princeton, NJ: Princeton University Press, 2007), 76.

136. Katerina Dalacoura, *Islamist Terrorism and Democracy in the Middle East* (Cambridge: Cambridge University Press, 2011), 13.

137 Khaled Abou El Fadl, "Islam and the Theology of Power," *Middle East Report* 221 (Winter 2001), http://www.merip.org/mer/mer221/221_abu_el_fadl .html, accessed June 10, 2009.

138. Azam Tamimi, "The Islamic Debate over Self-Inflicted Martyrdom," in Madawi al-Rasheed and Marat Shterin, eds., *Dying for Faith: Religiously Motivated Violence in the Contemporary World* (London: I. B. Tauris, 2009), 98.

139. Interview, Kholoud al-Masry, Nablus, November 7, 2007.

140. *The Covenant of the Islamic Resistance Movement—Palestine Filastin (Hamas)*, Article 12, "The Homeland and Patriotism from the Point of View of the Movement in Palestine," Muharram 1, 1409/August 18, 1988.

141. Tim McGirk, Jamil Hamad, and Aaron J. Klein, "Moms and Martyrs," *Time*, May 14, 2007, http://web/ebscohost.com/ehost/delivery?sid=89ccae7e-14cf -414e-816b-05de5a28c04, accessed June 20, 2011.

142. Ibid.

143. Interview, Osama Hamdan, Hamas representative in Lebanon, Beirut, May 4, 2007.

144. Paul Wood, "Just Married and Determined to Die," *BBC News*, October 13, 2008.

145. Barbara Victor, *Army of Roses: Inside the World of Palestinian Women Suicide Bombers* (London: Robinson, 2004), 8.

146. McGirk, Hamad, and Klein, "Moms and Martyrs."

147. Clara Beyler, "Messengers of Death—Female Suicide Bombers," International Institute for Counter-Terrorism, February 12, 2003, http://www.ict.org.il /Articles/tabid/66/Articlsid/94/Default.aspx, accessed January 24, 2011.

148. Ernshire, "Who Was Perpetrating the Terror?"

149. Linda Green, *Fear as a Way of Life: Mayan Widows in Rural Guatemala* (New York: Columbia University Press, 1999), 58.

150. Frances S. Hasso, "Discursive and Political Deployments by/of the 2002 Palestinian Women Suicide Bombers/Martyrs," *Feminist Review* 81 (2005): 24.

151. Anat Berko and Edna Erez, "'Ordinary People' and 'Death Work': Palestinian Suicide Bombers as Victimizers and Victims," *Violence and Victims* 20, no. 6 (December 2005): 606.

152. Anat Berko and Edna Erez, "Gender, Palestinian Women, and Terrorism: Women's Liberation or Oppression?" *Studies in Conflict and Terrorism* 30, no. 6 (2007): 493–519.

153. See Hala Jaber, "Inside the World of the Palestinian Suicide Bomber," *Sunday Times*, March 24, 2003; C. Ragavan, D. Pasternak, and R. Sharpe, "Femme Fatale? Al Qaeda's Mystery Woman," *US News and World Report*, April 7, 2003; O. Ward, "The Changing Face of Terror," *Toronto Star*, October 10, 2004; C. Dickey, "Women of Al Qaeda," *Newsweek*, December 12, 2005.

154. Beyler, "Messengers of Death," 7.

155. Terri Toles Patkin, "Explosive Baggage: Female Palestinian Suicide Bombers and the Rhetoric of Emotion," *Women and Language* 27, no. 2 (2004): 85.

156. Riaz Hassan, "What Motivates the Suicide Bombers?" Yale Global, September 3, 2009, http://yaleglobal.yale,edu, accessed January 28, 2010.

157. *Al Akhbar,* Beirut, 2002.

158. H. Hendawi, "Palestinian Father Expresses Shock over Daughter's Suicide Bombing," Associated Press Worldstream, April 13, 2002.

159. Quoted in Toles Patkin, "Explosive Baggage," 85.

160. Maria Holt, "The Unlikely Terrorist: Women and Islamic Resistance in Lebanon and the Palestinian Territories," *Critical Studies on Terrorism* 3, no. 3 (2010): 365–382.

7

The Way Forward

Works on Arab women in general tend to be limited in scope, if not number, and there are even fewer works that deal in any depth with Arab women and their roles and involvement in the rising up of Islamist resistance movements throughout the Arab world. In this book, we address this crucial lacuna by providing concrete evidence and analysis of the role of women in these resistance movements and in the current Arab spring revolutions. We highlight the struggles taking place in parts of the Arab world, with a particular focus on women in Palestine, in Lebanon, and in exile from Iraq who were or are still experiencing violent conflict as a result of foreign occupations and invasions. In these places, the resistance has assumed a politico-"religious" identity that is termed "Islamist." Our findings rely extensively on the personal narratives of women who themselves have lived through violent conflict. Our research reinforces the finding that the effects of violent conflict upon women vary widely, according to context, and have much to do with the existing social status of the women in question and the modalities of their agency, both within their specific communities and in society at large. In particular, we have looked at the various factors that influence the women's decisions to take part in the resistance, such as freedom of choice and the role of religion, in this case Islam, especially the manner in which sharia has been invoked as a means of encouraging everyone, including women, to participate and to sacrifice themselves, if necessary, in the face of external attacks and internal oppression.

This is not the place to analyze in depth the modalities of Arab resistance movements, as distinguished from Shiite political movements or the revolutions of the Arab spring. Instead what we can affirm and elucidate is the fact that when Islamic values are employed to galvanize resistance forces, the active participation of women in those societies increases to a hitherto unprecedented degree. Women's active participation in the resistance movements and their breaking away from the confines of the domestic sphere, is legitimized and justified by the "cause" of Islam, the call to struggle in the "path of God" (*fi sabil Allah*). As a positive corollary, women themselves feel more motivated to undertake this struggle and to participate more vigorously therein, invoking Islamic values as their justification. We observe that the degree to which this new or increased participation in the social sphere leads to a far-reaching and deep-rooted improvement of the social status of women seems to depend on the extent to which the male institutions of governance themselves have been transformed by Islamic ethical ideals. Where Islamic ideals shape the institutions of the movement, the advancement of women's social status appears to be genuine, but where the "Islamist" resistance movement has been puritanical, the gains appear short-term and superficial. Again, we must stress that this book is not the place to analyze the varying politico-religious underpinnings of the resistance movements; our aim is simply to illustrate how it is that religious symbolism can be employed to galvanize the resistance movement.

Khaled Abou El Fadl describes how the "powerful normative dynamics of the congregational prayers" in Tahrir Square in Cairo acted as "vehicles for moral and social solidarity, collective aspirations, and mobilization. These congregational performances affirmed a sense of solidarity that transcended the disparate economic statuses and divergent educational and cultural backgrounds of the revolutionaries," and, we would add, *gender boundaries.*[1] Such religious symbols, moreover, sustain people and allow them to maintain their struggle so that, in the case of military conflict and invasion, their resistance is underpinned by a religious belief that their mission is holy and sanctioned by the Divine to uphold rights, establish justice, and restore equilibrium. This feeds into the powerful concept of jihad, which is then employed in the context of armed resistance that "is quintessentially centered on the idea of just struggle," and encourages women (as well as men) to involve themselves in the resistance.[2] The concept of jihad gains momentum and becomes very attractive through another closely linked concept, "the idea of Shahada or bearing witness through martyrdom."[3] As Abou El Fadl goes on to explain, "Doctrinally, martyrdom is part and parcel of a moral status that grew out of and is corollary to the concept of jihad. For the most part, those who are considered martyrs first engage in a jihad and then are killed in the process. In other words, one first rises to the status of a *mujahid* (someone engaged in a jihad) before qualifying for the honoured status of martyrdom (*shahada*)."[4]

The important role these Islamic concepts play in mobilizing people to join the resistance in the context of invasions and attacks cannot be underestimated. However, what must be appreciated within the context of women's participation in these resistance movements is that genuine adherence to the spiritual ideals of Islam would necessitate the questioning and reappraisal of gender relations in light of patriarchal practices that have encroached upon these Islamic ideals. Since the spiritual depth or degree of genuine adherence to spiritual ideals of those spearheading these movements varies, taking part in violent conflicts very often leads to violence against the women themselves. Indeed, we have seen in our three case studies that women and children, although they are not usually combatants, tend to be disproportionately victimized. For example, our research indicates that women experience violence not only from the occupiers, whom the women have to confront, but also from the various militias that rise up during times of war and from within their families, especially from male members who feel hopeless in the face of their inability to fulfill their traditional roles during violent conflict situations.

Lines of demarcation between the public and the private domain become blurred or subsumed within the wider parameters of the struggle, whether domestic or international. Taking part in the resistance assumes the form of an attempted restoration of personal dignity as well as national dignity, both private and public here being merged into a fundamental reassertion of the dignity of women per se. As national identity has been battered, the Islamist resistance movements have sought to galvanize the population under the banner of Islam to challenge foreign invasion, injustice, and oppression, and our research has shown the role played by women in these movements cannot be dissociated either from the sociocultural process by which women are struggling to reinstate their rights within the Islamic context, or from the structural empowerment of women resulting from their engagement in social, economic, and political struggle. Such engagement, in and of itself, cannot but catapult women—and their conception of their role within an Islamic framework—to the very forefront of the struggle.

Our research has tested prevailing concepts of powerlessness and victimization by looking at women's own strategies of resistance. It suggests that, despite the impediments created by prevailing patriarchal structures, women have achieved a notable degree of success in overcoming these disadvantages, whether through negotiation or by defying hierarchies in the name of Islamic justice. Their strategies of resistance proliferated, ranging from political, educational, charity, and arts resistance to direct involvement in armed struggles. The result, as our three case studies clearly illustrate, has been an effective and expanded space for female participation. We also argue that the larger story of the Lebanese Shiite community has been one of learning and struggle. Both their own efforts and the inspiration provided by the heroes of Shiite history and the success of the Islamist resistance have challenged the political system, fought injustice, and expelled the Israeli occupiers from their land. As is made clear in numerous accounts, women played important roles in this struggle. We conclude that role models and doctrines from Shiite Islam have motivated women. That is, the female role models Fatima and Zaynab have encouraged and ultimately "sanctioned" the full participation of women in the struggle to achieve national liberation. Lebanese Shiite women speak with pride of their victory over aggression, exclusion, and injustice. In contrast to Palestinians and Iraqis, their "communal story" has had, up until now at least, a positive outcome.

In postwar Lebanon, Hizbullah has engaged in a process of reform employing particularly Shiite Islamic ideals, rather than global or western notions of modernization, and women have been included in this process. Sayyid Hasan Nasrallah, the current secretary-general of Hizbullah, stated the position very clearly:

> After the war, Lebanon engaged in reconstruction. It needs psychological and educational rehabilitation to keep the country out of future civil war. Women have a large role in this regard. The psychological and educational impact of women is larger than men, especially in Lebanon. Hizbullah works on encouraging this plan and trying to convince others who are hesitant. Women themselves need encouragement; it is not enough just to open the door. They must be prepared to advance and take the initiative.[5] A schoolteacher in the south echoed his sentiments: "Women's opportunities increased after liberation. Women should take more of a role in the political development of the country."[6]

The case of Iraqi women remains problematic. On the one hand, they seem optimistic that the Islamic values they adopted and that have played a significant role in the sacrifices they made have contributed, albeit partially, to the withdrawal of the occupying forces, thus boosting the integrity of their resistance; on the other hand, their efforts seem to fall short of achieving ultimate liberation. The occupation government is still in power and is not only riddled with political bickering over narrow personal ambitions but also laden with ethnic and sectarian strife that threaten to ravage the country again. For them, therefore, the struggle continues.

The outcome of the struggle for Palestinian women living under Israeli occupation in the West Bank or subjected to Israeli control in the Gaza Strip is also less clear-cut. Like Lebanese Shiite women, they have adopted Islamic values to empower their resistance; however, unlike them, Palestinians have seen their efforts and their sacrifices fail to bear fruit and, worse, their cause demonized by the international community as illegitimate and terrorist. Unlike in Lebanon, where women's roles were more clearly delineated, some Palestinian women have engaged in activities that appear nontraditional and even threatening to their society, such as suicide operations against Israeli civilians. While claiming to be "empowered" by Islamist resistance, many women show signs of weariness; for all their sacrifice, they have yet to see an even remotely satisfactory resolution to their struggle.

Armed conflict, as Eugenia Date-Bah and her colleagues note, "accentuates resourcefulness in adoption of coping and survival strategies which should be strengthened and sustained."[7] As Naila Nauphal argues in the same publication, women "were not passive victims of conflict." The war, she suggests, "opened new avenues for women by redefining their role and increased their role in public life. . . . In the gap created by the breakdown of family ties there is a potential for the development of a civil society as a base for democracy."[8] Many women have also been significantly empowered by their religion, which promotes activism and resistance against the enemy. The conflict situation heightens the underlying sense of injustice so that their preexisting grievances are conjoined to the new grievances generated by conflict, the result being a rediscovery of Islam—or of those dynamic and transformative Islamic ideals that were latent within the various forms of conventional "Islam" inherited from their past, but never before actualized.

Despite the trauma of losing family members and becoming the sole providers for their children, some women have experienced these challenges and difficulties as a source of strength. They have become stronger by having to survive in oppressive conditions and have been assisted by the confidence that resistance would eventually lead to liberation—not just from the aggressive enemies without, but also from oppressive structures within. Thanks to their desire for these modes of liberation and the surge of energy arising out of sheer necessity and a new sense of responsibility, women became instrumental in the creation of new support groups and innovative forms of communal organization that contributed significantly to the success of the resistance movement in Lebanon and also helped to some extent in Iraq and Palestine.

With regard to the influence of Islam, the ideals of the faith have legitimized women's involvement in armed resistance, and we conclude that overall it has enhanced the status of women. The experiences of some Shiite Muslim women in Lebanon, Palestinian women living in the West Bank and Gaza Strip, and women in postinvasion Iraq support the argument that, by deriving strength from their religion, women have been able to tap into what is considered to be an authentic mode of struggle against enemies who invade their society, whether militarily or culturally. They have found ways of participating in their community's struggle against inequality, occupation, and violence. In the process, some of them claim they have been able to expand the spaces in which they feel comfortable operating. However, some Palestinian women have felt more ambivalent about utilizing Islam as a source of strength in the same way (1) because their liberation struggle has been thwarted by circumstances outside their control and (2) because their political culture is rooted in secular rather than religious values, although some Palestinians argue that the abandonment of religion is responsible for the failure of their national movement.[9] Having heard the testimonies of a large number of narrators, we would like to offer three conclusions about women and violent conflict, in relation to women in the occupied Palestinian territories, Shiite women in Lebanon, and women in postinvasion Iraq. The first acknowledges the potentially empowering qualities that Islamist resurgence and Islamist-inspired action against oppressive regimes and intruders have upon women. Many of the women we interviewed during the course of our research spoke in glowing terms of the liberation they had experienced through their religion and of how they had been enabled to join in the battle wholeheartedly, confident that God was on their side. Such empowerment also translates into everyday terms, as women put on the veil, honor the rules of Islam, and bring their children up according to quranic injunctions. However, almost all such assertions came from Lebanese Shiite women. There is an impressive self-confidence about many of the women linked to Amal and Hizbullah. Their "grand narrative" is one of national assertion—the "nation," however, being defined not in nationalist terms but in the sense of the wider Islamic *ummah*; it is about feeling comfortable with Islam as a framework for life and political action.

But that is only one version of Islam among many, and as discussed earlier, it appears to be largely due to the politically significant female role models within Shiite culture. Overall, Muslim men in these regions have not had the power or the means to impose their will on women, and whether it be during the phase of resistance or postresistance institutionalization, the desire to restrict women's agency would appear both illogical and detrimental to the struggle. It is this reality that provides hope for the establishment of a more egalitarian political paradigm.

Second, we have observed the beginnings of a trend to reinterpret Islam in a way that is more in tune with the original ethical Islamic message; this reinterpretation crucially involves women. Third, the will of the international community, expressed in United Nations Security Council Resolution 1325, is supported by many Muslim and third world women who are not content to be excluded from processes of peacemaking and national reconstruction; they are confident they have a role to play.

It is our firm belief that Islam has been a genuinely empowering factor in the lives of large numbers of Muslim women, in Lebanon, Iraq, Palestine, and elsewhere. It is neither a temporary nor an imaginary phenomenon. On the contrary, women are laying claim to their perceived rights and entitlements given to them by Islam but withheld from them by generations of Muslim men. This activism has further been augmented by, and gained momentum from, the current Arab uprisings in which women—particularly those from tribal settings in places such as Yemen and Libya and also women from conservative and rural settings in both Egypt and Tunisia—played, and continue to play, important roles in the political and social transformations that are taking place in the Arab world. However, it is too early to ascertain whether this prominent role will continue and become institutionalized in Arab societies, especially when the dust of the struggle has settled down.

There is still a long way to go for Arab women to overcome ultraconservative social and political thinking, which still prevails among large sectors of the Arab population. Consider the following statement from a young Yemeni man when he was asked about the future role of Yemeni women: "Wait until the uprising is over and we will order them to go back to the kitchen!"[10] One can also mention the way some female Egyptian demonstrators were treated recently by the military: they were subjected to virginity tests, harassed, and beaten. The aim was to discourage them and force them to abandon their public role. Clearly, the existence of *boundaries* has the effect of constraining certain forms of behavior. Shame, as Friedman notes, "more than any laws or police is how a village, a society or a culture expresses approval and disapproval and applies restraints."[11] The extent to which this boundary of "shame" or the "shield" of Islam or any other prevailing norm retains its dominance will determine the extent of participation by women in the social, political, and religious spheres. The changes that have been championed by Arab women and have allowed political forces, especially the Islamists, to augment their power will put the Islamists and those who support them to the test in terms of respecting the rights of Arab women and appreciating the extent to which their services and sacrifices have enabled them to succeed in their cause. It remains to be seen how they use these newly acquired powers, and whether they will mount a serious effort to restore to women the rights they feel are theirs according to Islam. Underlying the participation of women in the various struggles of the Arab world was a largely implicit appeal to recognize the need for more equitable rights for women in Arab societies. As these struggles generate new power structures and dynamics in the Arab world, the tension between inherited patriarchal patterns of thought and behavior, on the one hand, and freshly articulated Islamic norms and principles, on the other, looks set to intensify further. The way in which this tension plays out will determine the degree to which women's participation in political struggle will translate into the recognition and institutionalization of women's rights in society.

Notes

1. Khaled Abou El Fadl, "The Language of the Age: Shari'a and Natural Justice in the Egyptian Revolution," *Harvard International Law Journal* 52 (April 2011): 312.

2. Ibid., 313.

3. Ibid.

4. Ibid.

5. Meeting with Sayyid Hassan Nasrallah, secretary-general of Hizbullah, Beirut, Lebanon, June 9, 2003.

6. Ibid.

7. Eugenia Date-Bah et al., "Gender and Armed Conflicts: Challenges for Decent Work, Gender Equity, and Peace Building Agendas and Programmes," Working Paper 2 (Geneva: Infocus Programme on Crisis Response and Reconstruction, Recovery and Reconstruction Department, International Labour Organization, March 2001), 1.

8. Naila Nauphal, "Women and Other War-Affected Groups in Post-War Lebanon," in Eugenia Date-Bah, et al., eds., "Gender and Armed Conflicts: Challenges for Decent Work, Gender Equity, and Peace Building Agendas and Programmes," Working Paper 2 (Geneva: Infocus Programme on Crisis Response and Reconstruction, Recovery and Reconstruction Department, International Labour Organization, March 2001), 56.

9. Islamist groups in the West Bank and Gaza Strip, for example, claim that only their determined resistance against the Israeli occupation caused the Israelis to withdraw from Gaza in August–September 2005.

10. Personal interview, Birmingham, November 2011.

11. Thomas L. Friedman, "War of Ideas, Part 1," *New York Times*, January 8, 2004.

Bibliography

Abou Atta, Iman. "The Occupation Goes On." Labour briefing online, April 23, 2011.

Abou El Fadl, Khaled. *The Great Theft: Wrestling Islam from the Extremists.* New York: Harper One, 2005.

———. "Islam and the Theology of Power." *Middle East Report* 221, http://www.mcrip.org/mer/mer221/221_abu_el_fadl.html, accessed June 10, 2009.

——— . "The Language of the Age: Shari'a and Natural Justice in the Egyptian Revolution." *Harvard International Law Journal* 52 (April 2011): 311–321.

Abu-Dayyeh Shamas, Maha. "The Second Palestinian Intifada: Social and Psychological Implications of the Israeli Escalation of Violence." Women's Centre for Legal Aid and Counselling (WCLAC), Jerusalem, August 2001.

Abu Fakh, Saqar, and Daud Faraj. "The File of the Female Martyrs." Beirut, undated.

Abu Khalil, Asad. "Druze, Sunni, and Shiite Political Leadership in Present-Day Lebanon." *Arab Studies Quarterly* 7, no. 4 (1985).

Abu-Lughod, Lila. "Do Muslim Women Really Need Saving? Anthropological Reflections on Cultural Relativism." *American Anthropologist* 104, no. 3 (September 2002): 783–790.

———, ed. *Remaking Women: Feminism and Modernity in the Middle East.* Princeton, NJ: Princeton University Press, 1998.

Abu-Odeh, Lama. "Crimes of Honour and the Construction of Gender in Arab Societies." In Mai Yamani, ed., *Feminism and Islam: Legal and Literary Perspectives.* Reading, Berkshire: Ithaca Press, 1996.

Abu Zeid, Nasr Hamid. "The Modernisation of Islam or the Islamisation of Modernity." In Roel Meijer, ed., *Cosmopolitanism, Identity, and Authenticity in the Middle East.* Richmond, Surrey: Curzon, 1999.

Accad, Evelyne. "Sexuality and Sexual Politics: Conflicts and Contradictions for Contemporary Women in the Middle East." In Chandra Talpade Mohanty, Ann

Russo, and Lourdes Torres, eds., *Third World Women and the Politics of Feminism*. Bloomington: Indiana University Press, 1991.

Ahmed, Akbar S. *Discovering Islam: Making Sense of Muslim History and Society*. London: Routledge and Kegan Paul, 1988.

———. *Islam Under Siege: Living Dangerously in a Post-Honor World*. Cambridge: Polity, 2003.

Ahmed, Leila. "Early Islam and the Position of Women: The Problem of Interpretation." In Nikki R. Keddie and Beth Baron, eds., *Women in Middle Eastern History: Shifting Boundaries in Sex and Gender*. New Haven, CT: Yale University Press, 1991.

———. *Women and Gender in Islam*. New Haven, CT: Yale University Press, 1992.

Ajami, Fouad. *The Vanished Imam: Musa al Sadr and the Shia of Lebanon*. London: I. B. Tauris, 1986.

al-Akiti, M. A. *Defending the Transgressed by Censuring the Reckless Against the Killing of Civilians*. Leicester: Aqsa Press, 2005.

Alarcón, Norma, Caren Kaplan, and Minoo Moallem. "Introduction: Between Woman and Nation." In Caren Kaplan, Norma Alarcón, and Minoo Moallem, eds., *Between Woman and Nation: Nationalisms, Transnational Feminisms, and the State*. Durham, NC: Duke University Press, 1999.

al-Ali, Nadje Sadig. *Secularism, Gender, and the State in the Middle East: The Egyptian Women's Movement*. Cambridge: Cambridge University Press, 2000.

al-Ali, Nadje Sadig, and Nicola Christine Pratt. *What Kind of Liberation? Women and the Occupation of Iraq*. Berkeley: University of California Press, 2009.

Allawi, Ali A. *The Occupation of Iraq: Winning the War, Losing the Peace*. New Haven, CT: Yale University Press, 2007.

Amit, Zalman, and Daphna Levit. *Israeli Rejectionism: A Hidden Agenda in the Middle East Peace Process*. London: Pluto Press, 2011.

Ang, Ien. "I'm a Feminist but . . . 'Other' Women and Postnational Feminism." In Reina Lewis and Sara Mills, eds., *Feminist Postcolonial Theory: A Reader*. Edinburgh: Edinburgh University Press, 2003.

Appleby, Joyce, Lynn Hunt, and Margaret Jacob. "Post-Modernism and the Crisis of Modernity." In *Telling the Truth About History*. New York: Norton, 1994.

Ashton, Catherine. "Women Are Essential to Democracy." *Guardian*, April 23, 2011.

Association of Muslim Scholars (AMS), Education and Media Section. "Activities of the Association of Muslim Scholars in Iraq." 2010.

———. "The Essence of the Statements of the AMS." Bas'ir Institute, 2007.

———. *Human Rights Annual Report, 2010–2011*.

———. "An Open Message to the Fighters in Iraq." 2007.

———. *Statements of the Association of Muslim Scholars*, compiled by Muhammad Bashar al-Fadhi. Part 1. Amman: Dar al-Jeel, Al-Arabi, 2008. All AMS statements can be found at www.iraq-amsi.org.

———. "Writings on the Association." 2007.

Ayubi, Nazih. *Political Islam: Religion and Politics in the Arab World*. London: Routledge, 1991.

Badran, Margot. "Egypt's Revolution and the New Feminism." *The Immanent Frame*, March 2011. http://blogs.ssrc.org/tif/2011/03/03/egypts-revolution-and-the-new-feminism/?disp=pr, accessed March 12, 2011.

———. *Feminism in Islam: Secular and Religious Convergences*. Oxford: Oneworld Publications, 2009.

Badran, Margot, and Miriam Cooke. "Introduction." In Margot Badran and Miriam Cooke, eds., *Opening the Gates: A Century of Arab Feminist Writing*. London: Virago, 1990.

Bailey, M. E. "Foucauldian Feminism: Contesting Bodies, Sexuality and Identity." In Caroline Ramazanoglu, ed., *Up Against Foucault: Explorations of Some Tensions Between Foucault and Feminism*. London: Routledge, 1993.

al-Banna, Hassan. "The Credo of the Muslim Brotherhood." In Anouar Abdel-Malek, ed., *Contemporary Arab Political Thought*. London: Zed, 1983.

Bar, Shmuel. "The Religious Sources of Islamic Terrorism: What the Fatwas Say." *Policy Review* (June–July 2004). Hoover Institution, Stanford University. http://www.hoover.org/publications/policy-review/article/6475, accessed October 6, 2009.

Barghouti, Mourid. "He Is the Son of All of You." *Guardian*, August 16, 2008.

Barrett, Michele, and Anne Phillips. "Introduction." In Michele Barrett and Anne Phillips, eds., *Destabilizing Theory: Contemporary Feminist Debates*. Cambridge: Polity, 1992.

Beaumont, Peter. "Hidden Victims of a Brutal Conflict: Iraq's Women." *Observer*, October 8, 2006.

Belhassen, Souhayr. "Femmes tunisiennes islamiste." *Annuaire de l'Afrique du Nord*. Paris: Editions CNRS, 1981.

Berko, Anat, and Edna Erez. "Gender, Palestinian Women, and Terrorism: Women's Liberation or Oppression?" *Studies in Conflict and Terrorism* 30, no. 6 (2007): 493–519.

———. "'Ordinary People' and 'Death Work': Palestinian Suicide Bombers as Victimizers and Victims." *Violence and Victims* 20, no. 6 (December 2005): 603–623.

Beyler, Clara. "Messengers of Death—Female Suicide Bombers." International Institute for Counter-Terrorism, Herzliya, February 12, 2003, http://www.ict.org.il/Articles/tabid/66/Articlsid/94/Default.aspx, accessed January 24, 2011.

Bock, Gisela. "Challenging Dichotomies: Perspectives on Women's History." In Karen M. Offen, Ruth Roach Pierson, and Jane Rendall, eds., *Writing Women's History: International Perspectives*. Basingstoke: Macmillan, 1991.

Bologh, Roslyn Wallach. "Feminist Social Theorizing and Moral Reasoning: On Difference and Dialectic." *Sociological Theory* 2 (1984): 373–393.

Douatta, Cherifa. "Feminine Militancy: *Moudjahidates* During and After the Algerian War." In Valentine M. Moghadam, ed., *Gender and National Identity: Women and Politics in Muslim Society*. Published for the United Nations University World Institute for Development Economics Research. London: Zed, 1994.

Boullata, Issa J. *Trends and Issues in Contemporary Arab Thought*. Albany: State University of New York Press, 1990.

Brahimi, Lakhdar. "Start Talking to Hezbollah." *New York Times*, August 18, 2006.

Brand, Laurie. *Women, the State, and Political Liberalization: Middle Eastern and North African Experiences*. New York: Columbia University Press, 1998.

Broning, Michael. *The Politics of Change in Palestine: State-Building and Non-Violent Resistance*. London: Pluto, 2011.

Brynen, Rex. "PLO Policy in Lebanon: Legacies and Lessons." *Journal of Palestine Studies* 18, no. 2 (Winter 1989): 48–70.

el-Bushra, Judy. "Transforming Conflict: Some Thoughts on a Gendered Understanding of Conflict Processes." In Susie Jacobs, Ruth Jacobson, and Jennifer Marchbank, eds., *States of Conflict*. London: Zed, 2000.

Carapico, Sheila. "Women and Public Participation in Yemen." In Suha Sabbagh, ed., *Arab Women: Between Defiance and Restraint*. New York: Olive Branch, 1996.

Christiansen, Connie Caroe. "Women's Islamic Activism: Between Self-Practice and Social Reform Efforts." In John L. Esposito and Francois Burgat, eds., *Modernizing Islam: Religion in the Public Sphere in Europe and the Middle East*. London: Hurst, 2003.

Cockburn, Cynthia. "The Gendered Dynamics of Armed Conflict and Political Violence." In Caroline O. N. Moser and Fiona C. Clark, eds., *Victims, Perpetrators, or Actors? Gender, Armed Conflict, and Political Violence*. London: Zed, 2001.

———. *The Space Between Us: Negotiating Gender and National Identities in Conflict*. London: Zed, 1998.

Cockburn, Cynthia, and Ann Oakley. "The Culture of Masculinity Costs All Too Much to Ignore." *Guardian*, November 25, 2011.

Cole, Juan, and Shahin Cole. "An Arab Spring for Women." *Nation*, April 26, 2011.

Conetta, Carl. *Vicious Circle: The Dynamics of Occupation and Resistance in Iraq*. Cambridge, MA: Project on Defense Alternatives, Commonwealth Institute, 2005.

Cook, David. "Women Fighting in *Jihad*?" In Cindy D. Ness, ed., *Female Terrorism and Militancy: Agency, Utility, and Organization*. London: Routledge, 2008.

Cooke, Miriam. "Arab Women, Arab Wars." In Fatma Muge Gocek and Shiva Balaghi, eds., *Reconstructing Gender in the Middle East: Tradition, Identity, and Power*. New York: Columbia University Press, 1994.

———. *War's Other Voices: Women Writers on the Lebanese Civil War*. Cambridge: Cambridge University Press, 1988.

———. *Women Claim Islam: Creating Islamic Feminism Through Literature*. London: Routledge, 2001.

———. *Women Write War: The Centring of the Beirut Decentrists*. Papers on Lebanon no. 6. Oxford: Centre for Lebanese Studies, July 1987.

The Covenant of the Islamic Resistance Movement—Palestine Filastin (Hamas). Article 12. "The Homeland and Patriotism from the Point of View of the Movement in Palestine." August 18, 1988.

Crooke, Alastair. *Resistance: The Essence of the Islamist Revolution*. London: Pluto, 2009.

Dalacoura, Katerina. *Islamist Terrorism and Democracy in the Middle East*. Cambridge: Cambridge University Press, 2011.

Danchev, Alex, and John Macmillan, eds. *The Iraq War and Democratic Politics*. London: Routledge, 2005.

Das, Veena. "Gender Studies, Cross-Cultural Comparison, and the Colonial Organization of Knowledge." *Berkshire Review* 21 (1986).

Date-Bah, Eugenia, et al. "Gender and Armed Conflicts: Challenges for Decent Work, Gender Equity, and Peace Building Agendas and Programmes." Working Paper 2. Geneva: Infocus Programme on Crisis Response and Reconstruction, Recovery and Reconstruction Department, International Labour Organization, March 2001.

Deeb, Lara. "Deconstructing a 'Hizbullah Stronghold.'" *MIT Electronic Journal of Middle East Studies* 6 (Summer 2006): 115–125.

———. "'Doing Good, Like Sayyida Zaynab': Lebanese Shi'i Women's Participation in the Public Sphere." In Armando Salvatore and Mark LeVine, eds., *Reli-

gion, Social Practice, and Contested Hegemonies: Reconstructing the Public Sphere in Muslim Majority Societies. New York: Palgrave Macmillan, 2005.
———. An Enchanted Modern: Gender and Public Piety in Shi'i Lebanon. Princeton, NJ: Princeton University Press, 2006.
De Groot, J. "Sex and 'Race': The Construction of Language and Image in the Nineteenth Century." In S. Mendus and J. Rendell, eds., Sexuality and Subordination. London: Routledge, 1989.
Dekmejian, R. Hrair. Islam in Revolution: Fundamentalism in the Arab World. Syracuse, NY: Syracuse University Press, 1985.
———. "Islamic Revival: Catalysts, Categories, and Consequences." In Shireen T. Hunter, ed., The Politics of Islamic Revivalism: Diversity and Unity. Bloomington: Indiana University Press, 1988.
Dickey, C. "Women of Al Qaeda." Newsweek, December 12, 2005.
Dodge, Toby. "War and Resistance in Iraq: From Regime Change to Collapsed State." In Rick Fawn and Raymond A. Hinnebusch, eds., The Iraq War: Causes and Consequences. Boulder, CO: Lynne Rienner, 2006.
Dowell, L. "Iraqi Women to Hang for Acts of Resistance." Above Top Secret, www.abovetopsecret.com/form/threat268429/pg1, accessed September 7, 2011.
Eid, Haidar. "Gaza 2009: Culture of Resistance vs. Defeat." Electronic Intifada, February 11, 2009.
Enloe, Cynthia. Bananas, Beaches, and Bases: Making Feminist Sense of International Politics. London: Pandora, 1989.
———. Does Khaki Become You? The Militarization of Women's Lives. London: Pandora, 1988 [1983].
Ernshire, Eliza. "Who Was Perpetrating the Terror? The Women of Beit Hanoun." Counterpunch, November 7, 2006. http://www.counterpunch.org/ernshire 11072006.html, accessed February 9, 2010.
Esposito, John L. "Islam and Civil Society." In John L. Esposito and Francois Burgat, eds., Modernizing Islam: Religion in the Public Sphere in Europe and the Middle East. London: Hurst, 2003.
——— The Islamic Threat: Myth or Reality? Oxford: Oxford University Press, 1992.
———. "Modernizing Islam and Re-Islamization in Global Perspective." In John L. Esposito and Francois Burgat, eds., Modernizing Islam: Religion in the Public Sphere in Europe and the Middle East. London: Hurst, 2003.
al-Fadhi, Muhammad Bashar. The Illusion. The Outcome of the Political Process Under the American Occupation of Iraq. Amman: Dar al-Jeel Al-Arabi, 2007.
Filiu, Jean-Pierre. The Arab Revolution: Ten Lessons from the Democratic Uprising. London: Hurst, 2011.
Fisher, Ian. "Women, Secret Hamas Strength, Win Votes at Polls and New Role." New York Times, February 3, 2006.
Fleischmann, Ellen L. The Nation and Its "New" Women: The Palestinian Women's Movement, 1920–1948. Berkeley: University of California Press, 2003.
Flint, Julie. "Crushed Hopes and Shattered Senses." Guardian, July 31, 1993.
Fluehr-Lobban, Carolyn. "The Political Mobilization of Women in the Arab World." In Jane I. Smith, ed., Women in Contemporary Muslim Societies. London: Associated University Presses, 1980.
Foucault, Michel. Power/Knowledge: Selected Interviews and Other Writings, 1972–1977. Edited by Colin Gordon. London: Harvester, 1980.

Friedl, Erika. "Ideal Womanhood in Postrevolutionary Iran." In Judy Brink and Joan P. Mencher, eds., *Mixed Blessings: Gender and Religious Fundamentalism Cross-Culturally*. New York: Routledge, 1997.

Friedman, Thomas L. "War of Ideas, Part 1." *New York Times*, January 8, 2004.

el-Gawhary, Karim. "An Islamic Women's Liberation Movement? An Interview with Heba Ra'uf Izzat." *Middle East Report* (November–December 1994): 26–27.

Gentry, Caron E. "Twisted Maternalism." *International Feminist Journal of Politics* 11, no. 2 (2009): 235–252.

Gerner, Debbie J. "Roles in Transition: The Evolving Position of Women in Arab-Islamic Countries." In Freda Hussain, ed., *Muslim Women*. London: Croom Helm, 1984.

Ghannoushi, Soumaya. "Rebellion: Smashing Stereotypes of Arab Women." Al Jazeera, April 25, 2011, http://english.aljazeera.net/indepth/opinion/2011/04/201142412303319807.html, accessed October 18, 2011.

El-Ghazali, Zaynab. *Ayyam min hayati (Days of My Life)*. Cairo: Dar Al Shurq, 1986.

Ghoussoub, Mai. "Feminism—or the Eternal Masculine—in the Arab World." *New Left Review* 161 (January–February 1987): 3–18.

———. *Leaving Beirut: Women and the Wars Within*. London: Saqi, 1998.

Gocek, Fatma Muge. "Introduction: Narrative, Gender, and Cultural Representation in the Constructions of Nationalism in the Middle East." In Fatma Muge Gocek, ed., *Social Constructions of Nationalism in the Middle East*. Albany: State University of New York Press, 2002.

Gole, Nilufer. "Close Encounters: Islam, Modernity and Violence." http://mb archives.blogspot.co.uk/2006/07/close-encounters-islam-modernity-and.html#!/2006/07/close-encounters-islam-modernity-and.html, accessed October 6, 2009.

Gonzalez-Perez, Margaret. "The False Islamization of Female Suicide Bombers." *Gender Issues* 28 (2011): 50–65.

Green, Linda. *Fear as a Way of Life: Mayan Widows in Rural Guatemala*. New York: Columbia University Press, 1999.

Greenfield, Liah. *Nationalism: Five Roads to Modernity*. Cambridge, MA: Harvard University Press, 1992.

el-Guindi, Fadwa. *Veil: Modesty, Privacy, and Resistance*. Oxford: Berg, 1999.

———. "Veiling Resistance." In Reina Lewis and Sara Mills, eds., *Feminist Postcolonial Theory: A Reader*. Edinburgh: Edinburgh University Press, 2003.

Gunning, Jeroen. *Hamas in Politics: Democracy, Religion, Violence*. London: Hurst, 2009.

———. "Hezbollah Reappraised: A Study into Hezbollah's Public and Hidden Transcripts in Post-Ta'if Lebanon." MSc thesis, School of Oriental and African Studies, University of London, September 1995.

Haddad, Yvonne Yazbeck. "Islam and Gender." In Yvonne Yazbeck Haddad, Byron Haines, and Ellison Banks Findly, eds., *The Islamic Impact*. Syracuse, NY: Syracuse University Press, 1984.

Hagopian, Patrick. "The Abu Ghraib Photographs and the State of America: Defining Images." In Louise Purbrick, Jim Aulich, and Graham Dawson, eds., *Contested Spaces: Sites, Representations, and Histories*. Hampshire: Palgrave Macmillan, 2007.

Halawi, Majed. *A Lebanon Defied: Musa al-Sadr and the Shi'a Community*. Boulder, CO: Westview, 1992.

Hall, Stuart. "Cultural Identity and Diaspora." In Patrick Williams and Laura Chrisman, eds., *Colonial Discourse and Post-Colonial Theory: A Reader.* New York: Harvester Wheatsheaf, 1993.

———. "Who Needs 'Identity'?" In Stuart Hall and Paul du Gay, eds., *Questions of Cultural Identity.* Thousand Oaks, CA: Sage, 1996.

Hamzeh, A. Nizar. "Lebanon's Hizbullah: From Islamic Revolution to Parliamentary Accommodation." *Third World Quarterly* 14, no. 2 (1993): 321–337.

Harding, Luke. "The Other Prisoners." *Guardian,* May 19, 2004, http://www.guardian.co.uk/world/2004/may/20/iraq.gender?INTCMP=SRCH.

Hassan, Riaz. "What Motivates the Suicide Bombers?" *Yale Global,* September 3, 2009. http://yaleglobal.yale.edu, accessed January 28, 2010.

Hasso, Frances S. "Discursive and Political Deployments by/of the 2002 Palestinian Women Suicide Bombers/Martyrs." *Feminist Review* 81 (2005): 23–51.

———. "The 'Women's Front': Nationalism, Feminism, and Modernity in Palestine." *Gender and Society* 12, no. 4 (August 1998): 441–465.

Heggy, Tarek. *The Arab Cocoon: Progress and Modernity in Arab Societies.* London: Valentine Mitchell, 2010.

Hendawi, H. "Palestinian Father Expresses Shock over Daughter's Suicide Bombing." Associated Press Worldstream, April 13, 2002.

Hizbullah. "Open Letter Addressed by Hizbullah to the Downtrodden of Lebanon and the World." February 16, 1985.

Hollander, Jocelyn A., and Rachel L. Einwohner. "Conceptualizing Resistance." *Sociological Forum* 19, no. 4 (December 2004): 533–554.

Holt, Maria. "The Unlikely Terrorist: Women and Islamic Resistance in Lebanon and the Palestinian Territories." *Critical Studies on Terrorism* 3, no. 3 (2010): 365–382.

hooks, bell. "Marginality as Site of Resistance." In Russell Ferguson, Martha Gever, Trinh T. Minh-ha, and Cornel West, eds., *Out There: Marginalization and Contemporary Cultures.* Cambridge, MA: MIT Press, 1990.

Hroub, Khaled. *Hamas: Political Thought and Practice.* Washington, DC: Institute for Palestine Studies, 2000.

Hudson, Michael C. *Arab Politics: The Search for Legitimacy.* New Haven, CT: Yale University Press, 1977.

Hunter, Shireen T. *The Politics of Islamic Revivalism: Diversity and Unity.* Bloomington: Indiana University Press, 1988.

Ibish, Hussein. "'Martyrs vs. Traitors' Myth Gains Currency in Gaza War's Wake." *Chicago Tribune,* January 25, 2009.

Ikram Centre for Human Rights. "Iraq After Seven Years of Occupation: Facts and Figures." 2010; contact the Ikram Centre at ikram2006@yahoo.com.

International Crisis Group. "Lebanon: Hizbollah's Weapons Turn Inward." *Middle East Briefing.* No. 23, May 15, 2008.

Ismail, Salwa. *Rethinking Islamist Politics: Culture, the State, and Islamism.* London: I. B. Tauris, 2006.

Jaber, Hala. *Hezbollah: Born with a Vengeance.* New York: Columbia University Press, 1997.

———. "Inside the World of the Palestinian Suicide Bomber." *Sunday Times,* March 24, 2003.

Jad, Islah. "Between Religion and Secularism: Islamist Women of Hamas." In Fereshteh Nouralie-Simone, ed., *On Shifting Ground: Muslim Women in the Global Era.* New York: Feminist Press at the City University of New York, 2005.

Jawad, Haifaa A. "Islamic Feminism, Leadership Role, and Public Representation." *Hawwa, Journal of Women of the Middle East and the Islamic World* 7, no. 1 (2009).

———. *The Rights of Women in Islam: An Authentic Approach*. Basingstoke: Macmillan, 1998.

Johnson, Nels. *Islam and the Politics of Meaning in Palestinian Nationalism*. London: KPI, 1982.

Johnson, Penny, and Eileen Kuttab. "Where Have All the Women (and Men) Gone? Reflections on Gender and the Second Palestinian Intifada." *Feminist Review*, no. 69 (Winter 2001): 21–43.

Joseph, Suad. "Women and Politics in the Middle East." *Middle East Report* (January–February 1986).

Kabbani, Rana. "Reclaiming the True Faith for Women." *Guardian*, May 23, 1992.

Kandiyoti, Deniz. "Contemporary Feminist Scholarship in Middle East Studies." In Deniz Kandiyoti, ed., *Gendering the Middle East: Emerging Perspectives*. London: I. B. Tauris, 1996.

———. "Gender, Power, and Contestation: Rethinking Bargaining with Patriarchy." In C. Jackson and R. Pearson, eds., *Feminist Visions of Development*. London: Routledge, 1998.

———. "Islam, Modernity, and the Politics of Gender." In Muhammad Khalid Masud, Armando Salvatore, and Martin van Bruinessen, eds., *Islam and Modernity: Key Issues and Debates*. Edinburgh: Edinburgh University Press, 2009.

———. "The Paradoxes of Masculinity: Some Thoughts on Segregated Societies." In A. Cornwall and N. Lindesfarme, eds., *Dislocating Masculinity: Comparative Ethnographies*. London: Routledge, 1994.

Karam, Azza M. *Women, Islamisms, and the State: Contemporary Feminisms in Egypt*. Basingstoke: Macmillan, 1998.

Keddie, Nikki R., and Juan Ricardo I. Cole. "Introduction." In Juan Ricardo I. Cole and Nikki R. Keddie, eds., *Shi'ism and Social Protest*. New Haven, CT: Yale University Press, 1986.

Kestler-D'Amours, Jillian. "Harsh Economic and Social Conditions Contribute to Violence Against Palestinian Women." *Electronic Intifada*, August 20, 2012.

Khalaf, Samir. *Beirut Reclaimed: Reflections on Urban Design and the Restoration of Civility*. Beirut: Dar an-Nahar, 1993.

———. *Civil and Uncivil Violence in Lebanon: A History of the Internationalization of Communal Conflict*. New York: Columbia University Press, 2002.

Khalidi, Rashid. "The Terrorism Trap." *New York Times*, July 22, 2006.

Khalili, Laleh. *Heroes and Martyrs of Palestine: The Politics of National Commemoration*. Cambridge: Cambridge University Press, 2007.

Kilcullen, David. "Twenty-Eight Articles: Fundamentals of Company-Level Counterinsurgency." *Small Wars Journal*. www.smallwarsjournal.com/documents/28artilces.pdf, accessed September 8, 2011.

Kocturk, Tahire. *A Matter of Honour: Experiences of Turkish Women Immigrants*. London: Zed, 1992.

Kramer, Gudrun. "Visions of an Islamic Republic: Good Governance According to the Islamists." In Frederic Volpi, ed., *Political Islam: A Critical Reader*. London: Routledge, 2011.

Lackner, Helen. "Women and Development in the Republic of Yemen." In Nabil F. Khoury and Valentine M. Moghadam, eds., *Gender and Development in the Arab World*. London: Zed, 1995.

Lal, Jayati. "Situating Locations: The Politics of Self, Identity, and 'Other' in Living and Writing the Text." In Sharlene Hesse-Biber, Christina Gilmartin, and Robin Lydenberg, eds., *Feminist Approaches to Theory and Methodology: An Interdisciplinary Reader.* Oxford: Oxford University Press, 1999.

Lazreg, Marnia. *The Eloquence of Silence: Algerian Women in Question.* New York: Routledge, 1994.

Leblance, Lauraine. *Pretty in Punk: Girls' Gender Resistance in a Boys' Subculture.* New Brunswick, NJ: Rutgers, 1999.

Lemu, Aisha B., and Fatima Heeren. *Women in Islam.* Leicester: Islamic Foundation, 1978.

Lutfi, Huda. "Manners and Customs of Fourteenth-Century Cairene Women: Female Anarchy Versus Male Shar'i Order in Muslim Prescriptive Treatises." In Nikki R. Keddie and Beth Baron, eds., *Women in Middle Eastern History: Shifting Boundaries in Sex and Gender.* New Haven, CT: Yale University Press, 1991.

Mahfouz, Asmaa. "Now Is the Time: Women and the Arab Awakening." *Economist,* October 15, 2011.

Mahmood, Saba. "Feminist Theory, Agency, and the Liberatory Subject." In Fereshteh Nouraie-Simone, ed., *On Shifting Ground: Muslim Women in the Global Era.* New York: Feminist Press at the City University of New York, 2005.

———. *Politics of Piety: The Islamic Revival and the Feminist Subject.* Princeton, NJ: Princeton University Press, 2005.

Mahmoud, Hozan. "An Empty Sort of Freedom." *Guardian,* March 8, 2004.

Majid, Anouar. "The Politics of Feminism in Islam." In Therese Saliba, Carolyn Allen, and Judith A. Howard, eds., *Gender, Politics, and Islam.* Chicago: University of Chicago Press, 2002.

Marcus, Julie. *A World of Difference: Islam and Gender Hierarchy in Turkey.* London: Zed, 1992.

Massad, Joseph. "Conceiving the Masculine: Gender and Palestinian Nationalism," *Middle East Journal* 49, no. 3 (Summer 1995): 467–483.

Mawdudi, Abu'l A'la. *Purdah and the Status of Women in Islam.* Lahore: Islamic Publications, 1981.

Mayer, Ann Elizabeth. "Cultural Particularism as a Bar to Women's Rights: Reflections on the Middle Eastern Experience." In Julie Peters and Andrea Wolper, eds., *Women's Rights, Human Rights: International Feminist Perspectives.* New York: Routledge, 1995.

———. *Islam and Human Rights: Tradition and Politics.* 2nd ed. Boulder, CO: Westview, 1995.

Mayer, Jane. "Ahmed Chalabi: The Manipulator." *New Yorker,* May 29, 2004, www.archive.truthout.org/article/ahmed-chalabi-the-man. Accessed May 19, 2013.

Mayer, Tamar, ed. *Women and the Israeli Occupation: The Politics of Change.* London: Routledge, 1994.

Mazrui, Ali. "Islam and the End of History." *American Journal of Islamic Social Sciences* 10, no. 4 (1993): 512–535.

McCarthy, Rory. "Sisters, Mothers, Martyrs." *Guardian,* December 5, 2006.

McClintock, A. "Family Feuds: Gender, Nationalism, and the Family." *Feminist Review* 44 (1993): 61–80.

McDowall, David. *Lebanon: A Conflict of Minorities.* London: Minority Rights Group, 1983, rev. ed. 1986.

McGirk, Tim, Jamil Hamad, and Aaron J. Klein. "Moms and Martyrs." *Time,* May 14, 2007, 48–50.

Melman, Billie. *Women's Orients: English Women and the Middle East, 1718–1918.* Ann Arbor: University of Michigan Press, 1992.

Merleau-Ponty, Maurice. *Humanism and Terror.* Boston: Beacon Press, 1969 [1947].

Mernissi, Fatima. *Islam and Democracy: Fear of the Modern World.* Translated by Mary Jo Lakeland. London: Virago, 1993.

———. *The Forgotten Queens of Islam.* Translated by Mary Jo Lakeland. Cambridge: Polity, 1993.

———. *Women and Islam: An Historical and Theological Enquiry.* Oxford: Basil Blackwell, 1991.

Miller, Judith. "The Bomb Under the Abaya." *Policy Review* (June–July 2007).

Milton-Edwards, Beverley. *Islamic Politics in Palestine.* London: Tauris Academic Studies, 1996.

Mir-Hosseini, Ziba. "We Need to Rethink Old Dogmas." Interview with Yoginder Sikand. Qantara.de—Dialogue with the Islamic World, October 28, 2010. http://en.qantara.de/We-Need-to-Rethink-Old-Dogmas9555c9654i1p660/.

al-Mofraji, Harith. "Al-Bas'ir: Story and History." Association of Muslim Scholars, Education and Media Section, 2010.

Moghadam, Valentine M. *Modernizing Women: Gender and Social Change in the Middle East.* Boulder, CO: Lynne Rienner, 1993, 2013.

———. *Women, Work, and Economic Reform in the Middle East and North Africa.* Boulder, CO: Lynne Rienner, 1998.

Moghissi, Haideh. *Feminism and Islamic Fundamentalism: The Limits of Postmodern Analysis.* London: Zed, 1999.

Mohanty, Chandra Talpade. "Cartographies of Struggle: Third World Women and the Politics of Feminism." In Chandra Talpade Mohanty, Ann Russo, and Lourdes Torres, eds., *Third World Women and the Politics of Feminism.* Bloomington: Indiana University Press, 1991.

———. "Under Western Eyes: Feminist Scholarship and Colonial Discourses." In Reina Lewis and Sara Mills, eds., *Feminist Postcolonial Theory: A Reader.* Edinburgh: Edinburgh University Press, 2003.

Mutahhari, Murtada. *The Rights of Women in Islam.* Tehran: World Organization for Islamic Services, 1981.

Naseef, Fatima Umar. *Women in Islam: A Discourse in Rights and Obligations.* Cairo: International Islamic Committee for Woman and Child, 1999.

Nasir, Jamal J. *The Status of Women Under Islamic Law.* 2nd ed. London: Graham and Trotman, 1994.

Nasser, Randa, Fidaa Barghouti, and Janan Mousa. "Feminist Attitudes and Praxis Among Palestinian Women Activists." *Feminist Formations* 22, no. 3 (Fall 2010): 146–175.

National Commission on Terrorist Attacks upon the United States. *The 9/11 Commission Report.* New York: Norton, 2004.

Nauphal, Naila. "Women and Other War-Affected Groups in Post-War Lebanon." In Eugenia Date-Bah, et al., eds., "Gender and Armed Conflicts: Challenges for Decent Work, Gender Equity, and Peace Building Agendas and Programmes." Working Paper 2. Geneva: Infocus, Programme on Crisis Response and Reconstruction, Recovery and Reconstruction Department, International Labour Organization, March 2001.

Nicholson, Linda J., and Nancy Fraser. "Social Criticism Without Philosophy: An Encounter Between Feminism and Postmodernism." In Linda J. Nicholson, ed., *Feminism/Postmodernism*. London: Routledge, 1990.

Norton, Augustus Richard. *Amal and the Shi'a: Struggle for the Soul of Lebanon*. Austin: University of Texas Press, 1987.

———. *Hezbollah: A Short History*. Princeton, NJ: Princeton University Press, 2007.

Ottaway, Marina. "The Limits of Women's Rights." In Thomas Carothers and Marina Ottaway, eds., *Uncharted Journey: Promoting Democracy in the Middle East*. Washington, DC: Carnegie Endowment for International Peace, 2005.

Peteet, Julie. "Icons and Militants: Mothering in the Danger Zone." In Therese Sabiba, Carolyn Allen, and Judith A. Howard, eds., *Gender, Politics, and Islam*. Chicago: University of Chicago Press, 2002.

———. *Landscape of Hope and Despair: Palestinian Refugee Camps*. Philadelphia: University of Pennsylvania Press, 2005.

———. "Male Gender and Rituals of Resistance in the Palestinian Intifada: A Cultural Politics of Violence." In Mai Ghoussoub and Emma Sinclair-Webb, eds., *Imagined Masculinities: Male Identity and Culture in the Modern Middle East*. London: Saqi, 2000.

Peters, Julie, and Andrea Wolper, eds. *Women's Rights, Human Rights: International Feminist Perspectives*. London: Routledge, 1995.

Peterson, V. Spike. "Gendering Informal Economics in Iraq." In Nadje Sadig al-Ali and Nicola Christine Pratt, eds., *Women and War in the Middle East: Transna tional Perspectives*. London: Zed, 2009.

Philipp, Thomas. "Feminism and Nationalist Politics in Egypt." In Luis Beck and Nikki R. Keddie, eds., *Women in the Muslim World*. Cambridge, MA: Harvard University Press, 1978.

Phillips, David. *Losing Iraq: Inside the Postwar Reconstruction Fiasco*. New York: Basic Books, 2005.

Philo, Greg, and Mike Berry. *More Bad News from Israel* London: Pluto, 2011.

Pratt, Nicola. *Democracy and Authoritarianism in the Arab World*. Boulder, CO: Lynne Rienner, 2007.

al-Qaradawi, Yousuf. "Women and the Islamic Movement." Crescent Life. http://www.crescentlife.com/thisthat/feminist%20muslims/women_and -islamic_movement.htm, accessed April 10, 2007.

Racioppi, Linda, and Katherine O'Sullivan See. "Engendering Nation and National Identity." In Sita Ranchod-Nilsson and Mary Ann Tetreault, eds, *Women, States, and Nationalism: At Home in the Nation?* London: Routledge, 2000.

Ragavan, C., D. Pasternak, and R. Sharpe. "Femme Fatale? Al Qaeda's Mystery Woman." *US News and World Report*, April 7, 2003.

Rahman, Fazlur. "A Survey of Modernization of Muslim Family Law." *International Journal of Middle East Studies* 2 (1980): 451–465.

Rao, Arati. "The Politics of Gender and Culture in International Human Rights Discourse. In Julie Peters and Andrea Wolper, eds., *Women's Rights, Human Rights: International Feminist Perspectives*. London: Routledge, 1995.

Rapoport, Yossef. *Marriage, Money and Divorce in Medieval Islamic Society*. Cambridge: Cambridge University Press, 2005.

al-Rashed, Hussein, and Saif al-Jubouri. "The Iraqi Scientific Competencies That Were Assassinated After the American Occupation of Iraq." Al-Umma Centre for Studies and Development, 2010.

Revkin, Mara. "Has Egypt's Revolution Left Women Behind?" *Foreign Policy*, December 8, 2011, http://mideast.foreignpolicy.com/posts/2011/12/08/has _egypts_revolution_left_women_behind.

Rice, Xan, Katherine Marsh, Tom Finn, Harriet Sherwood, Angelique Christafis, and Robert Booth. "Women Have Emerged as Key Players in the Arab Spring." *Guardian*, April 22, 2011.

Riverbend. "Baghdad Burning." http://riverbendblog.blogspot.com, accessed April 31, 2011.

Robinson, Glenn E. *Building a Palestinian State: The Incomplete Revolution.* Bloomington: Indiana University Press, 1997.

Roded, Ruth, ed. *Women in Islam and the Middle East: A Reader*. London: I. B. Tauris, 1999.

Rogers, Paul. *Iraq and the War on Terror*. London: I. B. Tauris, 2006.

———. *A War Too Far: Iraq, Iran, and the American Century*. London: Pluto, 2006.

Rosen, Ruth. "The Hidden War on Women in Iraq." ZNET online, July 13, 2006.

Roy, Sara. *Failing Peace: Gaza and the Palestinian-Israeli Conflict*. London: Pluto, 2007.

———. "The Transformation of Islamic NGOs in Palestine." *Middle East Report* 30, no. 1, Spring 2000.

Rubenberg, Cheryl A. *Palestinian Women: Patriarchy and Resistance in the West Bank*. Boulder, CO: Lynne Rienner, 2001.

Rubin, Jeffrey W. "Defining Resistance: Contested Interpretations of Everyday Acts." *Studies in Law, Politics, and Society* 15 (1996): 237–260.

Rupp, Leila J., and Verta Taylor. "Forging Feminist Identity in an International Movement: A Collective Identity Approach to Twentieth-Century Feminism." *Signs: Journal of Women in Culture and Society* 24, no. 21 (1999): 363–386.

Saad-Ghorayeb, Amal. *Hizbu'llah: Politics and Religion*. London: Pluto, 2002.

Sabawai, Samah. "Truth, Non-Violence, and the Palestinian Hills." Australians for Palestine. www.australiansforpalestine.com/22195, 2010.

Sabbagh, Suha. "Introduction." In Suha Sabbagh, ed., *Palestinian Women of Gaza and the West Bank*. Bloomington: Indiana University Press, 1998.

Sadiki, Larbi. "Reframing Resistance and Democracy: Narratives from Hamas and Hizbullah." *Democratization* 17, no. 2 (April 2010): 350–376.

Said, Edward W. *After the Last Sky*. London: Faber and Faber, 1986.

———. *Orientalism*. London: Routledge and Kegan Paul, 1978.

———. *Orientalism*, 2nd ed. New York: Vintage, 1994.

———. *The Politics of Dispossession: The Struggle for Palestinian Self-Determination, 1969–1994*. London: Vintage, 1995.

Salame, Ghassan. "'Strong' and 'Weak' States: A Qualified Return to the *Muqaddimah*." In Giacomo Luciani, ed., *The Arab State*. London: Routledge, 1990.

Saliba, Therese, Carolyn Allen, and Judith A. Howard. "Introduction." In Therese Saliba, Carolyn Allen, and Judith A. Howard, eds., *Gender, Politics, and Islam*. Chicago: University of Chicago Press, 2002.

Salibi, Kamal. *A House of Many Mansions*. London: I. B. Tauris, 1988.

Salvatore, Armando. "Tradition and Modernity Within Islamic Civilization and the West." In Muhammad Khalid Masud, Armando Salvatore, and Martin van Bruinessen, eds., *Islam and Modernity: Key Issues and Debates*. Edinburgh: Edinburgh University Press, 2009.

el-Sarraj, Shadia. "Screaming in Silence." In Marguerite R. Waller and Jennifer Rycenga, eds., *Frontline Feminisms: Women, War, and Resistance*. New York: Routledge, 2001.

Sayigh, Yezid. "War as Leveler, War as Midwife: Palestinian Political Institutions, Nationalism, and Society Since 1948." In Steven Heydemann, ed., *War, Institutions, and Social Change in the Middle East*. Berkeley: University of California Press, 2000.

Schwedler, Jillian. "Studying Political Islam." *International Journal of Middle East Studies* 43, no. 1 (February 2011): 135–137.

Scott, James C. *Weapons of the Weak: Everyday Forms of Peasant Resistance*. New Haven, CT: Yale University Press, 1985.

Segal, Lyne. *Is the Future Female? Troubled Thoughts on Contemporary Feminism*. London: Virago, 1987.

Sen, Amartya. *Identity and Violence: The Illusion of Destiny*. London: Penguin, 2006.

Shaaban, Bouthaina. *Both Right and Left Handed: Arab Women Talk About Their Lives*. London: Women's Press, 1988.

Shaery-Eisenlohr, Roschanack. *Shi'ite Lebanon: Transnational Religion and the Making of National Identities*. New York: Columbia University Press, 2008.

Shalhoub-Kevorkian, Nadera. "Liberating Voices: The Political Implications of Palestinian Mothers Narrating Their Loss." *Women's Studies International Forum* 26, no. 5 (2003): 391–407.

——. *Militarization and Violence Against Women in Conflict Zones in the Middle East: A Palestinian Case Study*. Cambridge: Cambridge University Press, 2009.

al-Shanti, Jameela. "We Overcame Our Fear." *Guardian*, November 9, 2006.

Shapira, Shimon. "The Imam Musa al-Sadr: Father of the Shiite Resurgence in Lebanon." *Jerusalem Quarterly*, no. 44 (Fall 1987): 121–144.

Sharoni, Simona, and Mohammed Abu-Nimer "The Israeli-Palestinian Conflict." In Jillian Schwedler and Deborah J. Gerner, eds., *Understanding the Contemporary Middle East*. 3rd ed. Boulder: Lynne Rienner, 2008.

Sharp, G. "The Intifadah and Nonviolent Struggle." *Journal of Palestine Studies* 19, no. 1 (1989).

Shaw, Martin. *The New Western Way of War*. Cambridge: Polity, 2005.

Shayegan, Daryush. *Cultural Schizophrenia: Islamic Societies Confronting the West*. London: Saqi, 1992.

Shepard, William. "The Diversity of Islamic Thought: Towards a Typology." In Suha Taji-Farouki and Basheer M. Nafa, eds., *Islamic Thought in the Twentieth Century*. London: I. B. Tauris, 2004.

Sh'hada, Nahda. "Women in Gaza." *Zmag*. www.zmag.org, November 27, 2000.

Sonbol, Amira El Azhary. "Law and Gender Violence in Ottoman and Modern Egypt." In Amira El Azhary Sonbol, ed., *Women, the Family, and Divorce Laws in Islamic History*. Syracuse, NY: Syracuse University Press, 1996.

Spellberg, Denise A. "Political Action and Public Example: A'isha and the Battle of the Camel." In Nikki R. Keddie and Beth Baron, eds., *Women in Middle Eastern History: Shifting Boundaries in Sex and Gender*. New Haven, CT: Yale University Press, 1991.

Stewart, Dona J. *The Middle East Today: Political, Geographical, and Cultural Perspectives*. London: Routledge, 2009.

Stowasser, Barbara Freyer. "Liberated Equal or Protected Dependent? Contemporary Religious Paradigms on Women's Status in Islam." *Arab Studies Quarterly* 9, no. 3 (Summer 1987).

———. "The Status of Women in Early Islam." In Freda Hussein, ed., *Muslim Women*. London: Croom Helm, 1983.

Strum, Philippa. *The Women Are Marching: The Second Sex and the Palestinian Revolution*. New York: Lawrence Hill, 1992.

Sullivan, Zohreh T. "Eluding the Feminist, Overthrowing the Modern? Transformation in Twentieth-Century Iran." In Lila Abu-Lughod, ed., *Remaking Women: Feminism and Modernity in the Middle East*. Princeton, NJ: Princeton University Press, 1998.

Tamimi, Azam. "The Islamic Debate over Self-Inflicted Martyrdom." In Madawi al-Rasheed and Marat Shterin, eds., *Dying for Faith: Religiously Motivated Violence in the Contemporary World*. London: I. B. Tauris, 2009.

Taraki, Lisa. "Introduction." In Lisa Taraki, ed., *Living Palestine: Family Survival, Resistance, and Mobility Under Occupation*. Syracuse, NY: Syracuse University Press, 2006.

———. "Mass Organizations in the West Bank." *Readings in Contemporary Palestinian Society*, vol. 2. Birzeit: Birzeit University Press, 1989, 125–142.

———. "Palestinian Society: Contemporary Reality and Trends." In *Palestinian Women: A Status Report*. Birzeit: Women's Studies Program, Birzeit University 1997.

Thabit, Abdullah. *Dictatorship, Imperialism, and Chaos: Iraq Since 1989*. London: Zed, 2006.

Thapar-Bjorkert, Suruchi, and Laura J. Shepherd. "Religion." In Laura J Shepherd, ed., *Gender Matters in Global Politics: A Feminist Introduction to International Relations*. London: Routledge, 2010.

Toles Patkin, Terri. "Explosive Baggage: Female Palestinian Suicide Bombers and the Rhetoric of Emotion." *Women and Language* 27, no. 2 (2004): 79–99.

Tucker, Judith. *Women, Family, and Gender in Islamic Law*. Cambridge: Cambridge University Press, 2008.

———. *Women in Nineteenth-Century Egypt*. Cairo: American University of Cairo, 1986.

Turner, Bryan S. *Orientalism, Postmodernism, and Globalism*. London: Routledge, 1994.

Umm Nader. "Palestinian Women Help Behind the Lines." November 13, 2000, indiainfo.com.

United Nations. *Women, Peace, and Security: Study Submitted to the Secretary-General Pursuant to Security Council Resolution 1325 (2000)*. New York, 2002.

United Nations Development Programme. *Arab Human Development Report 2004: Towards Freedom in the Arab World*. New York, 2005.

Utvik, Bjorn Olav. "The Modernizing Force of Islam." In John L. Esposito and Francois Burgat, eds., *Modernizing Islam: Religion in the Public Sphere in Europe and the Middle East*. London: Hurst, 2003.

Victor, Barbara. *Army of Roses: Inside the World of Palestinian Women Suicide Bombers*. London: Robinson, 2004.

Walther, Wiebke. *Women in Islam: From Medieval to Modern Times*. Princeton: Markus Wiener Publishers, 1993.

Ward, O. "The Changing Face of Terror." *Toronto Star*, October 10, 2004.

Waylen, Georgina. *Gender in Third World Politics*. Buckingham: Open University Press, 1996.

Weedon, Chris. *Feminism, Theory and the Politics of Difference*. Oxford. Black-well, 1999.

Weitz, Rose. "Women and Their Hair: Seeking Power Through Resistance and Accommodation." *Gender and Society* 15 (2001): 667–686.

Westervelt, Eric. "Female Activists a Force in Male-Dominated Gaza." National Public Radio, January 2, 2007, http://www.npr.org/templates/story/story.php?storyId=6725651, accessed March 26, 2009.

Women's Centre for Legal Aid and Counselling (WCLAC) and the Women's Studies Center (WSC). "A Report on the Situation of Women's Human Rights During the 'Second Intifada,'" presented to the United Nations Human Rights Commission Fact-Finding Mission on February 16, 2001.

Women's Centre for Legal Aid and Counselling. "The Second Palestinian Intifada: Social and Psychological Implications of the Israeli Escalation of Violence." National Public Radio, April 2001.

Wood, Paul. "Just Married and Determined to Die." *BBC News*, October 13, 2008.

Yaqub, Nadia. "Dismantling the Discourses of War: Palestinian Women Filmmakers Address Violence." In Moha Ennaji and Fatima Sadiqi, eds., *Gender and Violence in the Middle East*. London: Routledge, 2011.

Yeganeh, Nahid, and Nikki R. Keddie. "Sexuality and Shi'i Social Protest in Iran." In Juan Ricardo I. Cole and Nikki R. Keddie, eds., *Shi'ism and Social Protest*. New Haven, CT: Yale University Press, 1986.

Zangana, Haifa. *City of Widows: An Iraqi Woman's Account of War and Resistance*. New York: Seven Stories Press, 2007.

———. "Colonial Feminists from Washington to Baghdad: Women for a Free Iraq: A Case Study." In Jacqueline S. Ismeal and William W. Haddad, eds., *Barriers to Reconciliation: Case Studies on Iraq and the Palestine-Israel Conflict*. Lanham, MD: University Press of America, 2006.

———. "Foreword: Abu Ghraib: Prison as a Collective Memory." In Louise Purbrick, Jim Aulich, and Graham Dawson, eds., *Contested Spaces: Sites, Representations, and Histories*. Hampshire: Palgrave Macmillan, 2007.

———. "The Iraqi Resistance Only Exists to End the Occupation." *Guardian* online, April 12, 2007.

———. "The Message Coming from Our Families in Baghdad." *Guardian* online, April 3, 2003.

———. "There Is More Than One Triangle of Resistance." *Guardian* online, September 14, 2006.

———. "The Three Cyclops of Empire-Building: Targeting the Fabric of Iraqi Society." In Amy Bartholomew, ed., *Empire's Law: The American Imperial Project and the "War to Remake the World."* London: Pluto, 2006.

Index

About the Book

How are women in the Arab world negotiating the male-dominated character of Islamist movements? Is their participation in the Islamic political project—including violent resistance against foreign invasion and occupation—the result of coercion or of choice? Questioning assumptions about female powerlessness in Muslim societies, Maria Holt and Haifaa Jawad explore the resistance struggles taking place in Lebanon, Iraq, Palestine, and elsewhere in the Middle East from the perspectives of the women involved.

The authors make extensive use of vivid personal testimonies as they examine the influence of such factors as religion, patriarchy, and traditional practices in determining women's modes of participation in conflicts. In the process, they add to our knowledge not only of how women are affected by political violence, but also of how their involvement is beginning to change the rules that govern their societies.

Maria Holt is reader in the Department of Politics and International Relations at the University of Westminster, London. **Haifaa Jawad** is senior lecturer in Islamic and Middle Eastern studies at the University of Birmingham.